THE POWERFUL HAND OF GEORGE BELLOWS

Drawings from the Boston Public Library

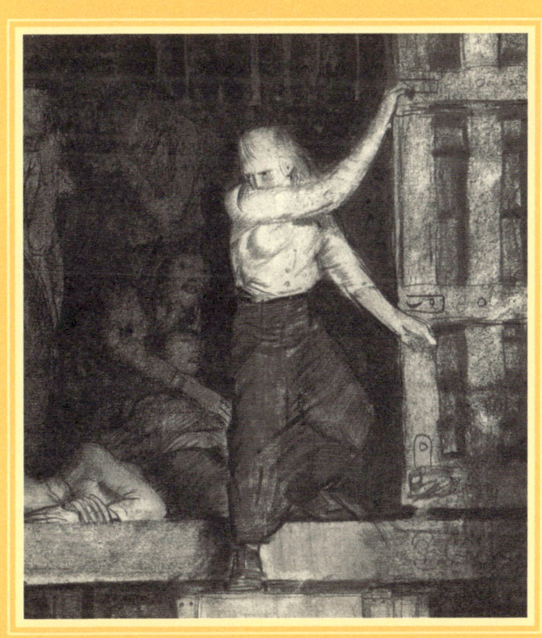

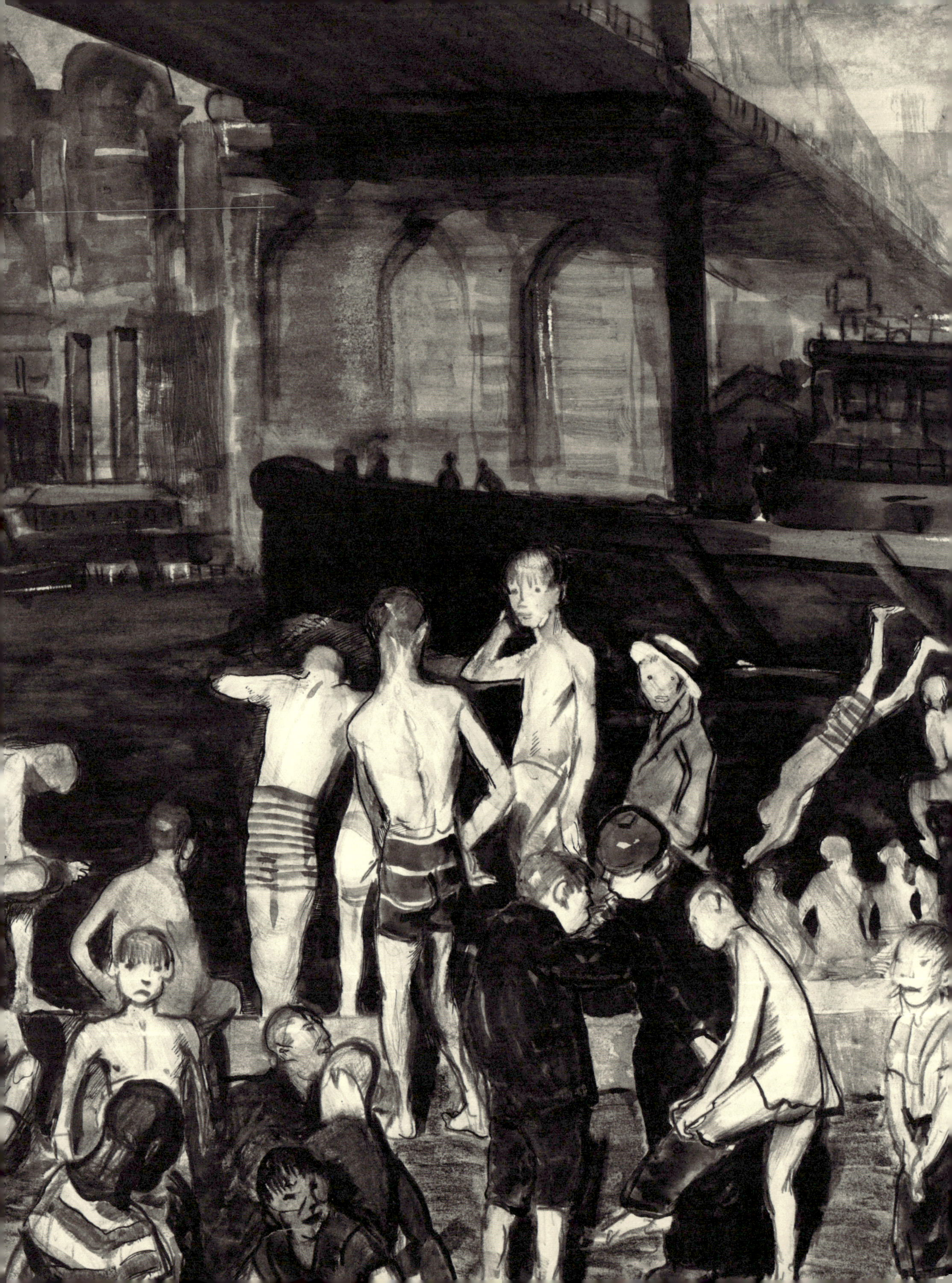

THE POWERFUL HAND OF GEORGE BELLOWS

Drawings from the Boston Public Library

ROBERT CONWAY, *Guest Curator*

TRUST FOR MUSEUM EXHIBITIONS
Washington, D.C.

IN COOPERATION WITH THE

BOSTON PUBLIC LIBRARY
Boston, Massachusetts

HALF TITLE: *Return of the Useless*, 1918, detail, cat. no. 18.
FRONTISPIECE: *Splinter Beach*, 1913, detail, cat. no. 2.

Trust for Museum Exhibitions
1250 Connecticut Avenue, N.W., Suite 200
Washington, DC 20036

202-745-2566
www.tme.org

ISBN: 978-1-882507-17-7

PHOTOGRAPHY BY:
Tom Blake, Boston Public Library

DESIGN BY:
Paul Hoffmann

PRINTED BY:
The Stinehour Press

EXHIBITION ITINERARY

THE FRICK ART & HISTORICAL CENTER
Pittsburgh, Pennsylvania
APRIL 21 – JUNE 17, 2007

THE COLUMBUS MUSEUM OF ART
Columbus, Ohio
JULY 12 – SEPTEMBER 23, 2007

THE MENNELLO MUSEUM OF AMERICAN ART
Orlando, Florida
OCTOBER 11 – DECEMBER 23, 2007

MILWAUKEE ART MUSEUM
Milwaukee, Wisconsin
JANUARY 10 – MARCH 23, 2008

PORTLAND MUSEUM OF ART
Portland, Maine
APRIL 10 – JUNE 1, 2008

SAN ANTONIO MUSEUM OF ART
San Antonio, Texas
JUNE 21 – AUGUST 31, 2008

BOSTON PUBLIC LIBRARY
Boston, Massachusetts
SEPTEMBER 22 – DECEMBER 1, 2008

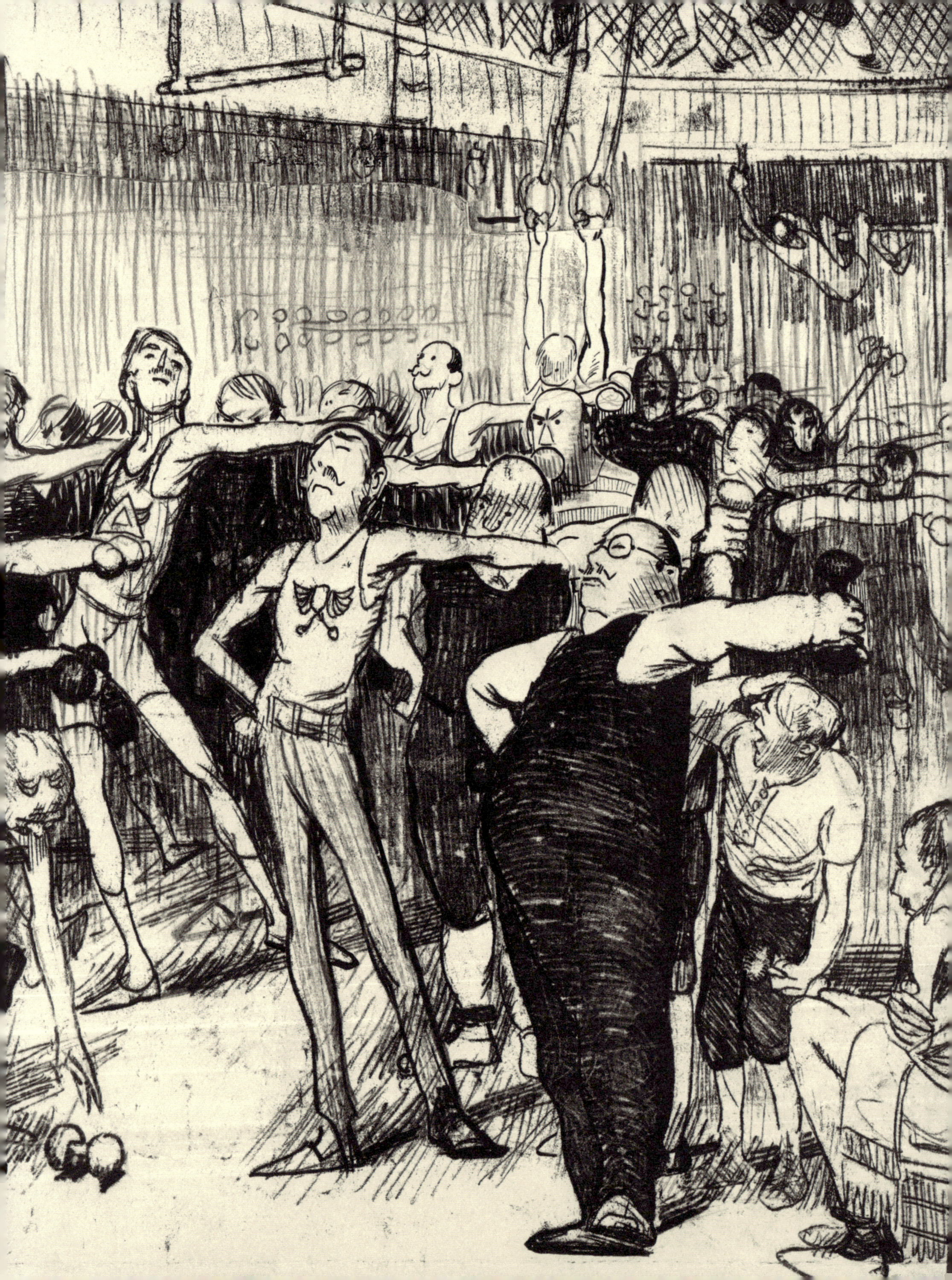

TABLE OF CONTENTS

Business Men's Class, 1913, detail, cat. no. 3.

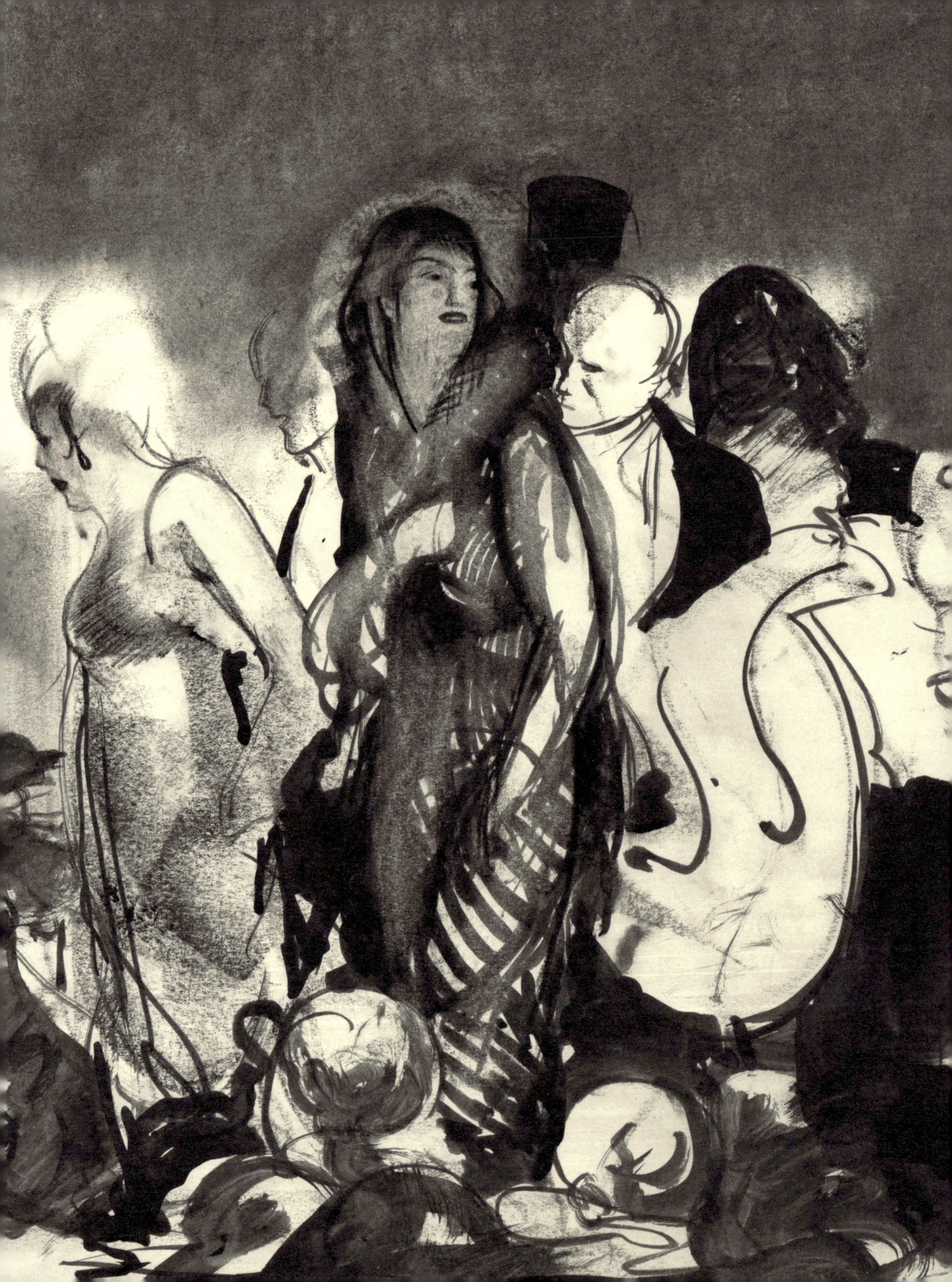

FOREWORD

JUST AFTER THE TURN of the last century, Albert H. Wiggin, who grew up in Boston and started his banking career in Boston before becoming President of Chase Bank in New York, began amassing an important collection of works of art, rich in Old Master prints and drawings as well as nineteenth and early twentieth century French, British and American works of art on paper. By the time of his donation of the entire collection to the Boston Public Library in 1941, the collection had grown to more than 5,000 works of art and included major holdings of notable drawings and prints by the English artist Thomas Rowlandson, major collections of prints by Francisco Goya y Lucientes, Honoré Daumier, Henri de Toulouse-Lautrec, Jean-Louis Forain, among many, many others. Among its most significant and notable parts is a remarkable group of prints, drawings, and books representing the extraordinary work of George Bellows.

The Trust for Museum Exhibitions approached the Boston Public Library in 2003 with a proposal to collaborate on a traveling exhibition bringing to light . . . and to new audiences . . . this especially appealing collection of Bellows drawings which have not been publicly exhibited for over 50 years. The Boston Public Library is honored to partner with the Trust for Museum Exhibitions in this exciting venture. The itinerary arranged by the Trust includes a group of distinguished museums from New England to the Southwest, from the Midwest to the South. When Albert Wiggin entrusted this collection to the Boston Public Library, it was with the expectation that these extraordinary works would be accessible to the Citizens of Boston through study and exhibition. We delight in this collaborative opportunity to present the extraordinary work of George Bellows to an even wider, though no less appreciative, audience.

BERNARD A. MARGOLIS
President, Boston Public Library

Preliminaries, 1916, detail, cat. no. 13.

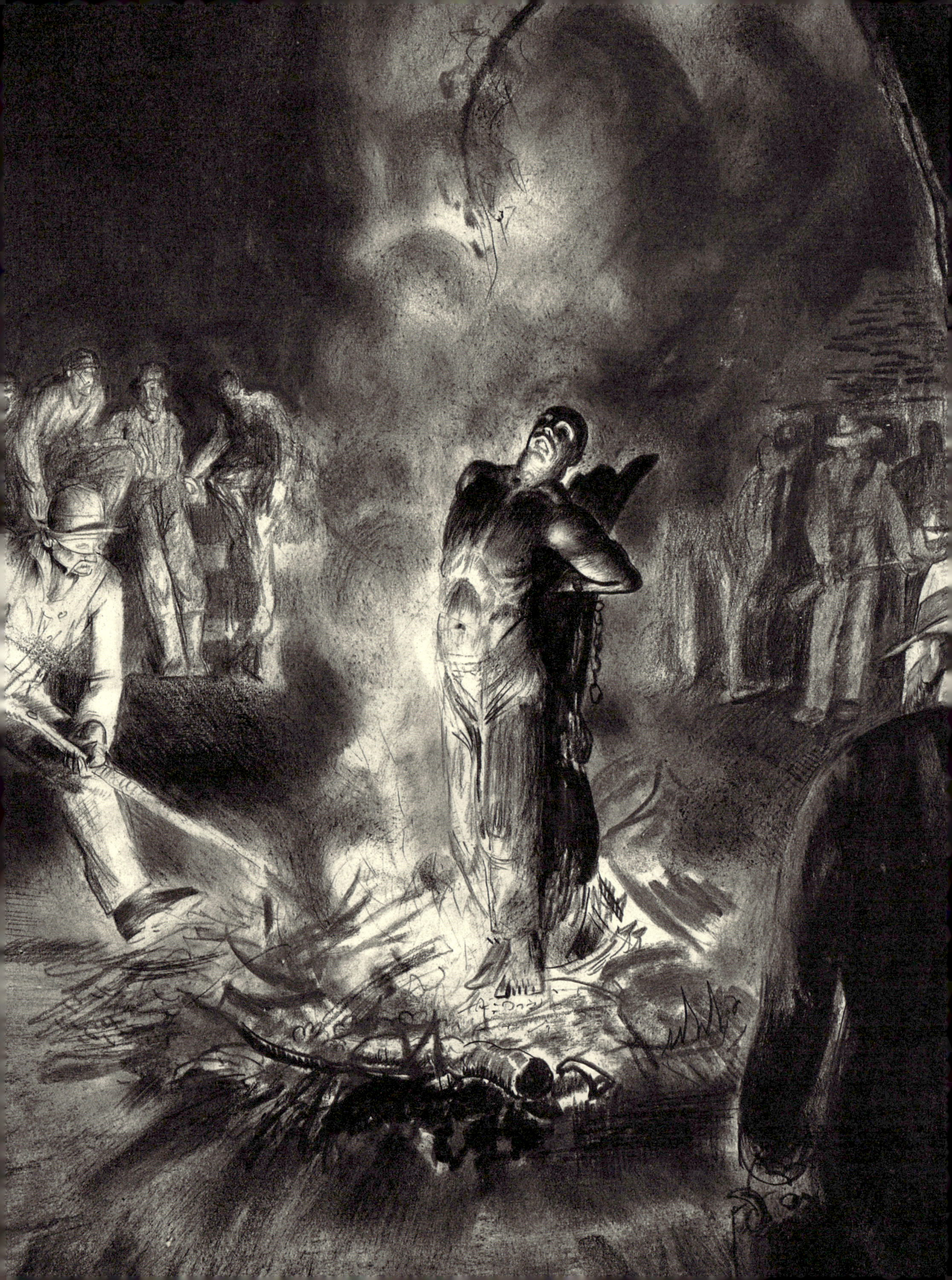

PREFACE

A little more than five years ago, in the summer of 2001, I wrote a letter to Clinton Adams asking him if he would contribute an essay to this exhibition catalogue on the drawings of George Bellows and their relationships to his lithographs. Clinton, as many readers already know, was an accomplished artist, lithographer, educator, author and this country's foremost print historian.

He answered my request in his characteristically concise and straightforward manner: he was sorry, but he couldn't write the essay because he was terminally ill with cancer. With the encouragement of a mutual friend, I dropped everything and traveled to Albuquerque to begin taping interviews with Clinton in his studio, so that we would have a first-person account of his life with lithography on which to base a catalogue raisonné.

With my attention directed to building a solid base of data before Adams died, I let the Bellows project slide. After his death, I let his project slide as well, in favor of starting another catalogue raisonné for yet another artist suffering from cancer. Now, in the winter of 2006, all three projects are nearing completion, and I look forward to closing the circle—actually more like an ellipse—started by my letter.

Along the way, I received assistance from a few key individuals. Sinclair Hitchings, then Keeper of the Print Department of the Boston Public Library, received my idea of doing an exhibition of the Wiggin Collection of Bellows drawings with a professional mix of caution and support which demanded of me a clearer idea of what I wanted to do and how I would do it. Katie Crum, then director of the Mills College Art Museum, pushed me to formalize this concept into a written proposal, and steered me to the Trust for Museum Exhibitions. There, a sequence of helpful staff culminating in Diane Salisbury, the real angel of this project, brought it along from idea to reality.

Several other friends and colleagues made my research and writing better than they otherwise would have been. Karen Shafts and her staff at the Library made the drawings and other Bellows material easily available. Sarah Riley, a paper conser-

The Law Is Too Slow, 1922–23, detail, cat. no. 39.

vator, examined the drawings with the professional exactitude I lack, and brought them to their current excellent condition. Daria D'Arenzio, head of Archives and Special Collections at the Amherst College Library, put her able staff at my disposal for a few intense days of reviewing their Bellows archive. Glen Peck of H. V. Allison & Co., the longtime representative of the Bellows estate and creator of the on-line Bellows catalogue raisonné, read my text carefully and critically, as did Jane Myers, Senior Curator of Prints and Drawings at the Amon Carter Museum and another expert on Bellows. It was a footnote in her and her colleague Linda Ayres' 1988 definitive work on Bellows' lithographs that first alerted me to the untapped riches of the Wiggin collection. Thanks also go to my collaborator Don Farnsworth for his reconstruction of the golden section.

Finally, I wish to thank Jean Bellows Booth and her daughters Laurie Booth and Emily Olmstead for granting permission to review the artist's record book and to reproduce both text and images from his archive. Many years ago I had the pleasure of visiting Jean in her home. There she showed me some cartoons her father had drawn for her and her older sister Anne when they were girls. The parental affection and good nature evident in those little drawings were reason enough to see this project through to completion.

Robert Conway

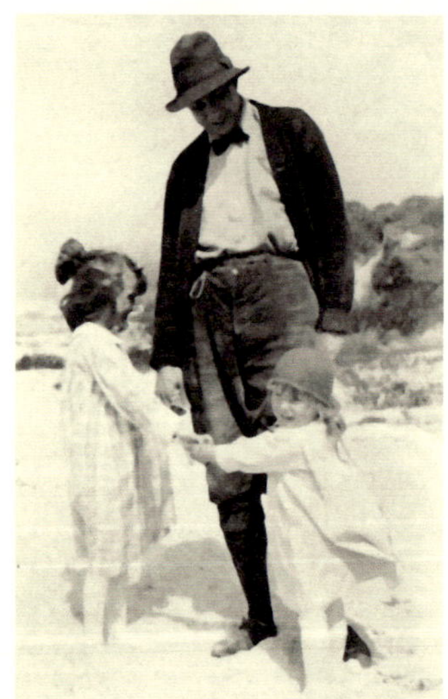

George, Anne and Jean Bellows, c. 1918.

ACKNOWLEDGMENTS

THE TRUST FOR MUSEUM EXHIBITIONS and the Boston Public Library have been working together since 2003—through renovations, moves and changes in personnel—to bring this beautiful exhibition of George Bellows' drawings to fruition. The Albert H. Wiggin Collection is a highlight of the rich treasures housed at the Boston Public Library, but the Wiggin Collection of drawings by George Bellows has never before been seen on tour.

The Trust is honored to have been selected for this special undertaking. We want to thank all at the Boston Public Library who have labored over the years to get these drawings ready for their inaugural tour: Bernard A. Margolis, President; Edward Maheigan, Acting Chief Financial Officer; Susan Glover Godlewski, Manager of Reference and Information Services who is currently over-seeing the Print Department; Tom Blake, Digital Imaging Production Manager; and Karen Shafts, Assistant to the Keeper of Prints.

The Library joins the Trust in thanking those in Washington, D.C. who have worked so tirelessly on this project: Diane C. Salisbury, Director of Exhibitions and project leader; and Christopher Whittington, Chief Registrar; as well as Richard Franklin, Ginger Crockett Hammer and Elizabeth Littlejohn.

Of course there would have been no catalogue without the scholarly text written by our Guest Curator, Robert Conway. Bob came to the project from a distinguished career in the field of prints and drawings, and, since 2000, he has devoted many hours to researching Bellows' work and career. He has been a joy to work with, always thorough, paying attention to deadlines and never requiring that much-dreaded editing. Thanks to Bob, in Oakland, California, and to Sarah Riley, in Arlington, Massachusetts, who has labored over the last several months to conserve all of the drawings and the related lithographs for this tour.

We would also like to thank Rick Yamada at Ely Inc. for packing and crating; Jack Ring at McCollisters Transportation Group for shipping; David Murphy and Jamie Griffith at Stanhope Framers for matting and framing; and Jennifer Schansburg, Contract Registrar.

Ann Van Devanter Townsend
Founding President, Trust for Museum Exhibitions

Bernard A. Margolis
President, Boston Public Library

ALBERT H. WIGGIN AND THE PRINT DEPARTMENT OF THE BOSTON PUBLIC LIBRARY

In his remarks at the time he presented his collection to the Boston Public Library, Albert Henry Wiggin (1868–1951)[1] stated:

> Some forty years ago a very dear friend gave to Mrs. Wiggin and myself an etching by Buhot known as "Country Neighbors." That was the start.[2]

From that gift over the next four decades, Wiggin went on to assemble one of the most important private print collections of the first half of the twentieth century.

Wiggin's collecting was far-reaching. When his collection came to the Library in 1941, among the more than 5,000 prints and drawings were woodcuts and engravings by Albrecht Dürer, including his Apocalypse series and an impression of "The Prodigal Son," impressions of Rembrandt van Rijn's "Three Trees" and "Christ with the Sick around Him, Receiving Little Children ("The Hundred Guilder Print")," and two of the four major series of etchings and aquatints by Francisco Goya y Lucientes, "Los Proverbios" and "La Tauromaquia." Also included were prints by masters of the European etching revival of the second half of the nineteenth century, among them Jean-François Millet, Charles Meryon, James Whistler, Frances Seymour Haden, Felix Buhot, and Auguste Lepère, and younger artists who were making their reputations during the early decades of the twentieth century: Muirhead Bone, James McBey, Gerald Brockhurst, Jean Louis Forain, and George Bellows. Wiggin developed personal relationships with a number of dealers, collectors, and, in many cases, with the artists themselves. Wiggin's goal, especially in collecting his contemporaries, was to be comprehensive. When possible, he not only collected the published state of a print, but also earlier states as well as preparatory drawings, a practice that he thought would be instructional for students and for other print connoisseurs.

In 1935, the Trustees of the Boston Public Library began discussions with Wiggin regarding their interest in the possibility of accepting Wiggin's collection.[3] By June of 1941, discussions were completed, and the collection was formally presented to the Library. Soon after, Arthur W. Heintzelman, an American printmaker with an international reputation as an etcher, was appointed the Library's first Keeper of Prints. The next ten years saw a remarkable collaboration. Heintzelman and Wiggin worked together to expand the collection, with Wiggin funding agreed-upon new acquisitions.

Between 1941 and 1951, through purchase and gift, many important acquisitions were made. The Print Department purchased first editions of Goya's "Los Caprichos" and "Los Disastres de la Guerra," the Maroni Collection of lithographs by Honoré Daumier and by Gavarni, and a major collection of lithographs by Henri Fantin-Latour. The collection of works by American artists was also increased by the donation of Frank W. Benson's own private collection of his prints and the donation of a complete set of prints by Charles H. Woodbury, given by the executors of the Woodbury estate. The American holdings also were increased by the acquisition of works by John W. Winkler, Letterio Calapai, and Asa Cheffetz. It was during this period that the Library's collection of drawings by George Bellows was acquired.

Prior to the presentation of his collection to the Library, Wiggin had acquired impressions of all but one of the lithographs that Bellows produced and four of his drawings. In 1943, through the auspices of H.V. Allison Galleries, the firm that had been responsible for inventorying the Wiggin Collection prior to its being given to the Library, arrangements were made under which Mrs. Bellows donated and Mr. Wiggin purchased a set of drawings from the Bellows estate for the Library. The acquisition of the drawings is yet another example of Wiggin's desire to make his collection, and subsequently that of the Library, instructional. The ability to study the drawings and the related lithographs makes the Library's collection, along with those of the Cleveland Museum of Art and the Amon Carter Museum, one of the three major repositories that scholars and students interested in Bellow's work must visit.

Since Wiggin's death in 1951 the Library's collection of prints and drawings has continued to grow, first under Arthur Heintzelman and then, after Heintzelman's retirement in 1960, under Sinclair Hitchings, who served from 1961 to 2005 as the Library's second Keeper of Prints. However, the primary focus of the collection has remained the same: French, British, and American prints and drawings from the last half of the nineteenth and the first half of the twentieth centuries. Today, visitors to the Print Department study the prints and drawings of George Bellows, as well as compare Bellows' work with that of the etcher and photographer Samuel Chamberlain, the wood engraver Thomas Nason, and the lithographer Stow Wengenroth. The Library also has continued Mr. Wiggin's interest in contemporary artists by developing its Collection of Works on Paper by Living Artists with Ties to Boston. That collection demonstrates that Boston continues to be a vital center of printmaking in all media that commands local, national, and international attention.

Raised in Massachusetts and especially in Boston, Wiggin chose to give his collection to the Boston Public Library as a way of giving something back to his native city. He also chose the Library because he thought it was where his collection would be most accessible to the public. The Library attempts to carry out the goals of access, instruction, and public service through the operation of a Print Study Room, a program of regular exhibitions in the Wiggin Gallery, and through loans to scholarly exhibitions organized by other institutions. We welcome the opportunity provided by the current exhibition and catalogue to look again at our collection of works by George Bellows and thus to gain further insight into Bellows as an artist.

Karen S. Shafts
Assistant to the Keeper of Prints
Boston Public Library

1. For a biography of Albert H. Wiggin, see: Marjorie Wiggin Prescott. *New England Son*. New York: Dodd Mead & Company, 1949.

2. Arthur W. Heintzelman. *The Tenth Anniversary of the Albert H. Wiggin Collection*. Boston: Trustees of the Boston Public Library, 1951, p. 3.

3. *Ibid*., p. 3.

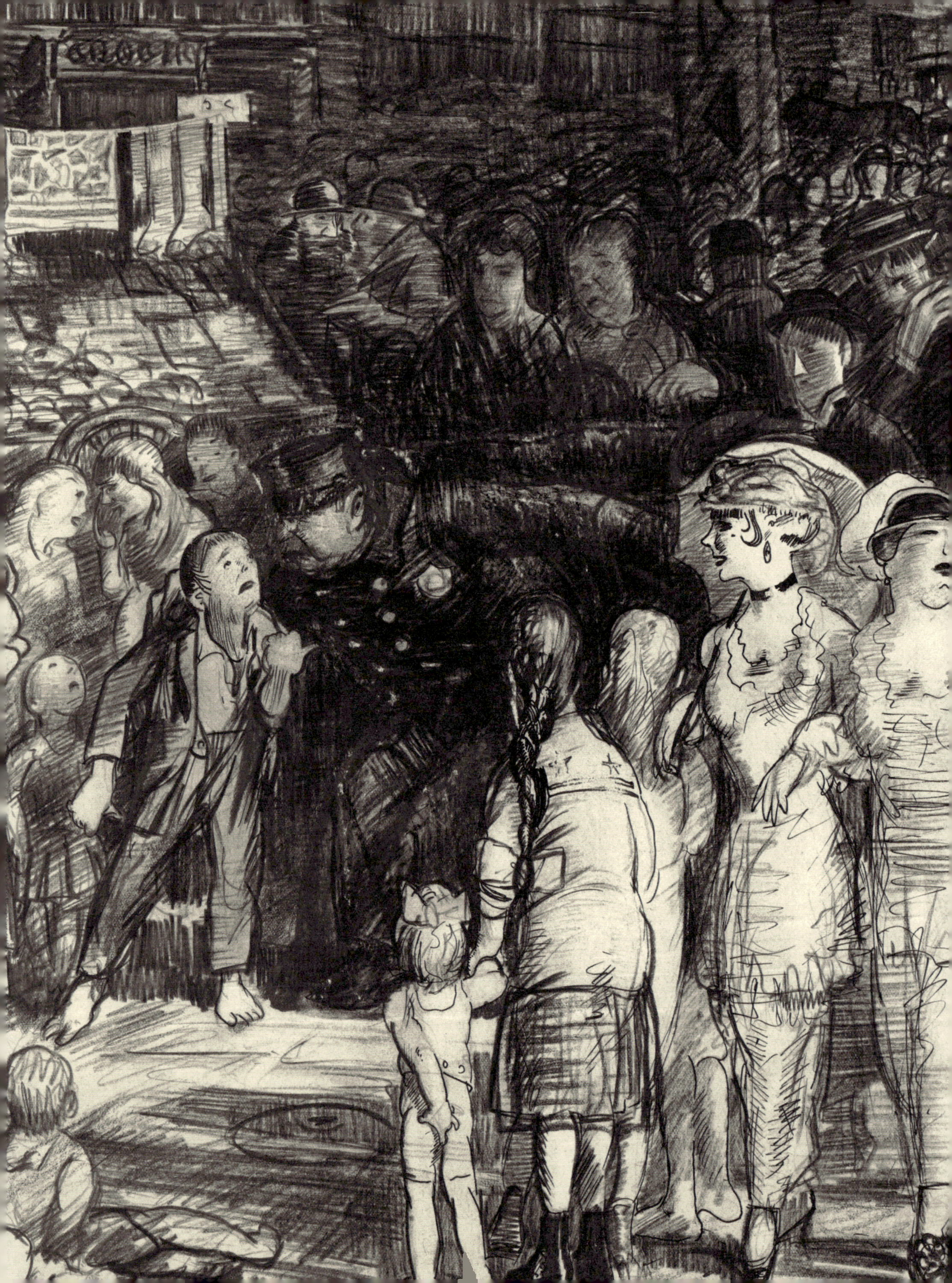

"A DISTINCTION BETWEEN FANCY AND IMAGINATION"

Learning from the Drawings of George Bellows

You must take care to distinguish between what immediately interests you and what sets your imagination to work. It is pretty hard to make a distinction between fancy and imagination, but the sooner you learn to make that distinction the better it will be for you.

- George Bellows writing to a young artist [1]

THE CAREER OF GEORGE BELLOWS is as well-documented as it was meteoric: college drop-out and beginning art student at twenty-two, member of the National Academy at twenty-seven, the country's most accomplished lithographer at thirty-five, and dead of appendicitis at forty-three. During his lifetime, he was given one-artist exhibitions at museums in Chicago, Detroit, Los Angeles, Worcester, Cincinnati, Columbus, Buffalo, and Rochester.[2] Following his premature death and continuing until the present, critics, curators and art historians have directed considerable attention to his life and art, beginning with the memorial exhibition at the Metropolitan Museum of Art in 1925 and its many attendant reviews and tributes in the contemporary press. In no fewer than sixteen major exhibitions between then and 1992, the year of the definitive retrospective organized by the Amon Carter Museum and the Los Angeles County Museum of Art, this country's most important collections of American painting have granted Bellows a place among our most important artists.[3] We have Charles Morgan's anecdotal biography, three catalogues raisonnés of his lithographs and a host of more recent thematic exhibitions and publications.[4] Most recently, H.V. Allison Galleries, the artist's dealer for over eighty years, has completed an on-line, fully searchable catalogue raisonné of his paintings.[5]

The reasons for the attention given to the paintings and lithographs are obvious. An enormously popular and successful painter whose large, engaging personality matched his canvases, Bellows produced hundreds of paintings of consistently

Pinched, 1914, detail, cat. no. 7.

high quality that in subsequent decades his heirs and representatives carefully placed in public collections of all sizes and locations. A pioneer of American lithography, he and his collaborating printers, the best in the business, completed nearly two hundred editions that sold well in his lifetime and have continued to do so ever since. Every important public and private collection of modern American art owns examples of his work, and there is a consistent commercial and curatorial demand for reliable data and fresh insight regarding both the prints and the paintings.

Within this rich body of scholarship there is a noticeable gap: not one exhibition, substantial book or even scholarly essay is dedicated solely to his drawings. Over the years, the drawings have not developed the constituencies that have gathered around both the paintings and the prints. With a few exceptions, they do not directly relate to the paintings. Bellows rarely used drawings in the traditional manner as preliminary studies for finished works,[6] and we are not obliged to consider them when we consider the paintings. Paradoxically, they are very closely related to the prints. As the Wiggin Collection definitively demonstrates, many are the direct sources for lithographs. While many writers have noted the obvious connections between lithographs and drawings, few have moved outside the culture of printmaking to study the drawings in their original contexts, not as preparatory studies but as complete works of art themselves. A shift in perspective is needed to do justice to the drawings. They are not related to the prints as much as the prints are related to them.[7]

DRAWING AND LITHOGRAPHY

Bellows' lithographs connect to his drawings in several ways, all of which are more completely explained in the catalogue's entries. Some pairs of drawings and prints are what we would expect, more-or-less literal transfers of an image from paper onto stone so that it then could be printed in an edition. Whether Bellows made a specific drawing in order to test an idea for an edition before committing it to stone is not always clear. He may have drawn with this purpose in mind, or may have just as easily drawn something that caught his interest and only later decided to turn into a lithograph. In other pairs, the drawing is clearly the original work and the

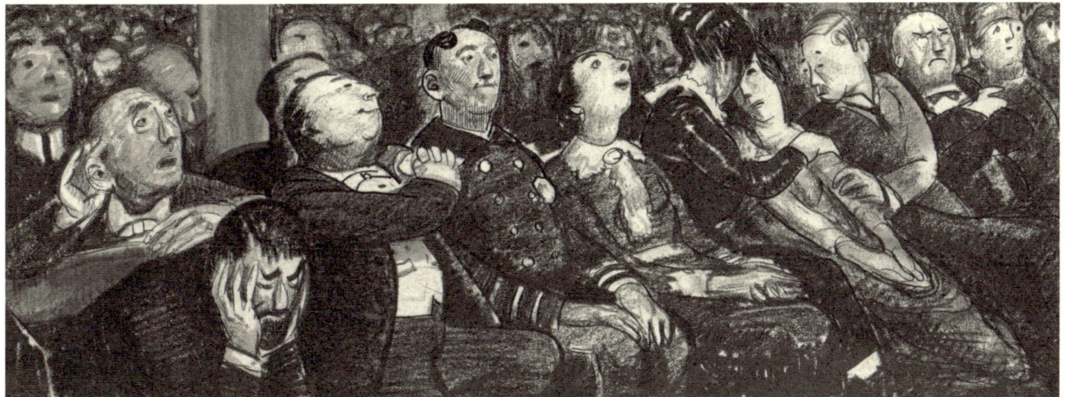

Fig. 1. *Preaching*, 1915, detail, cat. no. 9.

print an afterthought, well-done and justifiably notable in the history of American printmaking but a revision of the original nonetheless. Some of his most popular prints—*Splinter Beach, Business-Men's Class, The Sawdust Trail*—derive from stunning drawings made years earlier, well before Bellows began making lithographs. Only when we see the images alongside each other do we understand how accomplished Bellows was in both media, yet how the later print pales in comparison to its source.[8]

The Wiggin Collection of Bellows drawings was formed to complement the already existing Wiggin Collection of Bellows lithographs at the Boston Public Library. One of only two complete collections of his prints, its importance understandably influenced those involved in the selection and donation of the drawings.[9] From its inception, therefore, the drawings in this collection were chosen for their relationships to the much larger collection of prints and viewed subsequently from this viewpoint. Given this reason for being, the Wiggin Collection predictably contains many crayon drawings, crayon being the artist's medium of choice for drawing both on paper and on litho stones.[10] Fortunately, it contains just enough examples of other media to give us a sense of Bellows' fluency and even virtuosity with graphite, collage, and especially ink and wash. The Collection also favors a certain size and degree of finish: large, complete images most closely resembling the lithographs that followed them. There are relatively few small ink or graphite sketches, the quick records of the artist's ideas in their earliest forms. Although Bellows did not rely on sketches as part of his development of his paintings, he did use them for this purpose with his lithographs, an important choice of method which deserves closer study beyond the limited examples found in the Wiggin Collection.

ILLUSTRATION

A large number of the Wiggin drawings, certainly the most impressive examples, were done by Bellows on commercial assignment. While quickly becoming a celebrated painter, he also pursued a parallel career as a successful illustrator. The combination of the two was a natural one without the stigma we might attach to it today. Prior to coming to New York to study art, Bellows' body of work consisted only of illustrations, facile cartoons done for college yearbooks and fraternity house living rooms. Once in New York, he worked in the company of Robert Henri and his circle of Ashcan realists, older artists who began their careers as newspaper illustrators in Philadelphia and who deliberately bridged what they considered the artificial separation between the concerns of fine art and the subject matter of popular culture. Later in his career, Bellows continued to accept commissions from book publishers for illustrations to short stories and novels. The major venues for his commercial output between 1913 and 1924, for example *The Masses*, *Harper's Weekly*, and *Vanity Fair*, are all represented in the Wiggin Collection. The details of his work for them are contained in individual catalogue entries.

Immersed as we are in mechanical and electronic media, we have to remind ourselves that photography was not always the chosen method of journalistic illustration. When the editors of *Metropolitan Magazine* sent reporter John Reed to Philadelphia in January 1915 to cover the revival meeting of evangelist Billy Sunday, they didn't ask a photographer to go with him. They asked an artist. They didn't choose an artist who specialized in precise illustration, but one best known for his cartoons.[11] Bellows' strength as a commercial illustrator was caricature, ". . . the illusion of life which can do without any illusion of reality. . . ."[12] His best illustrations, those of small groups at the Y.M.C.A. and large ones on the lower East Side, of preachers, boxers and other athletes at work, immediately convince us of their vitality. On closer examination, we notice that there are very few faces in Billy Sunday's audi-

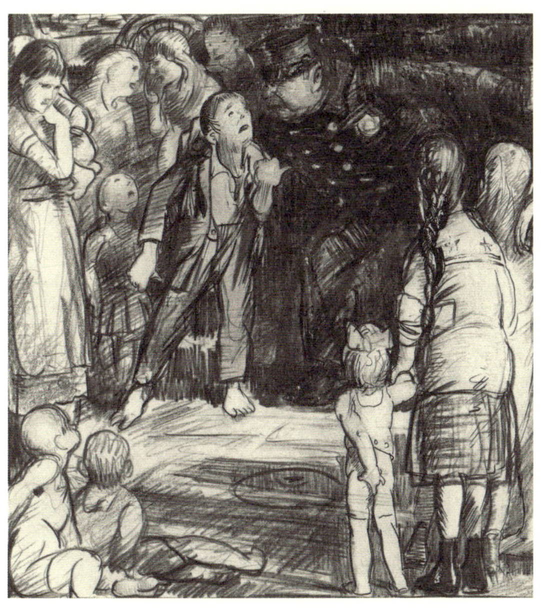

Fig. 2. *Pinched*, 1914, detail, cat. no. 7.

ence that meet any standard of realistic portraiture (Fig. 1). The people in his illustrations are quickly drawn, simplified, mildly exaggerated caricatures.

In his most ambitious illustrations, Bellows built complicated arrangements out of these simplified figures, constructions that successfully evoke emotional validity. They express a good-natured, sympathetic satire coming from an observer who had both a sense of humor and an understanding of the general truths of human interaction operating beneath the specific scenes and actions he recorded or invented. Take the beat cop in *Pinched*, along with the boy he pinched and the little girl in front of them scratching her bottom (Fig. 2). With sure lines and skillful placement, including his handling of the spaces between his characters, Bellows delivers to us the experience of the policeman's scolding, the boy's protestations and the girl's idle curiosity.

Bellows' facility carried a price. His engaging touch of humor kept him skating across the surface of the world he illustrated, only rarely digging into its substance. Even in his drawings of Billy Sunday, for whom he expressed unrestrained antipathy, the passion of these images lies more in Sunday's spellbinding performance than in the viewpoint of the artist. Unlike Goya, Hogarth and Daumier, his distinguished predecessors, Bellows did not invest his satirical illustrations with the strength of his convictions. He kept his distance. He was not one of them, nor did he pour much of himself into their lives. He existed in a separate stratum of society, from which he observed and recorded with expert artistry but without deep commitment.[13]

Within the Wiggin Collection there are examples of the two notable, even profound exceptions to this lack of connection: images of his family and friends, and his depictions of the atrocities visited upon Belgian citizens during the German invasion of 1914. In the former category we lack any of the very moving portraits of his two daughters, in which his great affection and insight are clear for all to see. We do have, however, a quietly touching image of his wife sewing (Fig. 3), a pair of sketches of Elsie Speicher, the wife of his best friend and fellow artist Eugene Speicher, for whom his younger daughter Jean was named, and an antiquated portrait of Auntie Mason and her husband. Even in this last image, which appears to have been taken from an old family daguerreotype, Bellows established a connection with his subjects missing from his images of city life.

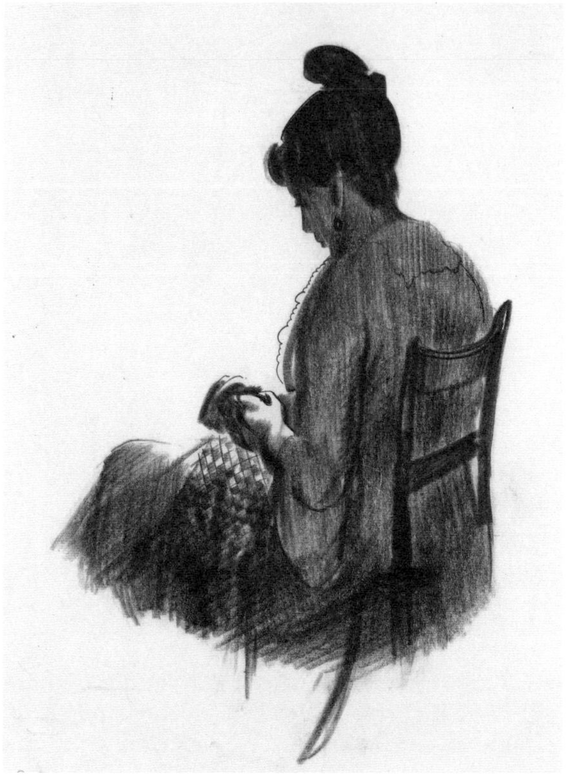

Fig. 3. *Girl Sewing*, 1923, cat. no. 40.

In the latter category we have three tough pictures: *The Barricade*, *The Last Victim* and *Return of the Useless*. In them, as in many of the illustrations of the Great War published in 1918, Bellows let loose with unrestrained outrage and condemnation. The results are problematic. If we view them in the context of our own responses to the horrors of our own wars, we find a common spirit. If we judge them for their success as works of art, we may question the wisdom of Bellows' aesthetic decisions as numerous critics have, generally taking the position that an artist in an emotional state is not fully in control of his creative faculties. Judging from the images themselves, this dichotomy does not seem relevant. The content of the most brutal scenes may be disturbing, but what bothers our eyes is not their strength. It is their peculiar composition, the artificial, overly dramatic arrangement of the characters and their awkwardly placed and elongated limbs (Fig. 4). The oddities of these scenes have little to do with their content and the artist's emotional commitment to it, and much to do with his recent affinity for a particular compositional theory.

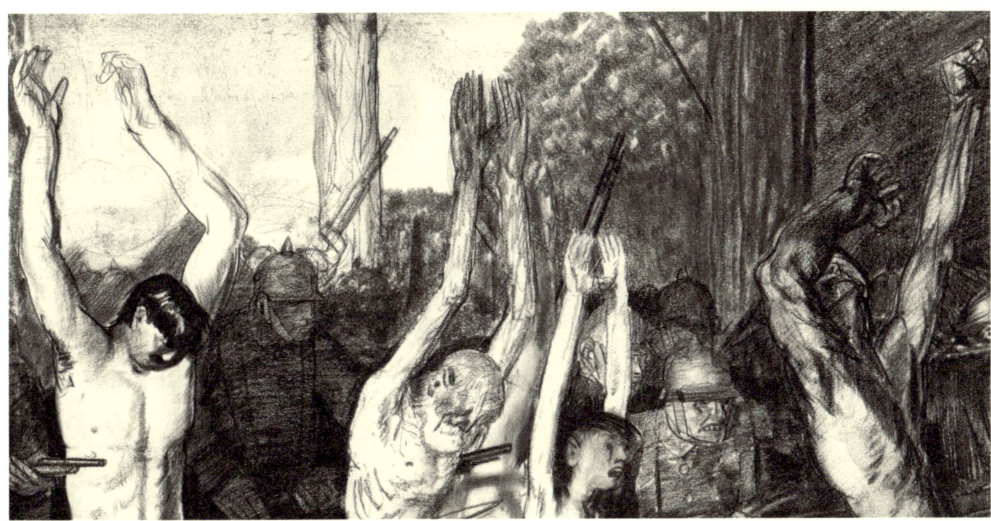

Fig. 4. *The Barricade*, 1918, detail, cat. no. 19.

COMPOSITION

Bellows encountered Dynamic Symmetry and its creator, the classical archaeologist Jay Hambidge, toward the end of 1917. He used it steadily though not exclusively until his death in 1925. The war images of 1918 are among the first to be based on the system's numerous ratios between the shorter and longer sides of a rectangle that generate vertical, horizontal and diagonal lines and their many points of intersection. These lines and points serve the artist as guides to establishing his composition.

Bellows' emphatic opinions about Dynamic Symmetry can be found in several published articles, including a 1920 interview in *The American Architect*:

> Hambidge has shown me a great many things that are profoundly true. . . . Ever since I met Mr. Hambidge and studied with him I have painted very few pictures without at the same time working on his theory. I believe it to be as profound as the law of the lever or the law of gravitation.[14]

Eugene Speicher saw his friend's use of the system differently:

> George had a natural feeling for a lively and well-conceived composition. It is therefore rather surprising that he should have been taken in by the mechanical and uninspiring system of Jay Hambidge. Fortunately for George, his style was

> already well matured by the close of the war, when he met Hambidge. While he thereafter made elaborately rectangle and diagonaled designs for many of his more serious paintings, he actually used these designs as a springboard for a creative effect. A few of his works . . . are dynamically symmetrical to a somewhat painful degree, but he rarely allowed the system to over-assert itself.[15]

The disparity that Spiecher identified between Bellows' natural talent and his use of a mechanical system went unresolved for decades, although many critics and curators put forth possible explanations. In 1946, writing about his museum's retrospective exhibition, Daniel Catton Rich, director of the Art Institute of Chicago, sympathetically suggested a motivation for Bellows' susceptibility to theory:

> Why, with such remarkable gifts, did Bellows slowly but unmistakably surrender a number of them and become a self-conscious stylist? The answer is not only to be found in his ambition (no one was more ambitious) but in his response to the revolutionary doctrines exposed in the Armory Show. Much has been written of the public's amazement at this revelation of advanced European art, but how did the artist feel?
>
> How did a man like Bellows, brought up on what he believed to be the most advanced tendency of his day, self-expression applied to the problems of contemporary life, react when suddenly confronted with the fauvism of Matisse and Rouault, the cubism of Picasso and Braque? We can imagine the bewilderment, self-questioning, the determination not to be swept off one's feet. . . . So we find Bellows turning away from the organic vigor of his early work and seeking theories and formulas which would resolve the conflict.[16]

Rich's connection of Bellows' attraction to theory with a presumed crisis of confidence laid the foundation for later critical opinion, a conjunction of history, psychology and the equation of modernism with progress that was soon regarded as fact.[17] Whether or not Bellows was flummoxed by the Armory Show—anecdotal accounts suggest he wasn't—our task is to determine whether the evidence at hand, the Wiggin drawings, supports a connection between the events of 1913 and his use of geometrical frameworks. In doing so, we are following the lead of Michael Quick, whose essay on technique and theory in the 1992 Fort Worth / Los Angeles catalogue challenged sixty years of critical misunderstanding.[18]

In his examination of paintings from beginning to end of Bellows' career, Quick identified the use of four different compositional systems: rebatement, the

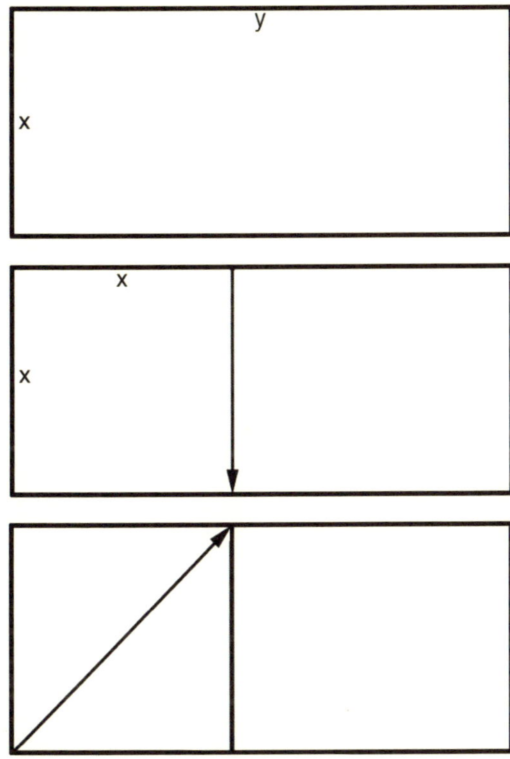

Fig. 5. Constructing vertical and diagonal lines by means of Rebatement.

golden section, the Maratta system and Dynamic Symmetry. The Maratta system was based on an internal web of equilateral triangles.[19] The other three all involve the subdivision of the rectangular field of the work of art according to the relationship between its shorter and longer sides. Rebatement, the simplest of these, creates a square within a rectangle whose sides are equal to the shorter side of the rectangle, and then extends a diagonal across this square (Fig. 5). Quick found evidence of this system in paintings dating as early as 1909.

The golden section is a more sophisticated version of rebatement that subdivides the sides of a rectangle based on the ratio of 1:1.618. A golden rectangle is one whose sides already have this ratio. Bellows did not construct canvases with these proportions, but Quick found that he did subdivide them using this ratio between 1912 and 1916. After establishing two points on all four sides, Bellows would further divide the sides in half and calculate the ratio on these halves, ending up with seven points from which to connect vertical, horizontal and diagonal lines (Fig. 6).

Dynamic Symmetry is the most complex of the three and yielded for Bellows the most stilted results. It involves the subdivision of the sides of a rectangle according to several set ratios, the square roots of 2, 3, 5 and the golden section. It appears in Bellows' paintings after the fall of 1917. Dynamic Symmetry is too complicated to summarize in a few diagrams. The one shown here is taken from Bellows' schema for his 1920 group portrait of his aunt, daughter and mother, *Elinor, Jean and Anna*, as published in Hambidge's 1923 survey of how various artists applied his system, *Dynamic Symmetry in Compostion* (Fig. 7).[20]

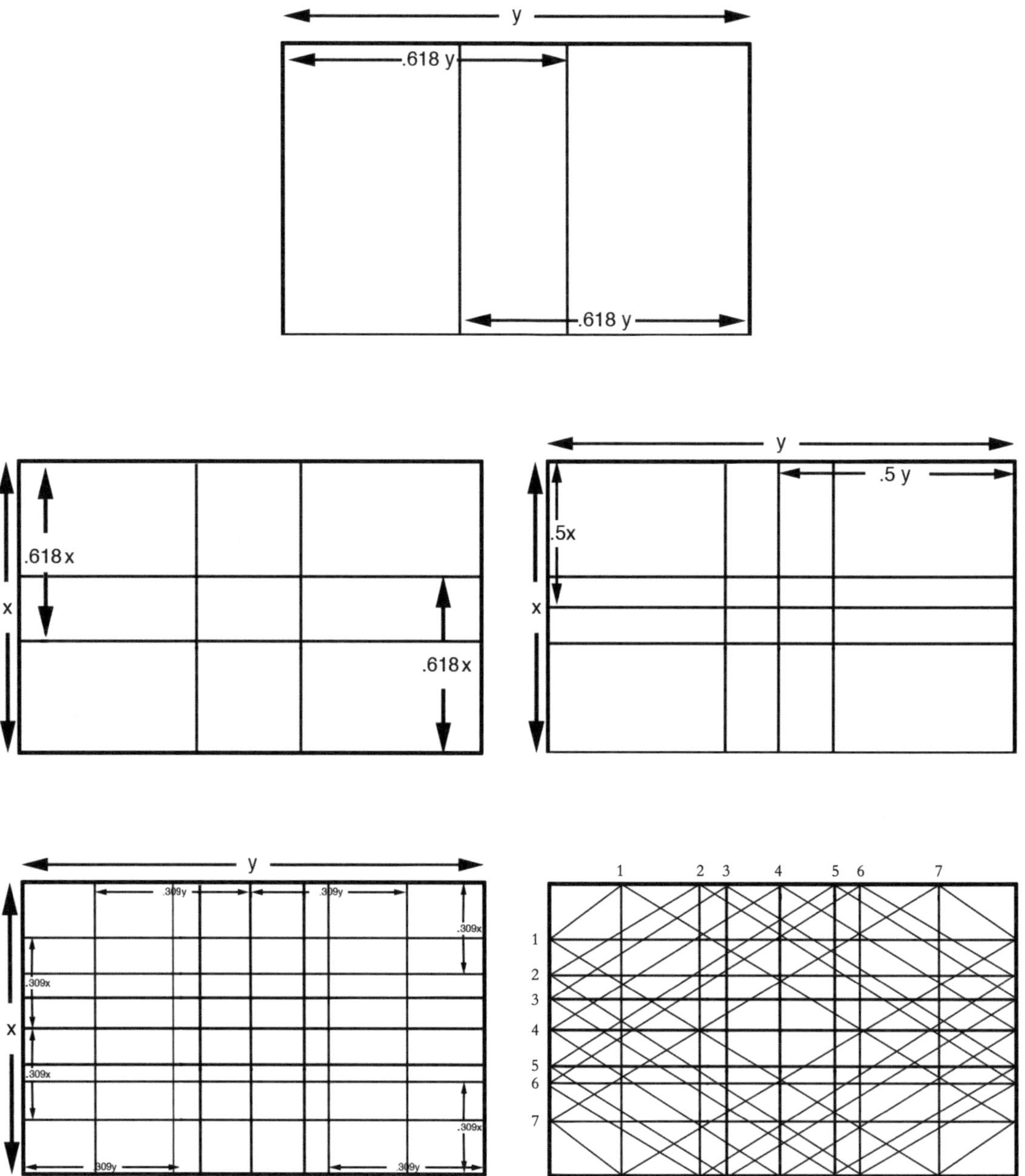

Fig. 6. Constructing vertical and diagonal lines by means of the Golden Section.

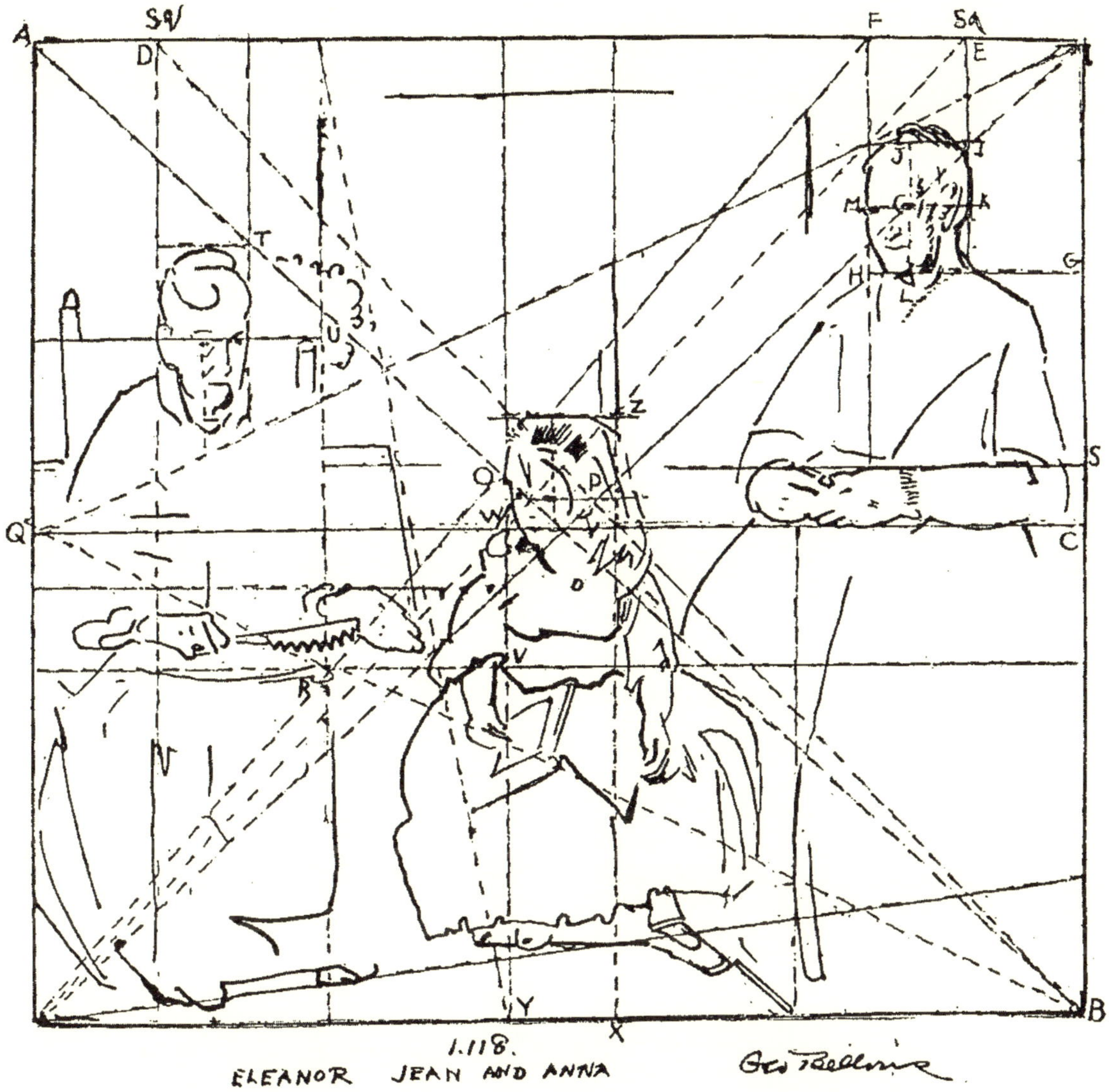

Fig. 7. Schematic of Elinor, Jean and Anna According to Dynamic Symmetry.

Quick does not dispute directly the inference that Bellows embraced Dynamic Symmetry as an alternative to the challenges of European modernism. He simply demonstrates that the artist knew and used similar systems well before the Armory Show and that his affinity for theories had no causal link to the events of 1913. Analysis of the drawings in the Wiggin Collection supports his findings with a surprising degree of clarity and consistency.

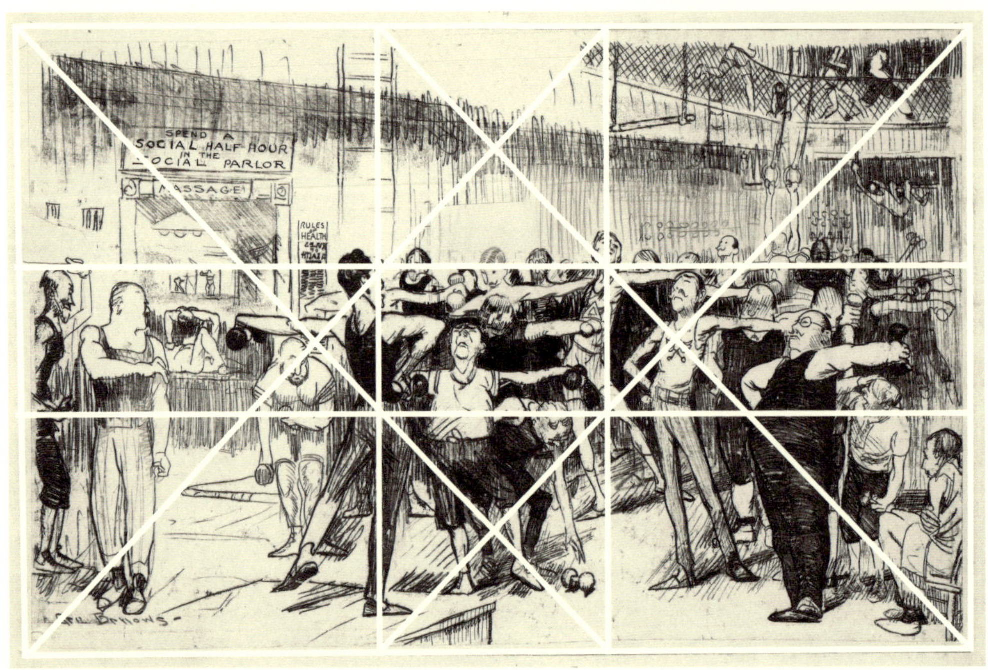

Fig. 8. *Business Men's Class*, 1913, cat. no. 3.

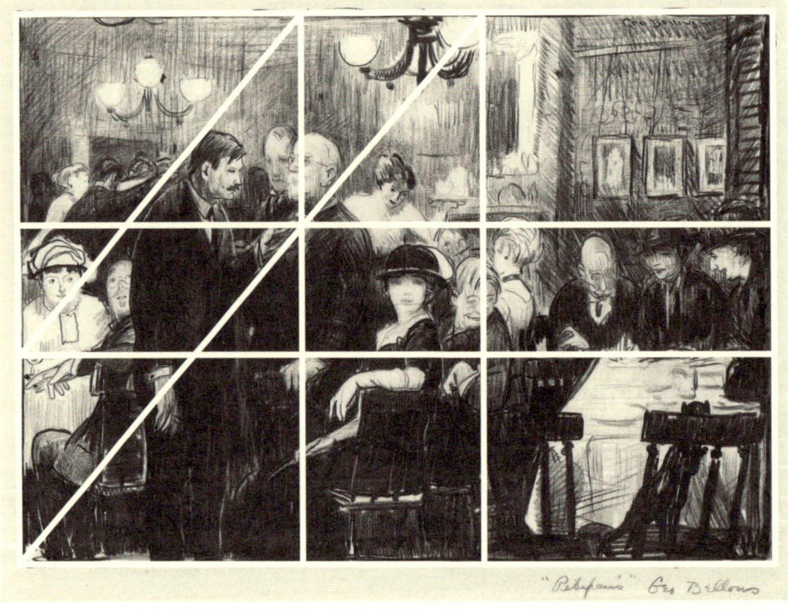

Fig. 9. *Night at Petitpas*, 1914, cat. no. 6.

There is in the Wiggin Collection a core of master drawings done between 1912 and 1916, eight large, highly finished sheets, some of which were published in contemporary journals and all of which the artist later selected as models for lithographs:

1912 - *Splinter Beach*
1913 - *Business Men's Class*; *The Strugglers*
1914 - *Petitpas'*; *Pinched*
1915 - *Billy Sunday*; *Preaching*
1916 - *Preliminaries*

The horizontal compositions of all eight are based upon the golden section. One, *Business Men's Class*, approximates a golden rectangle. Two others, *Preaching* and *Preliminaries*, contain golden rectangles. The rest all conform to the subdivision of their sides according to the ratio of 1:1.618. As seen in diagrams for four of these drawings, Bellows anchored the important elements of his compositions to lines generated by golden section segments.

He divided his pictorial space according to the golden section. In the Y.M.C.A gym, the businessmen are below the line and the walls and track above (Fig. 8). In the French restaurant, the area between the two horizontal lines holds the faces of all the seated figures, above them the faces of all those standing. Emma Bellows looks at us from dead center (Fig. 9). In the cavernous space of Madison Square Garden, all the standing figures cluster to the right of a vertical, all the seated figures below a horizontal (Fig. 10). Within these spatial divisions, he aligned his important figures along verticals dropped from points across the top edge: the calisthenics leader in *Business Men's Class*, the artist John Butler Yeats in *Petitpas'*, the leading lady in *Preliminaries*. In *Preaching*, Billy Sunday projects his message from his pulpit into the audience along a spiral generated by successive golden rectangles (Fig. 11).[21]

In every case, the geometry of the composition does not intrude upon our experience of the image. There is nothing artificial about these scenes to suggest a system underlying them. It appears as if Bellows had internalized these proportions and didn't need to plot them before composing his images. Consider *Prayer Meeting*, 1913, one of the few compositional preparatory sketches in the Wiggin Collection, probably drawn on site in a little church on Monhegan Island. In it Bellows organized his space just as he did in *Business Men's Class* and *Petitpas* (Fig. 12).

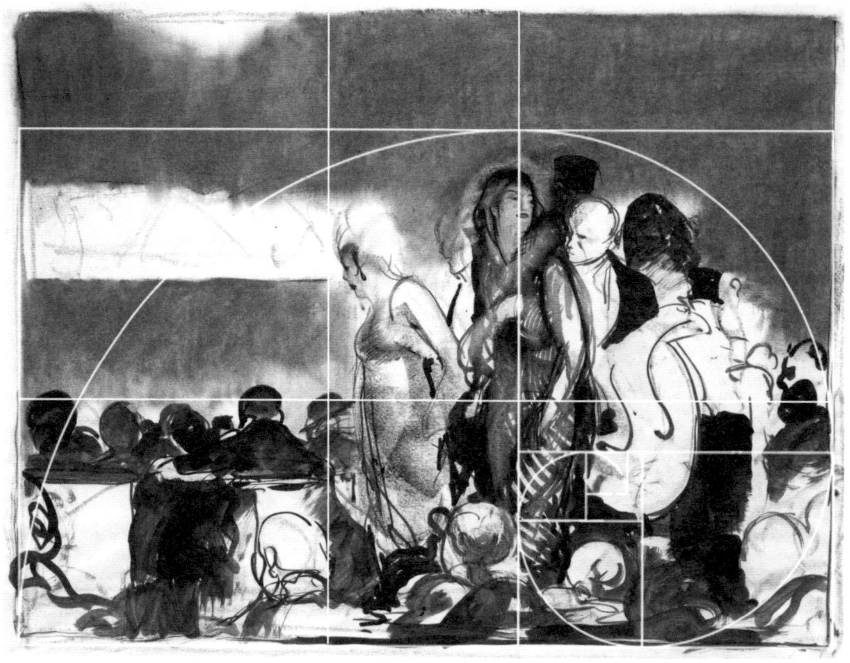

Fig. 10. *Preliminaries*, 1916, cat. no. 13.

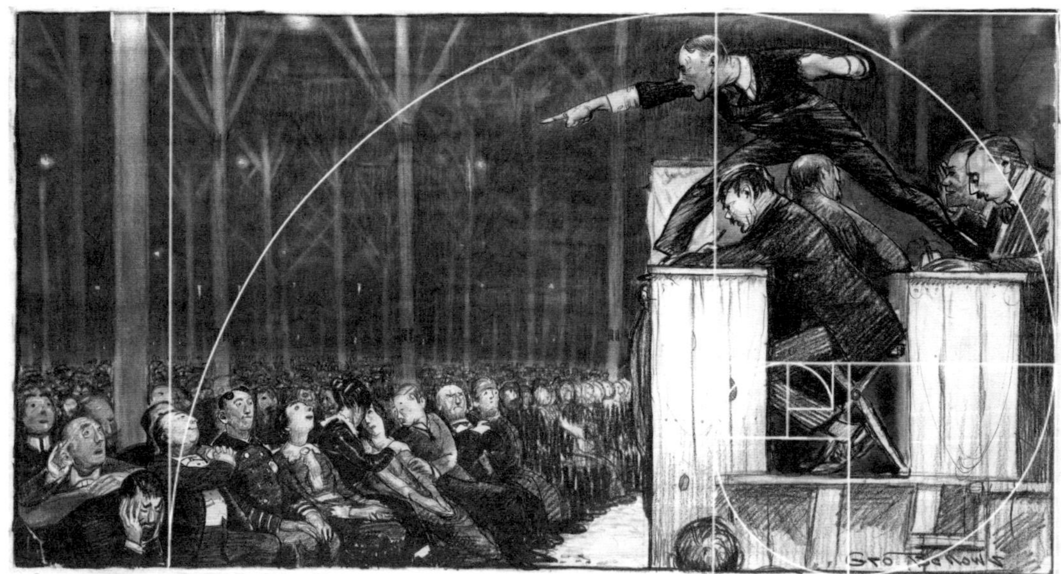

Fig. 11. *Preaching*, 1915, cat. no. 9.

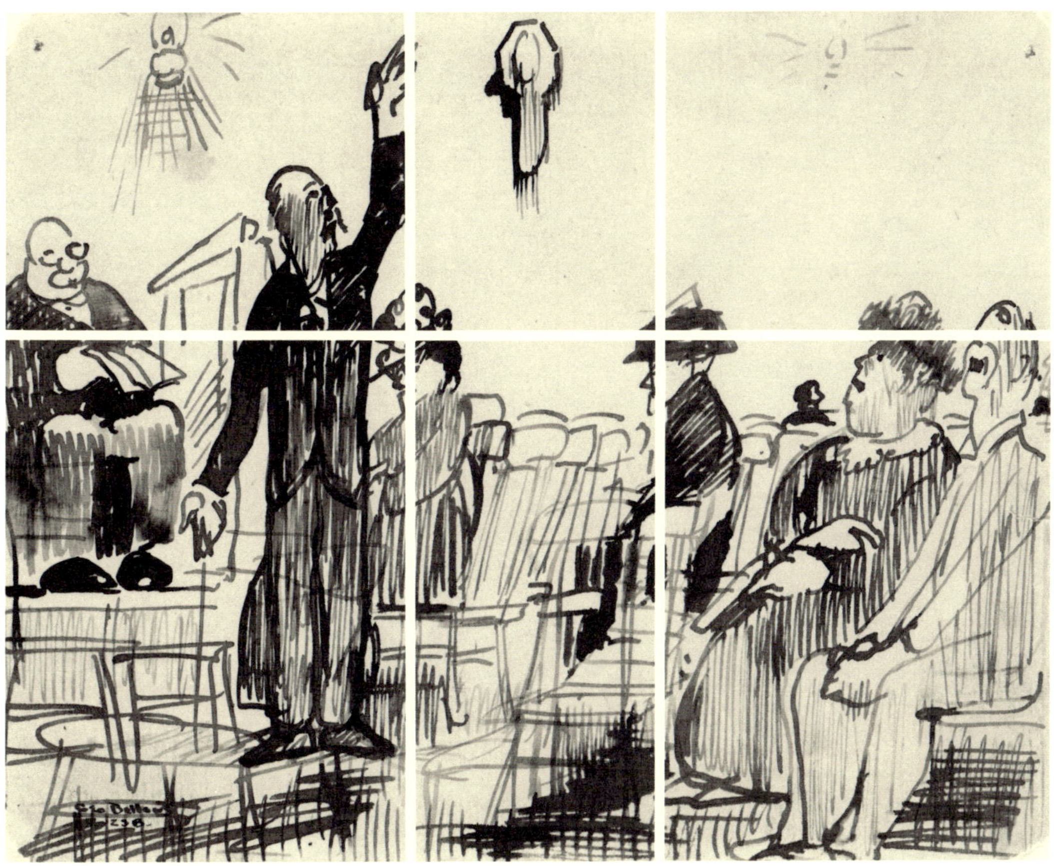

Fig. 12. *Prayer Meeting*, 1913, cat. no. 5.

In his drawings through 1916, Bellows struck a perfect balance of planning and spontaneity. After his encounter with Hambidge in 1917, he occasionally lost this balance. One of the most egregious examples in the Wiggin Collection is *The Battle*, an illustration commissioned by *Hearst's International Magazine* in 1923 to illustrate H. G. Wells' novel, *Men Like Gods* (Fig. 13).

Examples of distended limbs and awkward angles can be found in other illustrations from *Men Like Gods* as well as in the earlier drawings from the *War Series* of 1918 mentioned above. On the other hand, we have enough examples of his "natural feeling for a lively and well-conceived composition" after 1917—*The Beach*, 1919, *Introducing Georges Carpentier*, 1921, *The Law Is Too Slow*, 1923—to rule out any

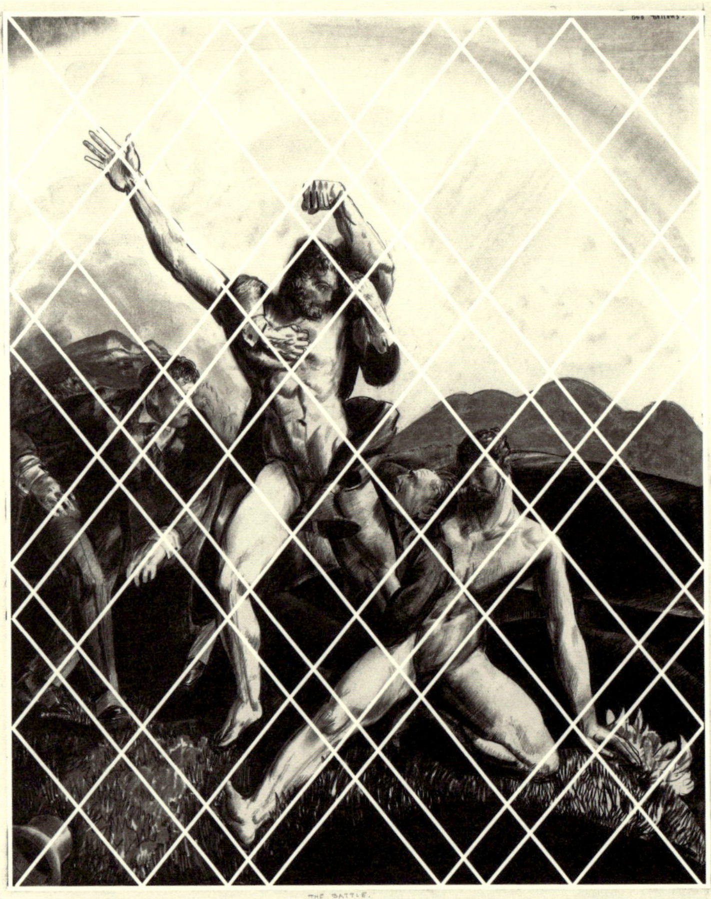

Fig. 13. *The Battle*, 1923, cat. no. 36.

generalizations about Bellows permanently succumbing to some crack-pot theory. Judging from the limited sampling offered by the Wiggin Collection, we might propose the opposite. Despite some flirtation with an extreme example of compositional theory after 1917, Bellows reasserted his own habits of ordered composition: a loose division of space according to the golden section (Fig. 14) or an even simpler scheme dividing his vertical and horizontal dimensions in halves and quarters (Fig. 15). Although even the master himself struggled with the distinction between fancy and imagination, he never lost his instinct for the right choice.

ROBERT CONWAY

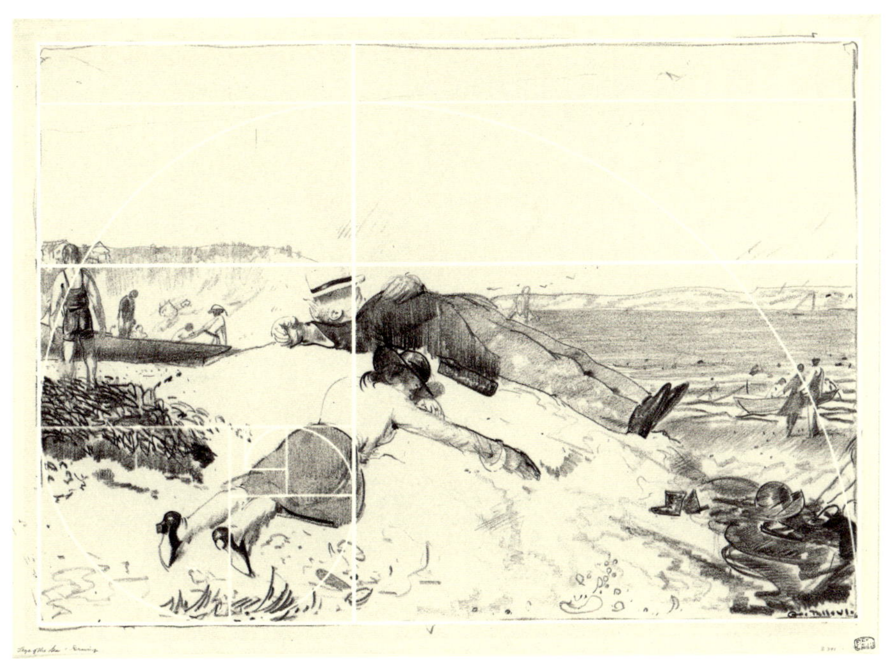

Fig. 14. *The Beach*, 1919, cat. no. 23.

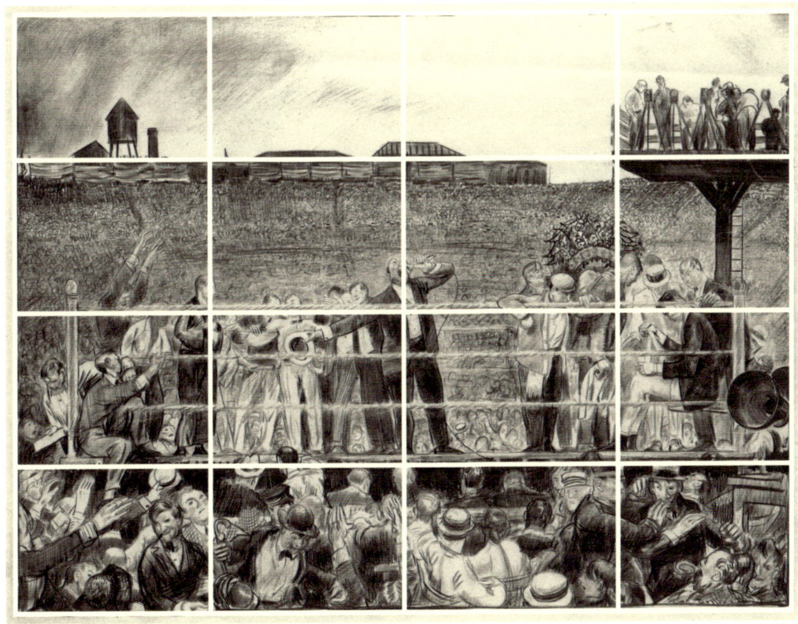

Fig. 15. *Introducing Georges Carpentier*, 1921, cat. no. 29.

ESSAY NOTES

1. George Bellows "in a letter to a young artist," quoted in Thomas Beer and Emma S. Bellows, *George W. Bellows: His Lithographs*, New York, 1927, 22.

2. For details of these exhibitions, see Trinket Clark, "Chronology," in E. A. Carmean, Jr., John Wilmerding, Linda Ayres and Deborah Chotner, *Bellows The Boxing Pictures*, National Gallery of Art, Washington, 1982, 101–106.

3. Memorial exhibitions were held in New York, Worcester and Rochester in 1925, in Buffalo, Cleveland and San Diego in 1926, and in St. Louis in 1927. The Columbus Gallery of Fine Arts produced four major exhibitions in the artist's hometown in 1931, 1940, 1957 and 1979. Other retrospectives include those at The Art Institute of Chicago, 1946, the National Gallery of Art in 1957 and the Gallery of Modern Art, New York, in 1966. See Clark, 106–108.

4. Charles H. Morgan, *George Bellows Painter of America*, New York: 1965. The three catalogues of lithographs are: Thomas Beer and Emma S. Bellows, *George W. Bellows: His Lithographs*, New York, 1927, Lauris Mason, *The Lithographs of George Bellows A Catalogue Raisonné*, San Francisco, 1977, and Jane Myers and Linda Ayres, *George Bellows, The Artist and His Lithographs 1916–1924*, Amon Carter Museum, 1988. Thematic studies include *Bellows The Boxing Pictures* cited above, and Rebecca Zurier, *Art for the Masses (1911–1917): A Radical Magazine and its Graphics*, Yale University Art Gallery, 1985, Marianne Doezma, *George Bellows and Urban America*, Yale University Press, 1992, Rebecca Zurier, Robert W. Snyder and Virginia Mecklenburg, *Metropolitan Lives The Ashcan Artists and Their New York*, National Museum of American Art, 1996, David Setford and John Wilmerding, *George Bellows: Love of Winter*, Norton Museum of Art, 1997, and Marjorie B. Searl and Ronald Netsky, *Leaving for the Country / George Bellows at Woodstock*, Memorial Art Gallery of the University of Rochester, 2003.

5. H. V. Allison & Co., George Bellows' Catalogue Raisonné, http://hvallison.com/home.aspx

6. Bellows' mentor Robert Henri advocated direct painting, without the traditional use of preliminary drawings. See Frederick Sweet, "Bellows: Twenty-three Years after Dempsey and Firpo," *Artnews*, 44, 19 (January 15–31, 1946), 13.

7. See George Eggers, *George Bellows*, American Artists Series, New York: Whitney Museum of American Art, 1931, 12 for one of the few assessments of the importance of drawings to Bellows and their primacy vis-à-vis the lithographs.

8. Carl O. Schniewind referred to the lithographs taken from drawings as "afterthoughts to powerful, origial compositions which have preceded them." See his essay in Art Institute of Chicago, *George Bellows / Paintings, Drawings and Prints*, January 31 – March 10, 1946, 13.

9. The principals involved were the artist's widow, Emma Bellows, the dealer Gordon Allison, the collector Albert Wiggin, and the curator Arthur Heintzelman.

10. Bellows may have started using litho crayon before 1910, although he didn't start drawing on litho stones until 1916. See Mason, 11.

11. Rebecca Zurier has established connections between Bellows' cartoons and contemporary comics. See "Hey Kids: Children in the Comics and the Art of George Bellows," *Print Collector's Newsletter*, 18, 6 (January – February 1988): 196.

12. Ernst Gombrich, *Art and Illusion*, New York, 1961, 336.

13. John Wilmerding described Bellows as having ". . . the flexibility to be social observer, journalist and occasional critic." See "The Art of George Bellows and the Energies of Modern America," his

introduction to Michael Quick, Jane Myers, Marianne Doezema and Franklin Kelly, *The Paintings of George Bellows*, Amon Carter Museum and Los Angeles County Museum of Art, 1992, 1. Milton Brown considered this approach to be journalism but not art. See *American Painting, from the Armory Show to the Depression*, New York, 1970, 21–22.

14. George Bellows, "The Relation of Painting to Architecture," *The American Architect*, 118, 2349 (December 29, 1920): 851.

15. Eugene Spiecher, personal reminiscence recorded in F. Seiberling Jr., "George Bellows, 1882 – 1925 / His Life and Development as an Artist," Ph.D. dissertation, The University of Chicago, 1948, 218.

16. Daniel Catton Rich, "Bellows Revalued," *Magazine of Art*, 39 (April, 1946): 140–41.

17. See Milton Brown, "Twentieth-Century Nostrums: Pseudo-Scientific Theory in American Painting," *Magazine of Art*, 41, 3 (March, 1948): 98, introductory essays by Lee Malone and Philip R. Adams in Columbus Museum of Art, *George Wesley Bellows, Paintings, Drawings and Prints*, 1979, and Suzanne Boorsch, "The lithographs of George Bellows," *Artnews*, 75, 3 (March 1976): 60.

18. Michael Quick, "Technique and Theory: The Evolution of George Bellows's Painting Style," in Quick, Myers, Doezema and Kelly, 9–95.

19. Robert Henri began studying color and compositional theory with Hardesty Maratta in 1910, and was most likely the source of Bellows' involvement. I have not yet found convincing evidence of Bellows' using the Maratta compositional system in the Wiggin drawings. See William Innes Homer, *Robert Henri and His Circle*, Ithaca: Cornell University Press, 1969, 184.

20. Jay Hambidge, *Dynamic Symmetry in Composition as Used by Artists*, New York, 1923, 24.

21. There is no evidence that Bellows constructed this spiral. I include it because the correspondence between its curve and the preacher's dramatic pose is too intriguing to ignore. However, we know that Robert Henri wrote an unpublished manuscript on Dynamic Symmetry after 1917 in which he presented a "whirling square" based on the golden section ratio. See Homer, 192.

This device may generate a spiral curve like that I have superimposed on *Preaching* and *The Beach*. The overlapping geometries of rebatement, the golden section and Dynamic Symmetry, the shared interest about compositional theory among members of Henri's circle, and the chronology of who used what when require further examination.

CATALOGUE OF THE EXHIBITION

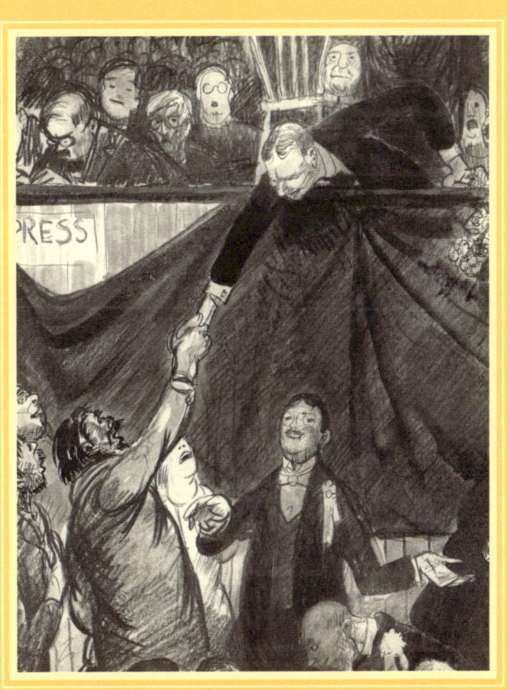

INTRODUCTORY NOTES TO THE CATALOGUE

CATALOGUE NUMBER AND DATE

The drawings are listed in chronological order, as best as can be determined from existing records and inscriptions. In cases where there is not enough information to specify a month and year, dating is established by stylistic comparisons to other drawings and to related lithographs.

TITLE

Titles used are, whenever possible, those given by the artist, either in his Record Books or as inscribed on the drawing itself. In the years between their creation and their sale, some of the drawings were given the same title as their corresponding lithographs. When this is significantly different than the original title, it is included in parentheses. Other titles, either alternate titles given by the artist or captions from published versions, are also noted.

MEDIA

A work's media are described in order of most used. Type of paper and watermark, when present, are included.

DIMENSIONS

Measurements are taken for both image and sheet size, height preceding width, in both inches and millimeters.

SIGNATURE

Where available, information regarding signature, title, date and other annotations is included. Collector's marks are noted.

REFERENCE NUMBERS

Bellows Record Book: Bellows interspersed entries for some of the drawings in his record books of his paintings. There are three volumes (A, B and C); each page is numbered; many but not all of the entries are numbered.

Weinhardt: Carl Weinhardt, an intern at the Boston Public Library in 1973, compiled a handwritten, unpublished checklist for the collection, *The Drawings of George Bellows in the Boston Public Library*.

Boston Public Library: the Library's accession number.

Bellows: the first catalogue raisonné of the lithographs—Thomas Beer and Emma S. Bellows, *George W. Bellows: His Lithographs*, New York: Alfred A. Knopf, 1927.

Mason: the revised edition of the second catalogue raisonné of the lithographs—Lauris Mason, *The Lithographs of George Bellows A Catalogue Raisonné*, revised edition, San Francisco: Alan Wofsy Fine Arts, 1992.

Myers & Ayres: the third catalogue raisonné of the lithographs—Jane Myers and Linda Ayres, *George Bellows, The Artist and His Lithographs 1916–1924*, Amon Carter Museum, 1988.

WORKS INCLUDED IN THE EXHIBITION

Forty-three of the forty-eight sheets in the Wiggin Collection and described in this catalogue are included in the exhibition. The following five, all from 1923–24 are not:

38. *Nude Child, c. 1923*
42. *Auntie Mason and her Husband, c. 1923*
43. *Study of Mary, 1923*
44. *Study of Mary, 1923*
48. *Study of a Girl (Miss Tate), 1924*

Forty-six of the drawings are related to lithographs. Fourteen of these prints, all from the collection of the Boston Public Library, are included in the exhibition alongside the relevant drawings:

3. *Business-Men's Class*, 1916, M.20
5. *Prayer Meeting, First Stone*, 1916, M.13
11. *Standing Nude Bending*, 1916, M.4 iii
13. *Prelininaries to the Big Bout*, 1916, M.24
15. *Two Girls*, 1916, M.41
16. *The White Hope*, 1921, M.96
21. *Hail to Peace*, 1918, M.68
22–23. *Legs of the Sea*, 1921, M.85
24–25. *Bathing Beach*, 1921, M.86
26. *Indoor Athlete, First Stone*, 1921, M.81
30–31. *Elsie Emma and Marjorie*, 1921, M.103
32. *The Irish Fair*, 1922, M.153
33–34. *Punchinello in the House of Death*, 1922, M.151
39. *The Law Is Too Slow*, 1923, M.147

PAGE 41: *Billy Sunday and the Sawdust Trail*, 1915, detail, cat. no. 8.

1. DOGS, EARLY MORNING (Hungry Dogs)

Spring 1907. Graphite, pen and ink and crayon on heavy weight cream wove paper, spray varnished, 13 5/16 x 9 7/8 in., 338 x 250 mm (image and sheet). Signed in ink in the lower left corner of the sheet: *Geo Bellows—.*

Bellows Record Book A, p. 34, no. 40, described by the artist as *Dogs nosing in rubbish in a deserted street.* Weinhardt 18, Boston Public Library 1943.1.10. Published as *A New York Street Before Dawn* in *Harper's Weekly*, September 6, 1913, 21.

SOURCE FOR: *Hungry Dogs*, 1916. Lithograph, 13 1/8 x 9 13/16 in., 333 x 250 mm. Bellows 98, Mason 1. Described by the artist as *Early morning factory district, New York. The first lithograph made by George Bellows. From an early drawing.*[1]

Sold by H. V. Allison Galleries to A. H. Wiggin, June 1943, as *Hungry Dogs.*

Dogs, Early Morning is one of four drawings Bellows submitted to the Independent Artist Exhibition organized in 1910 by his mentor and close friend, Robert Henri. Reacting against what they considered conservative and exclusionary decisions made by the National Academy of Design for its semi-annual exhibition, Henri, Bellows, John Sloan, Walt Kuhn and others established a policy of no jury and no rejections. Each entering artist made his or her own decisions as to what would be included. The resulting show of over six hundred entries attracted thousands of visitors and generally favorable press. A contemporary editorial in *The Nation* declared:

> *For sheer drastic character, Jerome Myer's and George Bellows's slum sketches are extraordinary. Mr. Bellows, in fact, forces expression to the danger point.*[2]

Bellows' expressive imagery was a source for the label "Ash Can School" given to him and other artists of Henri's circle then working in the New York realist style. The specific association in print between them and ash cans came six years later, in 1916, in reference to their work for *The Masses*, a progressive journal to which Bellows and many of his colleagues were contributors.[3]

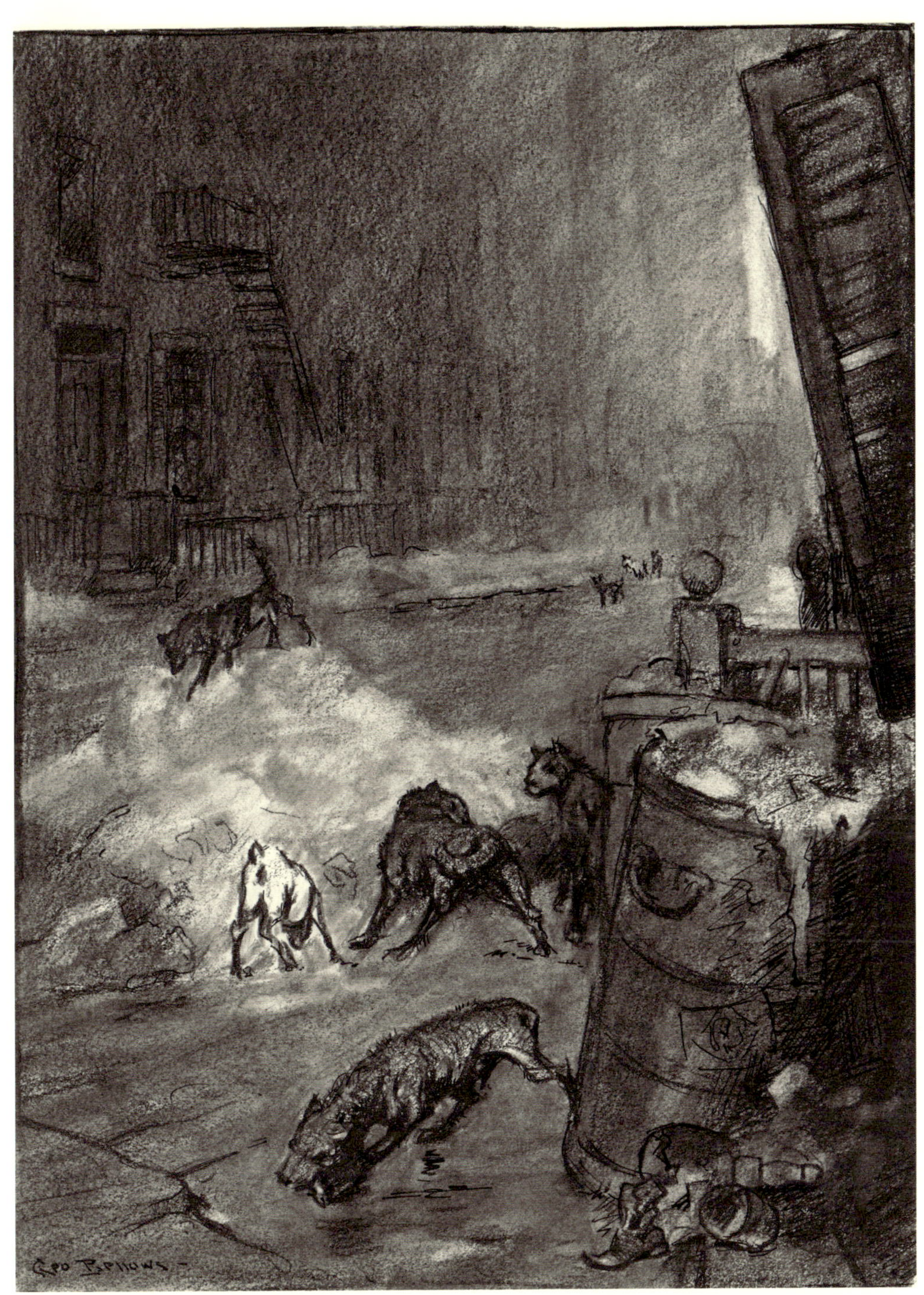
Geo Bellows

2. SPLINTER BEACH

February 1912. Crayon, pen and ink, brush and ink wash, with graphite underdrawing and ruling, and scratchwork on cream colored, smooth surfaced, medium weight paper, 16¾ x 22¾ in., 427 x 576 mm (image); 21 ⅝ x 27 1/16 in., 550 x 689 mm (sheet). Signed in ink in the lower left corner of the image: *Geo Bellows –*. Collector's mark: BPL/MB black ink stamp in lower right corner.

Record Book A, p. 132, no. 161, given by the artist the additional title *Wharf Rats*.[4] W.41, BPL 1942.1.1. A very similar drawing, also titled *Splinter Beach*, was drawn sixteen months later in reverse to the Wiggin image (Record Book A, p. 160, no. 206, June 1913), and was published in *The Masses*, July 1913, 10–11.[5]

SOURCE FOR: *Splinter Beach*, 1916. Lithograph, 14⅞ x 19⅝ in., 378 x 500 mm. B.63, M.28, Myers & Ayres 14. Described by the artist as *Bathing urchins under the Brooklyn Bridge. An open Brooklyn Public Dock from which many artists have gathered material for pictures.*

Sold by H. V. Allison Galleries to A. H. Wiggin, April 1942.

In this large, richly drawn sheet Bellows demonstrates both his fluency with a complex mixture of media and his sympathetic representation of city life that made him so popular in his own lifetime.

The dramatic background of a tugboat passing under a bridge comes almost verbatim, although drastically reduced in scale, from his 1911 painting, *Snow Dumpers*, now in the Columbus Museum of Art. A similar combination of boat and bridge can be seen also in an earlier painting, *The Bridge, Blackwell's Island*, 1909, now in the Toledo Museum of Art. In all, five pictures (two paintings, two drawings and one print) produced by the artist over a period of seven years utilize the same, very effective stage set: the tug anchors the middle ground while the arc of the bridge carries our view deep into the background, where a wall of densely placed buildings acts as a backdrop for the equally animated human activity in the foreground.

Repeating this successful compositional strategy allowed Bellows to refine his image. As he progressed from paintings to drawings to print, his range of tones narrowed, his background sky disappeared and the entire urban space closed around the kids swimming in the river.[6]

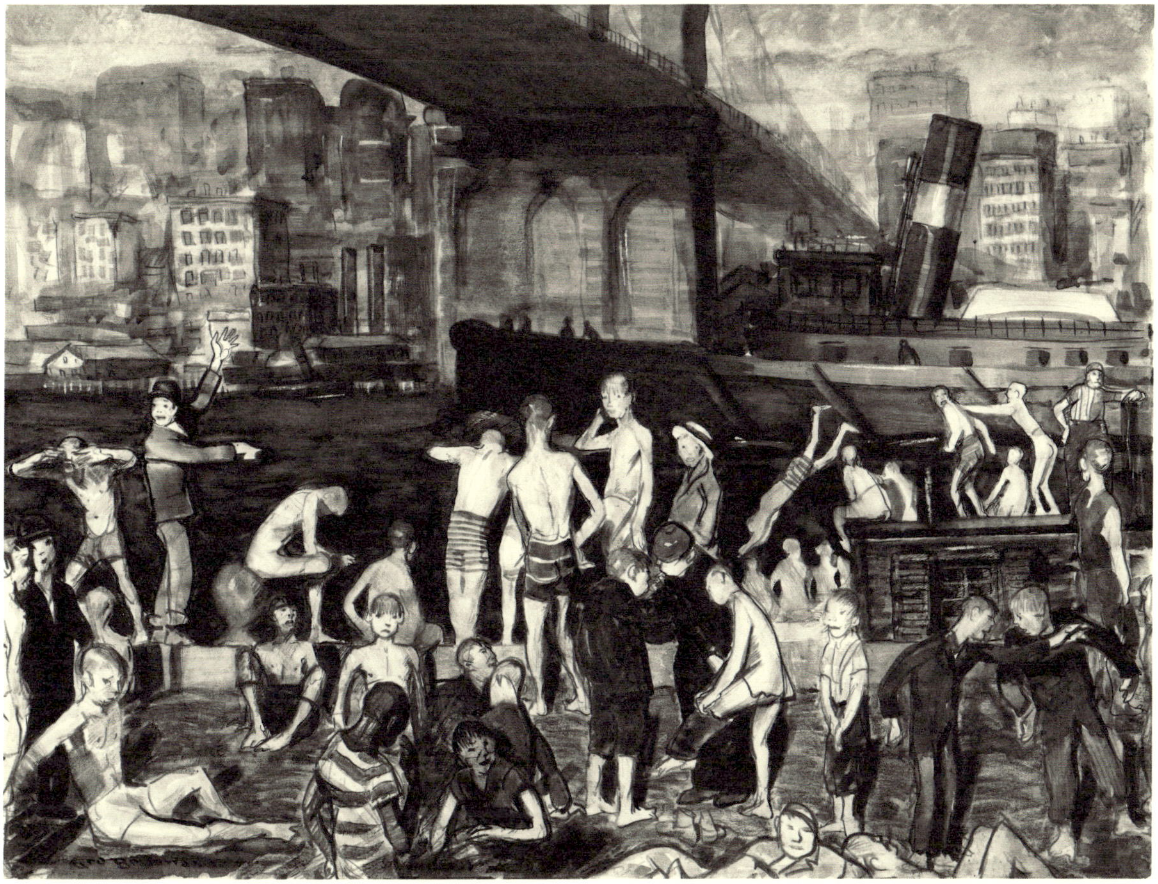

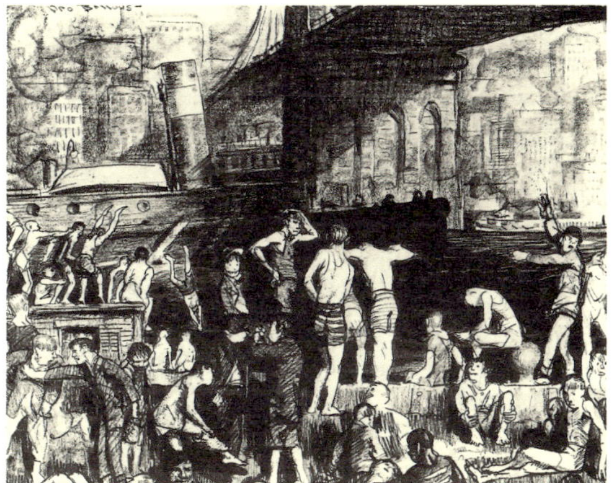

Splinter Beach, 1913, crayon, ink and wash, Private Collection.

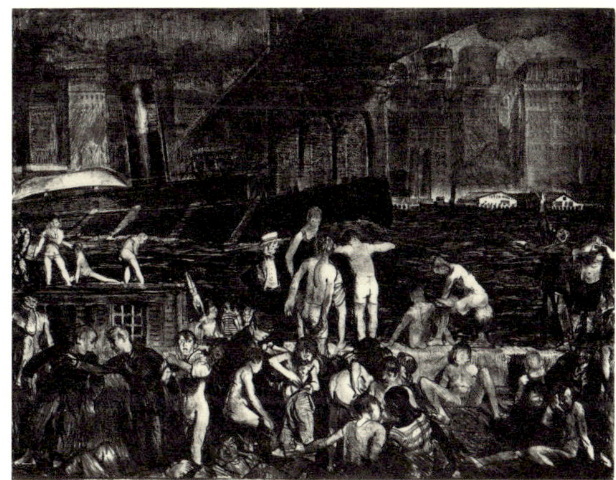

Splinter Beach, 1916, lithograph.

3. BUSINESS MEN'S CLASS

April 1913. Monoprint on cream colored, smooth wove paper mounted on paper faced wood-pulp, one ply card, with graphite, crayon, pen and ink, and scratchwork on both the monoprint and the mount,[7] 15 13/16 x 25 1/8 in., 403 x 640 mm (image and sheet); 22 3/16 x 28 in., 564 x 713 mm (mount). Signed in crayon in the lower left corner of the image: *Geo Bellows –*, titled *Business Men's Class* on the reverse. Collector's marks: Wiggin black ink stamp in lower left corner, BPL/MB black ink stamp in lower right corner.

Record Book A, p. 158, no. 201. W.11, BPL 1943.1.7. Published as *Superior Brains The Businessmen's Class*, in *The Masses*, April 1913, 10–11.

SOURCE FOR: *Business-Men's Class*, 1916. Lithograph, 11 5/8 x 17 1/8 in., 293 x 438 mm. B.128, M.20, M.&A.4. Described by the artist as *Brain workers taking their exercise*.

Sold by H. V. Allison Galleries to A. H. Wiggin, June 1943, as *Business Men's Class, Y.M.C.A.*

In early September 1904, a few weeks after his twenty-second birthday, George Bellows left home and family in Columbus, Ohio, to pursue a career as an artist in New York City. He moved into the West Side Y.M.C.A., a few blocks down 57th Street from The New York School of Art, where he soon met his mentor Robert Henri.[8]

Although Bellows left the "Y" the next spring for a series of flats shared with friends and fellow art students, his affection for his first lodgings in the city found expression in his graphic art for almost twenty years. These images are what he called "humoresques," his own personal conflations of generalized caricature and journalistic observation that owed much of their good-natured bite to the late-nineteenth-century lithographs of Honoré Daumier.[9]

Business Men's Class is the first of a group of five large, ambitious drawings Bellows produced in the spring of 1913 to be published that summer and fall in *The Masses*, then at its height as a journalistic community of politically involved writers and artists. A flattering comment in the *Chicago Evening Post*, excerpted in the October 1913 issue of the magazine, stated that "The liveliest art in America is finding a place between the covers of *The Masses*. . . . It is the liveliest because it most fully expresses the reaction of real minds to our contemporary life."[10]

There is no more succinct expression of George Bellows the draughtsman and illustrator: a real mind reacting to real life. Following the examples of older realists like Henri and his colleague John Sloan, then art editor of *The Masses*, Bellows applied his prodigious natural talent to amused and amusing records of urban life. His illustrations synthesized commercial and fine art as successfully as those published a generation earlier by Winslow Homer, an artist he admired greatly.[11]

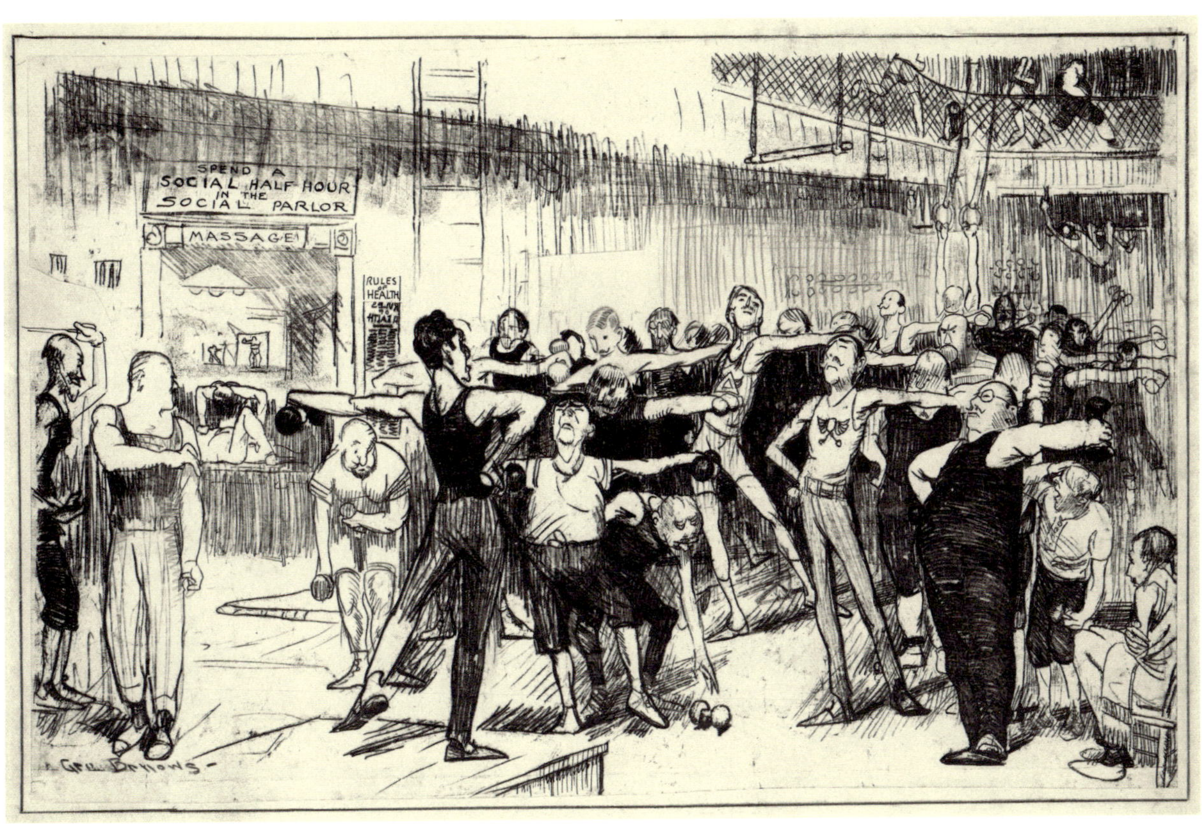
SPEND A
SOCIAL HALF HOUR
IN THE
SOCIAL PARLOR
MASSAGE
RULES
OF
HEALTH
Geo. Bellows

4. THE STRUGGLERS (Solitude)

June 1913. Crayon, pen and ink, brush and ink wash, scratchwork and collage on Strathmore Drawing Board, 22½ x 17½ in., 570 x 448 mm (image); 27⅝ x 23 in., 703 x 585 mm (sheet). Signed in black ink at the center of the bottom edge of the image: *Geo Bellows,* titled *The Strugglers* in crayon; annotated *don't thin out!* in colored graphite.

Record Book A, p. 160, no. 205, as *Park Benches*. W.40, BPL 1943.1.25. Published as *Solitude* in *The Masses*, September 1913, 14.

SOURCE FOR: *Solitude*, 1917. Lithograph, 17 x 15 ⅜ in., 435 x 393 mm. B.61, M.37, M.&A.22. Described by the artist as *Central Park on a Spring night. Love genuine and make believe.*

Sold by H. V. Allison Galleries to A. H. Wiggin, June 1943, as *Solitude.*

The Strugglers reprises the subject of an earlier painting, *Summer Night, Riverside Drive*, 1909, now in the Columbus Museum of Art. By shifting his location to Central Park and bringing us much closer to the action, Bellows created a noticeably less elegant, less romantic scene, one more appropriate to the socialist sentiments of *The Masses*, in which it was published in the fall of 1913.[12]

Like the four other drawings Bellows made for publication that year, this one shows his technical flair. He worked and reworked the surface of the paper with crayon and pen, adding shading and then scratching it away to achieve a convincing sense of bright streetlight filtered through trees. The lone figure on the far right, in summer suit and straw boater, was drawn on a separate sheet, cut out and pasted onto the bench. Since the drawing would be reproduced photographically in the magazine, this cut-and-paste technique would not be visible to the reader.

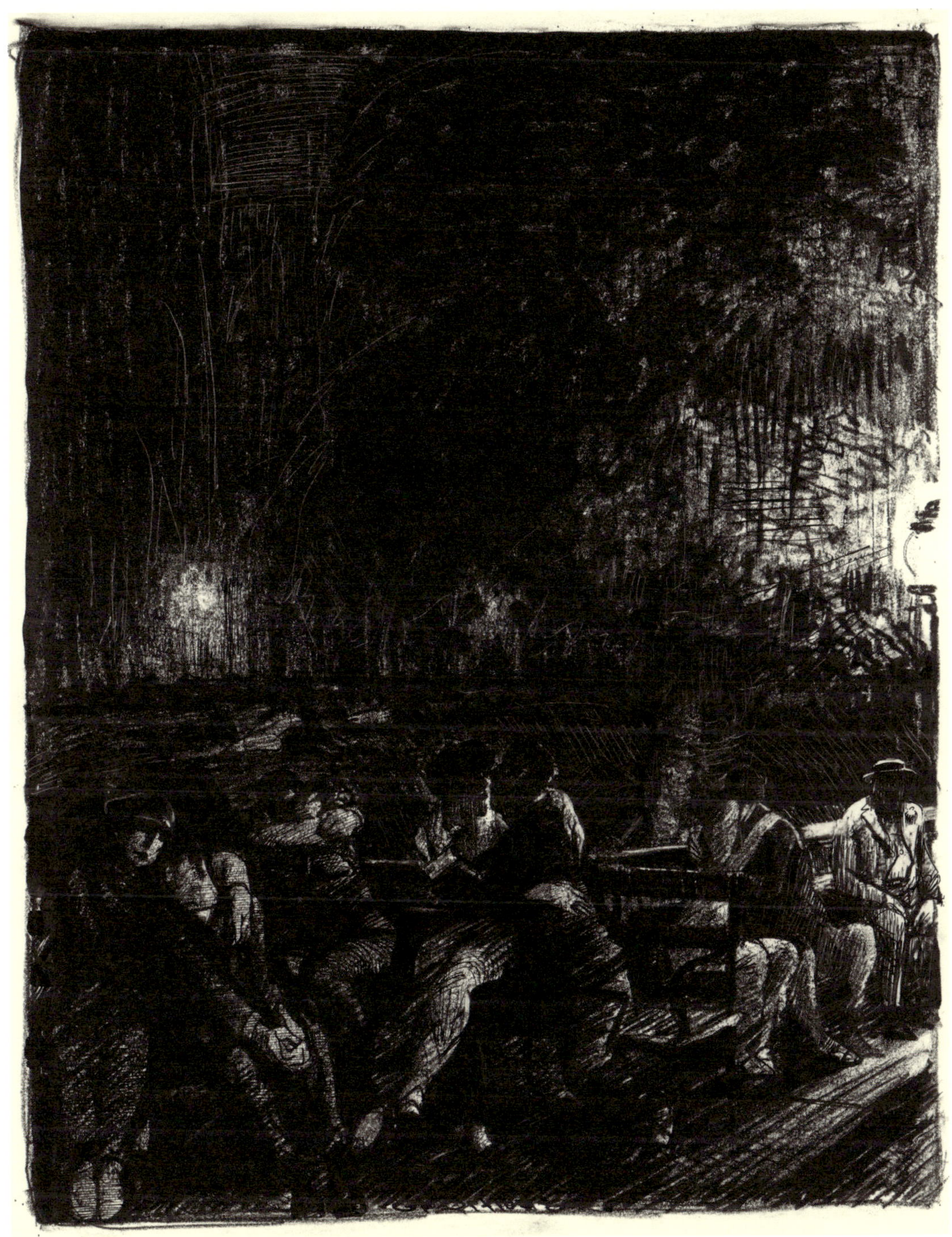

5. PRAYER MEETING (Prayer Meeting No. 1)

Summer–Fall 1913. Pen and ink on light weight cream wove paper, 5 1/16 x 6 5/8 in., 131 x 167 mm (image and sheet). Signed in ink in the lower left corner of image: *Geo Bellows / ESB.*

Record Book A, p. 279. W.31, BPL 1943.2.7.

STUDY FOR: a more finished drawing published in *Harper's Weekly*, January 3, 1914, 16–17 as *Deponent Testifies That He Is No Longer a Sinner*. This second drawing is the SOURCE FOR: *Prayer Meeting, First Stone*, 1916. Lithograph, 18 x 21 3/4 in., 457 x 552 mm. B.38, M.13. Described by the artist as *Humoresque of Deacon Smith on a Wednesday night at Monhegan Island.*

Given by Emma S. Bellows to the Boston Public Library, June 1943, as *Prayer Meeting No. 1.*

In the summer of 1913, Bellows traveled to Monhegan Island, off the coast of Maine, for the second time. A previous visit, in the summer of 1911, had been without his wife Emma, who was then expecting their first child. This time he took her and their baby daughter Anne. Most of his prodigious output of one hundred and seventeen paintings that summer concerned the land- and seascapes all around him.[13]

This sketch records his visit to a small Methodist church on the island. It became the basis for a larger drawing published early in 1914. Although by its small size and quick lines it appears to have been done on the scene, Bellows had a reputation for his prodigious verbal and visual memory, and reportedly had no need to make sketches on site. It could, then, have been drawn after the fact, most likely on the island that summer, but possibly even back in New York between the end of October when the family returned home and the beginning of January when the final version appeared in *Harper's*.[14]

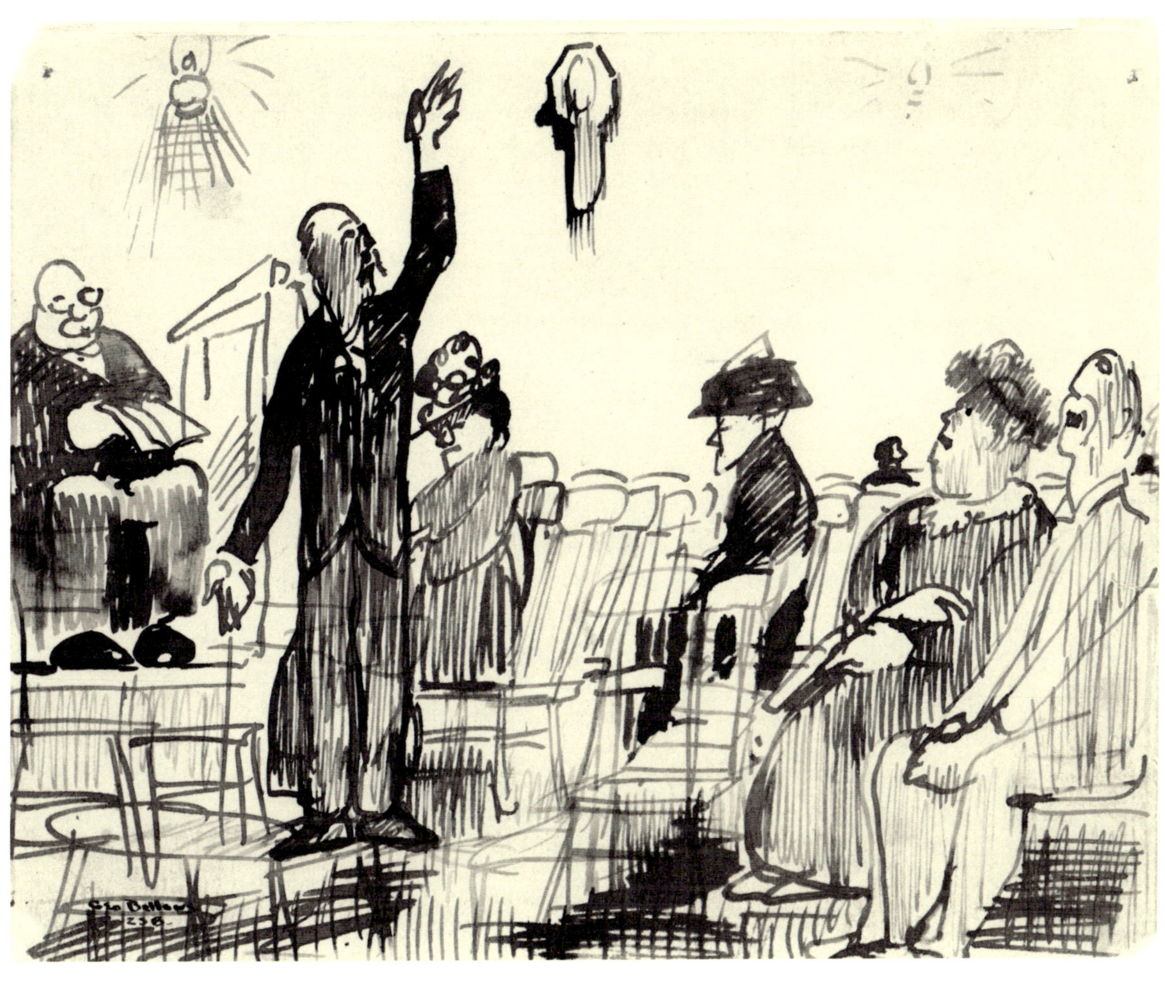

6. NIGHT AT PETITPAS (Artists' Evening Petitpas)

February 1914. Crayon and graphite on cream wove paper, mounted on paper faced, two ply woodpulp board, 8 9/16 x 12 1/8 in., 217 x 307 mm (image and sheet); 13 1/4 x 16 1/2 in., 336 x 417 mm (mount). Signed in crayon in the top right corner of the sheet *Geo Bellows*—; signed in crayon on the mount in the lower right below the image *'Petitpa's' Geo Bellows.*

Record Book A, p. 282, no. 310, with a note by Emma Bellows giving the alternate title, *Artist's Evening*. W.30, BPL1943.1.17.

SOURCE FOR: *Artist's Evening*, 1916. Lithograph, 8 7/8 x 12 1/8 in., 225 x 310 mm. B.34, M.19, M.&A. 51. Published as *At Petitpa's*, in *The Masses*, July 1916, 6.

Sold by H. V. Allison Galleries to A. H. Wiggin, June 1943, as *Artists' Evening Petitpas.*

As the caption to the lithograph published in *The Masses* tells us, *Mlle. Petitpas* was a restaurant and rooming house on West 29th Street between 8th and 9th Avenues owned and run by three Frenchwomen. In the center of the scene, we see Robert Henri conversing with the Irish artist John Butler Yeats, father of two famous sons, William the poet and Jack the painter.[15] Behind and between them Bellows himself hovers, and seated in front and to their side, Emma Bellows looks directly at us. Marjorie Henri is seated at the table in the right corner, drawing on a pad of paper.

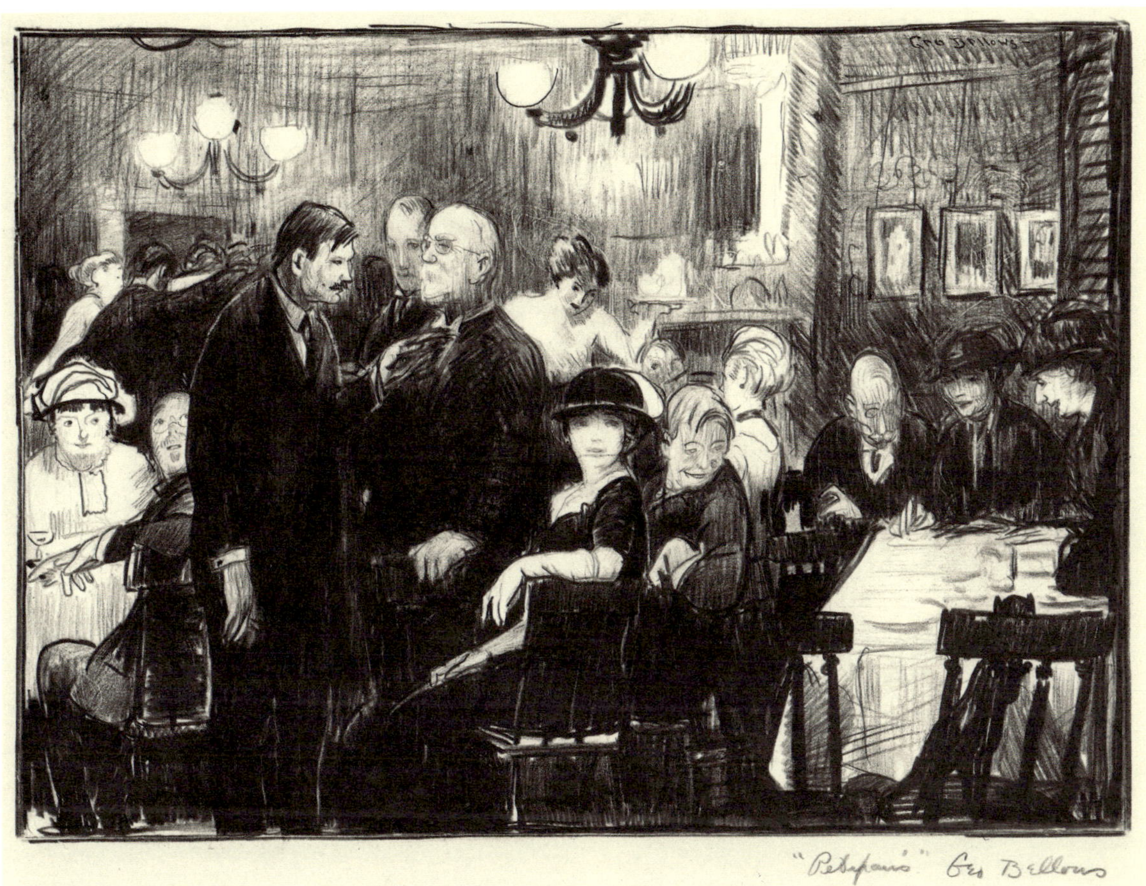

7. PINCHED (The Street)

March–April 1914. Graphite, crayon, and pen and ink, and scratchwork on paper-faced wood-pulp two-ply board, spray varnished, 20 x 15⅜ in., 510 x 390 mm (image); 26⁵⁄₁₆ x 19⁹⁄₁₆ in., 670 x 497 mm (sheet). Signed in crayon in the lower right corner of the image: *Geo Bellows—*, titled *Pinched* lower center, and with an alternate title in crayon crossed out in ink, ~~*I was punchin' his face*~~.

Record Book A, p. 284, no. 313, as *No 1* of two drawings with the title *I was Beatin his face*. Drawing *No 2*, now in the collection of the Nelson-Atkins Museum of Art, Kansas City, MO, was commissioned in March 1914, for $100 and published in *Harper's Weekly*, April 11, 1914, 18–19 as *I was Beatin' 'is Face*. It illustrated *Fixing the Responsibility* by Curt Hanson, a story about children of different ethnicities living on the lower East Side of New York City.[16] W.44, BPL1943.1.3.

SOURCE FOR: *The Street*, 1917. Lithograph, 19 x 15¼ in., 485 x 387 mm. B.9, M.47, M.&A.24. Published as *The Street* in *The Masses*, July 1917, p. 15. Described by the artist as *Under the elevated, lower east side in mid-summer.*

Sold by H. V. Allison Galleries to A. H. Wiggin, June 1943, as *The Street*.

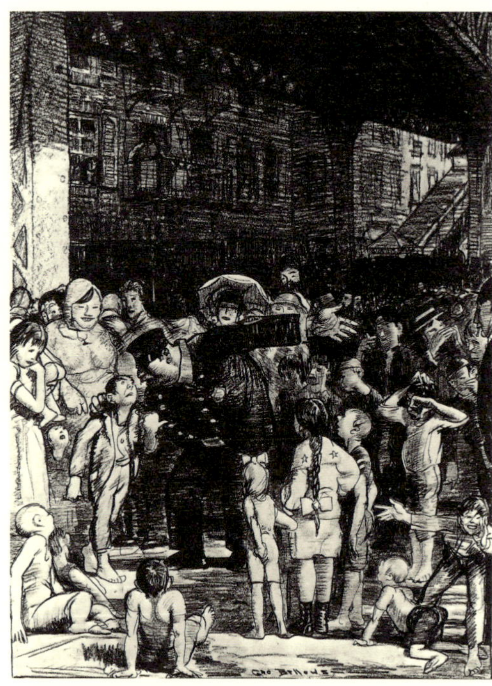

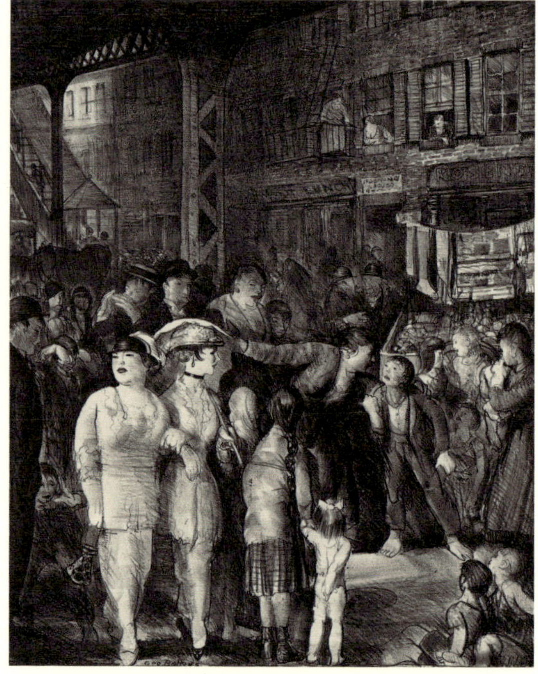

(LEFT): *I Was Beatin' 'is Face*. Crayon, ink, and graphite on paper, 24½ x 18 inches (61.59 x 45.72 cm). The Nelson-Atkins Museum of Art, Kansas City, Missouri. Gift of Mr. and Mrs. Herbert O. Peet, 58-31. (RIGHT): *The Street*, 1917, lithograph.

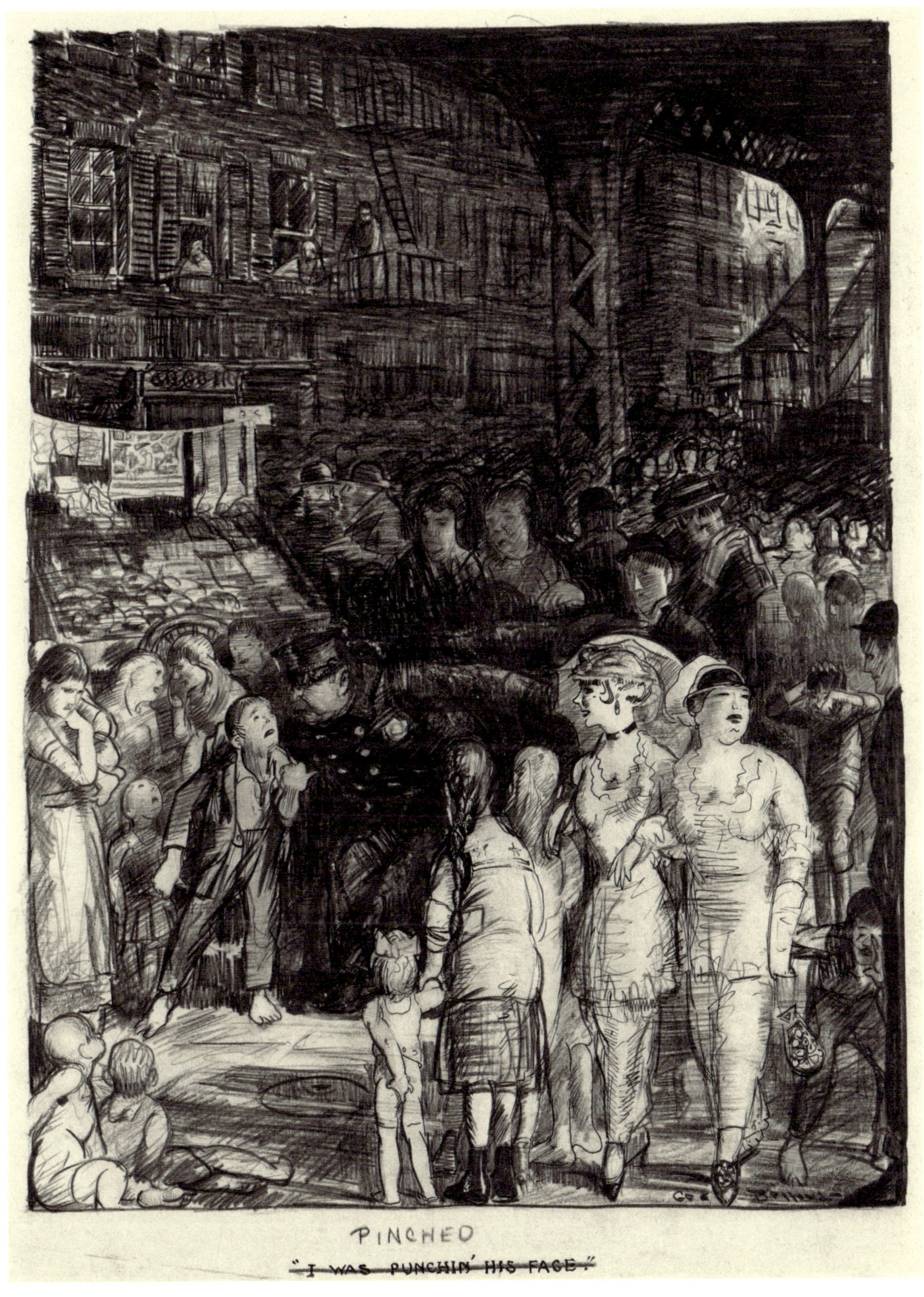
PINCHED
~~"I WAS PUNCHIN' HIS FACE."~~

In all three versions of this scene, two drawings and one print, Bellows rearranged the players in his neighborhood drama. All of them offer us the same basic narrative, but with differences in emphasis.

The Nelson-Atkins drawing, the version Bellows chose for *Harper's Weekly*, tells the story most directly: the three main characters, two boys and the policeman who breaks up their fight, are well-lit and clearly visible in the middle ground. The children gathered in front of them all look at their interaction, especially the argument between the apparent winner of the fight and the cop, and the gesturing boy in the lower right corner is an obvious device used by the artist to direct our attention to the central event.

In the Wiggin drawing, a pair of very stylish young women has strolled into view. The sunlight falls most dramatically on them; the policeman and boy are now in half-shadow, the other boy is much less noticeable, and the important narrative gesture of the policeman's arm connecting the two boys is interrupted by one woman's parasol.[17]

In the lithograph, the storyline has receded further into the general ambience of the street. The crying boy is now difficult to find, and the policeman has been replaced by a woman.[18] The protagonists are now treated with the same grey tones used for all the other figures in the scene, except for the foreground women and the three girls with their backs to us.

His decisions to shift our attention away from one specific action *(I was beatin' 'is face)* to the many interactions of a crowded tenement neighborhood (*The Street*) demonstrate how well Bellows balanced the demands of commercial illustration and his own standards of directly observed realism. Life "under the El" didn't stop artificially for a minor scrape between two urchins. It flowed continuously in and around uncountable numbers of glances, gestures and conversations, a reality the artist captured progressively through his three versions of the scene.

8. BILLY SUNDAY AND THE SAWDUST TRAIL
(The Sawdust Trail)

March 1915. Crayon, pen and ink, and brush and ink wash, spray and brush varnished on Strathmore Drawing Board, mounted on paper-faced, woodpulp, two ply board. Independent of, and in places on top of the varnish is an overlay of grayish/white pigment, applied irregularly and unevenly over the surface of the image, 26⅝ x 19$^{15}/_{16}$ in., 677 x 507 mm (image); 28 x 22$^{1}/_{16}$ in., 713 x 560 mm (sheet). Signed in crayon in the upper right corner of the image: *Geo Bellows —*, with an alternate title *March to Zion* in graphite lower right. Collector's mark: BPL/MB black ink stamp in the lower right corner.

Record Book B, p. 11, no. 341, W.38, BPL 1943.1.21. Commissioned in January, and published in *Metropolitan* magazine, May 1915, 9 as an illustration to John Reed's article "Back of Billy Sunday."

STUDY FOR: *The Saw Dust Trail*, February 1916. Oil on canvas, 63 x 45⅛ in., 1600 x 1146 mm; Record Book B, p. 43. Milwaukee Art Museum, WI.

SOURCE FOR: *The Sawdust Trail*, 1917. Lithograph, 25½ x 20⅛ in., 646 x 511 mm. B.76, M.48, M.&A.20. Described by the artist as *The artist "hits the trail" and signs up during the Philadelphia revival. The fact is noted in the morning papers, the reason is in the lithograph.*

Sold by H. V. Allison Galleries to A. H. Wiggin, June 1943, as *The Sawdust Trail.*

In January 1915, Bellows and reporter John Reed went on assignment from *Metropolitan Magazine* to cover the "Christ for Philadelphia—Philadelphia for Christ" rally.[19] The organizer and star of the event was the evangelist Billy Sunday, then in his eighteenth year of preaching against what he saw as the evils of an intemperate life.

"Sow a card party and you'll reap gamblers. Sow dances and you'll reap prostitutes."[20]

Calling on the audience to "hit the Sawdust Trail," Sunday would reach down to shake the hand of every convert as they filed beneath the podium, down the center aisle and back to their seats. Behind him stands his wife "Ma" Sunday and on the right with his back to us, choir director and soloist Homer Rodeheaver. Both had worked the trail with Sunday for years.[21]

In the foreground, just behind and to the left of the woman being carried away, we see one of Sunday's staff greeting a tall, lanky young man. In the lithograph derived from the drawing two years later, this fellow is obviously bald. Since Bellows was in the habit of slipping self-portraits into his scenes that emphasized both his height and lack of hair, this figure is most likely the source for his comment about the artist hitting the trail.

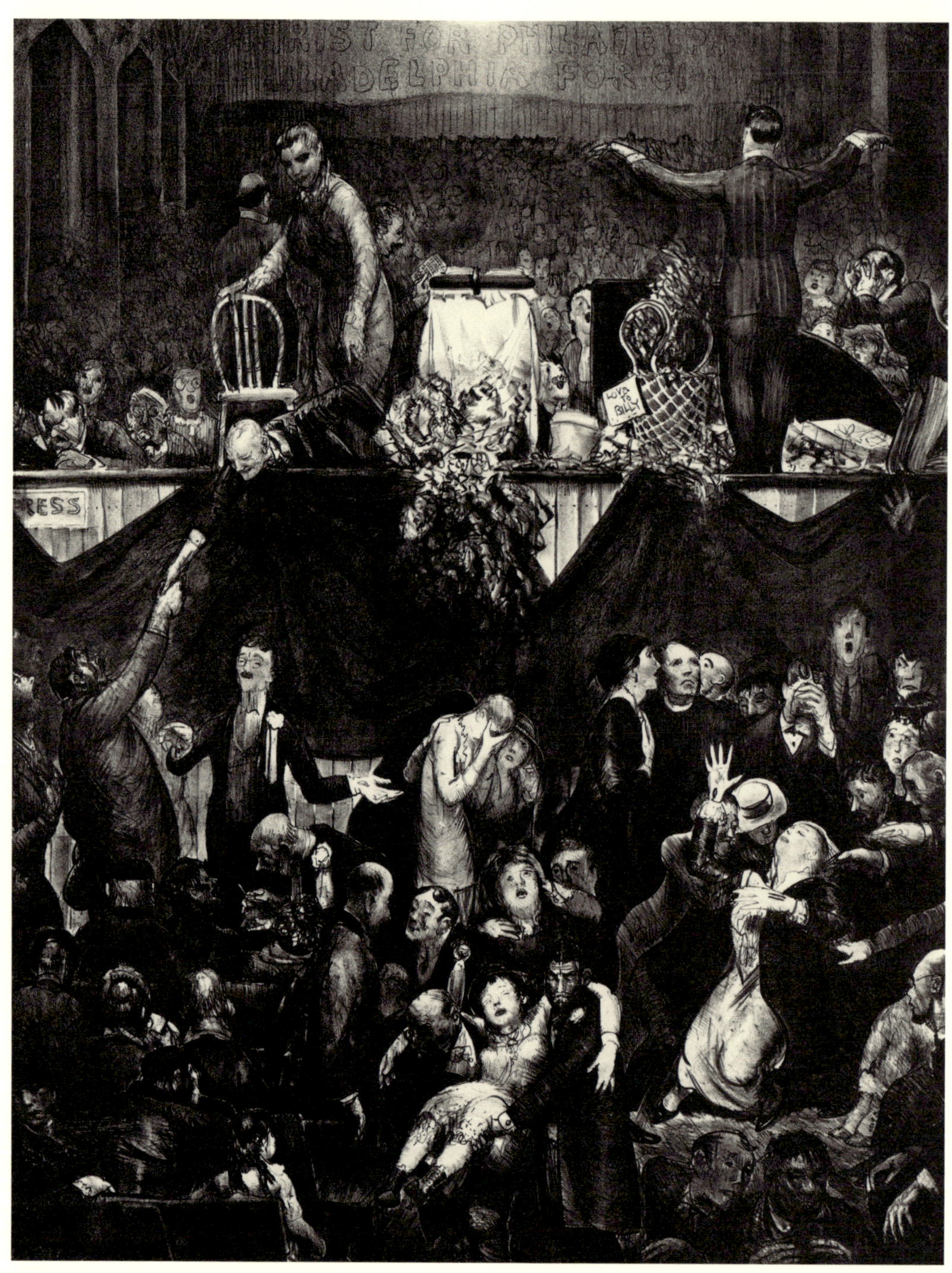

The Sawdust Trail, 1917, lithograph.

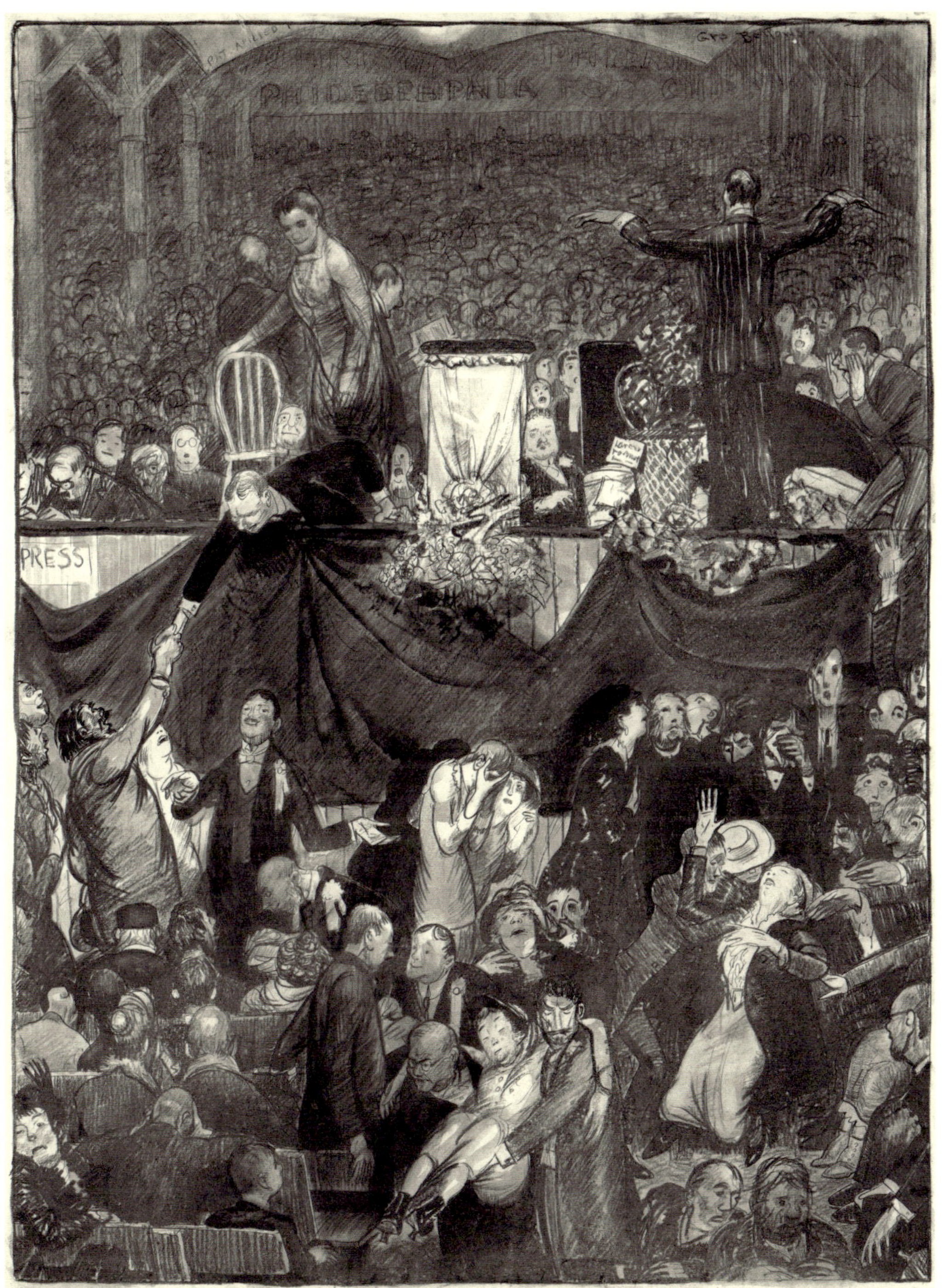
PRESS

9. PREACHING (Billy Sunday)

March 1915. Crayon, pen and ink, brush and ink wash and scratchwork, spray and brush varnished, on Strathmore Drawing Board, $14\frac{7}{16}$ x $27\frac{15}{16}$ in., 367 x 712 mm (image); $14\frac{13}{16}$ x $28\frac{5}{16}$ in., 376 x 721 mm (sheet). Signed in crayon in the lower right of the image: *Geo Bellows*. Collector's mark: Wiggin black ink stamp in lower left corner verso.

Record Book B, p. 11, no. 341, W.48, BPL1943.1.6. Commissioned in January and published in *Metropolitan* magazine, May 1915, 9 as an illustration to John Reed's article "Back of Billy Sunday."

SOURCE FOR: *Billy Sunday*, 1923. Lithograph, 9 x $16\frac{1}{8}$ in., 226 x 411 mm. B.III, M.143, M.&A.59.

Sold by H. V. Allison Galleries to A. H. Wiggin, June 1943, as *Billy Sunday*.

Bellows' opinions about Billy Sunday were unequivocal:

> *I like to paint Billy Sunday, not because I like him, but because I want to show the world what I do think of him. Do you know, I believe Billy Sunday is the worst thing that ever happened to America? He is death to imagination, to spirituality, to art. Billy Sunday is Prussianism personified. His whole purpose is to force authority against beauty. He is against freedom, he wants a religious autocracy, he is such a reactionary that he makes me an anarchist. You can see why I like to paint him and his devastating "saw-dust-trail." I want people to understand him.*[22]

Although he rejected Sunday's politics, Bellows recognized the satirical opportunities the athletic preacher offered. In the winter of 1914, exactly a year before he covered Sunday's rally in Philadelphia, he wrote his former college professor and close friend, Joe Taylor:

> *Did you see my prayer meeting in recent Harper's. That's what I wanted to do to Billy Sunday and didn't get a look. This I will allways* (sic) *regret.*[23]

Preaching is another excellent example of Bellows' ability to blend caricature and journalistic illustration. While the faces of the potential converts in the front row are quick cartoon sketches, the figure of Sunday in action is remarkably faithful to photos of him in his trademark poses, leaping forward to deliver his message.[24]

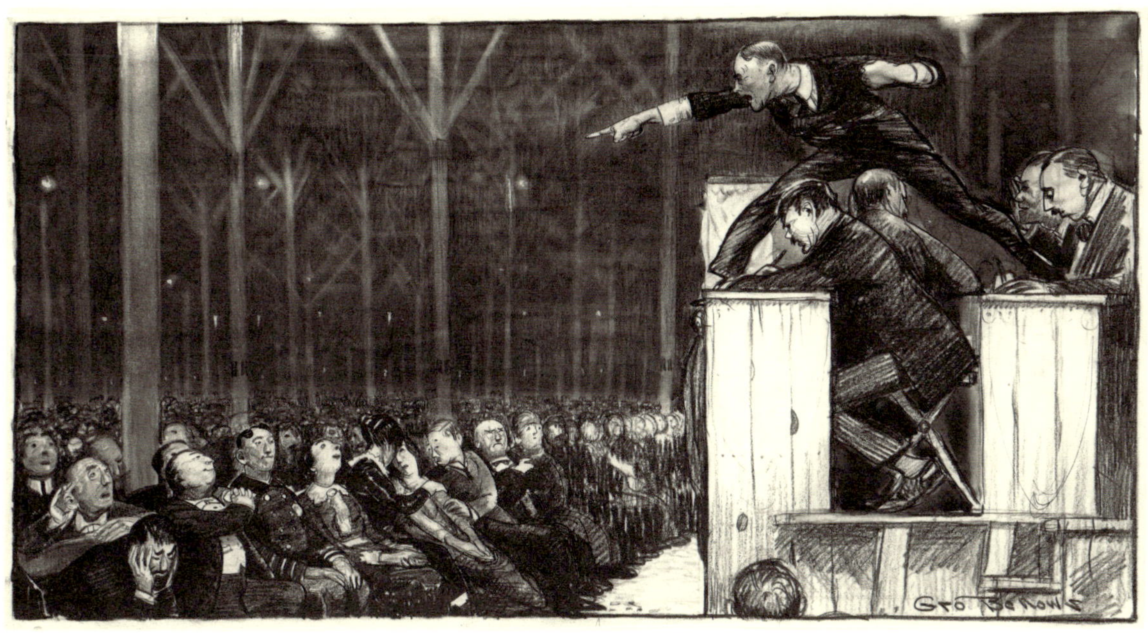

10. MATINICUS

Fall 1916. Crayon on lightweight wove paper (Watermark: DIANA, with a partial figure of the goddess below), 6⅝ x 9 in., 168 x 230 mm (image); 8³⁄₁₆ x 10¹⁄₁₆ in., 207 x 256 mm (sheet). Signed in graphite in lower left corner below image: *Geo Bellows E.S.B.*

W.27, BPL 1943.1.15.

SOURCE FOR: *Matinicus*, 1916. Lithograph, 7 x 9 in., 178 x 229 mm. B.121, M.15

Sold by H. V. Allison Galleries to A. H. Wiggin, June 1943.

While spending their second summer together on Monhegan Island, George and Emma together with three friends traveled with a fisherman to the smaller island of Matinicus for the night. The Bellowses returned for a month at the end of the summer of 1916. Since the very similar lithograph was printed in the winter of 1916, we can reasonably date this drawing to their second visit that fall.

Although the drawing and print are the same size and orientation, the print is not a direct copy of the drawing. Differences between the two include the shading on the tarp on the right edge of the composition and the cross-hatching on the lobster pots in the left foreground. They tell us Bellows redrew the scene on a lithographic stone. Lithographs made after drawings are usually oriented in reverse. An artist normally redraws an image onto the stone in the same direction as the original drawing he is using as a model. Transferring that image from printing surface to printed surface, from stone to paper, reverses it.

In this case, the drawing's and print's being in the same orientation prompts us to wonder how and why this happened. Bellows, a talented, facile draughtsman, could have drawn the image on the stone in reverse, so that the second reversal taking it from stone to paper would have put it back into the orientation of his original drawing. Since the image was of an actual location, he may have wanted his edition of prints to portray the village correctly, rather than backwards.[25]

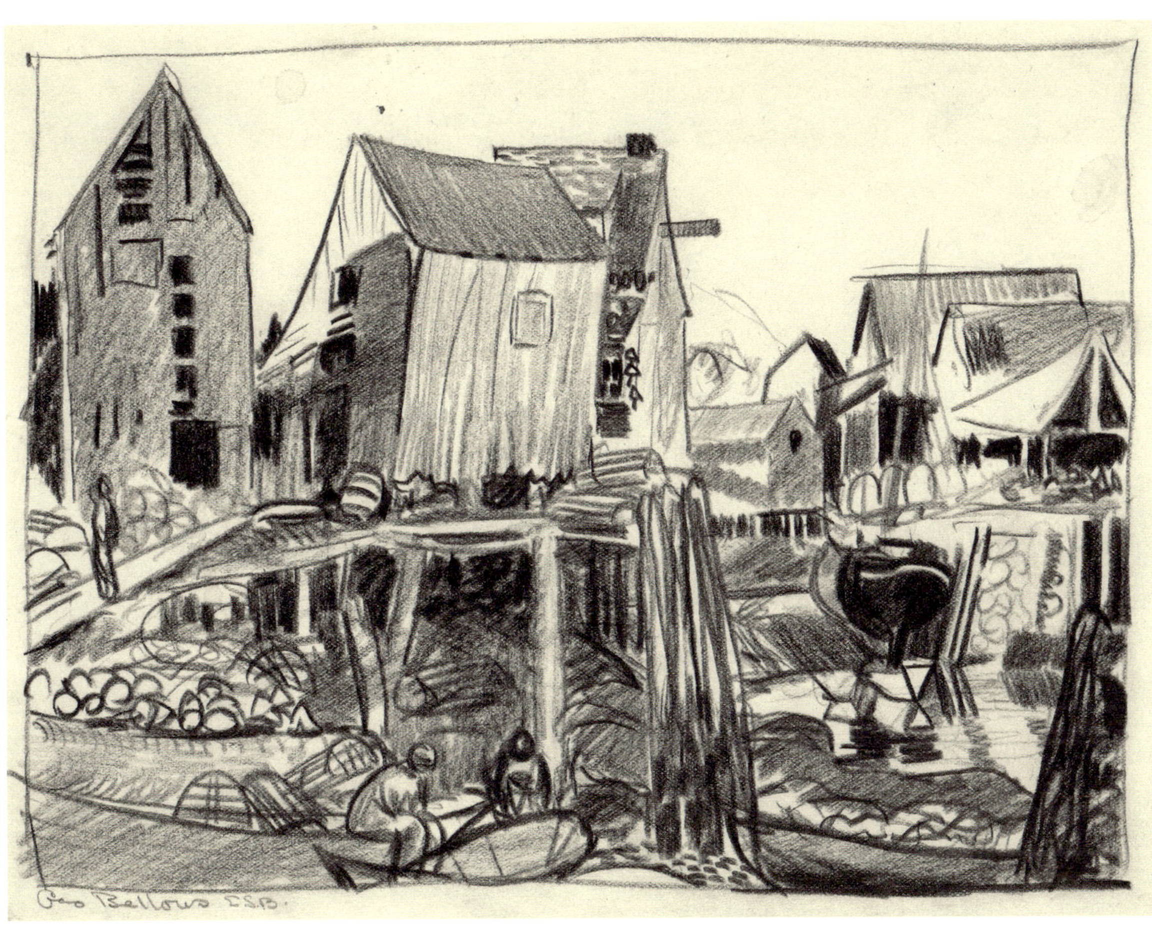
Geo Bellows ESB.

11. STANDING NUDE BENDING FORWARD (Standing Nude)

Winter 1916. Crayon on tracing paper, 13 7/16 x 11 1/4 in., 341 x 285 mm (sheet). Signed in graphite in lower right corner of sheet: *Geo. Bellows E.S.B.*

W.43, BPL 1943.1.24

SOURCE FOR: *Standing Nude Bending Forward*, 1916. Lithograph, 12 3/4 x 10 1/8 in., 324 x 257 mm. B.29, M.4.

Sold by H. V. Allison Galleries to A. H. Wiggin, June 1943.

Bellows' earliest lithographs, with the notable exceptions *Hungry Dogs* and *Prayer Meeting* (see cat. nos. 1 and 5), were all relatively sketchy nude studies. Often printed in several different states documenting his reworking the stone, they are generally accepted as exercises in which the artist found his way around a new medium by trial and error.[26]

This drawing is the source for what was most likely the first of these nudes, very close in scale and in the same orientation as the lithograph. In this case, their being in the same direction suggests that in the beginning of his involvement with lithography Bellows drew his images on transfer paper. For an artist unaccustomed to the texture and great weight of limestone, transfer paper offers a familiar surface for drawing. The printing of a lithograph from an image on transfer paper involves two reversals, the first from the paper to the stone, and the second from the stone to the sheets of paper on which the edition is printed. Going through two reversals brings the image back to its original orientation.

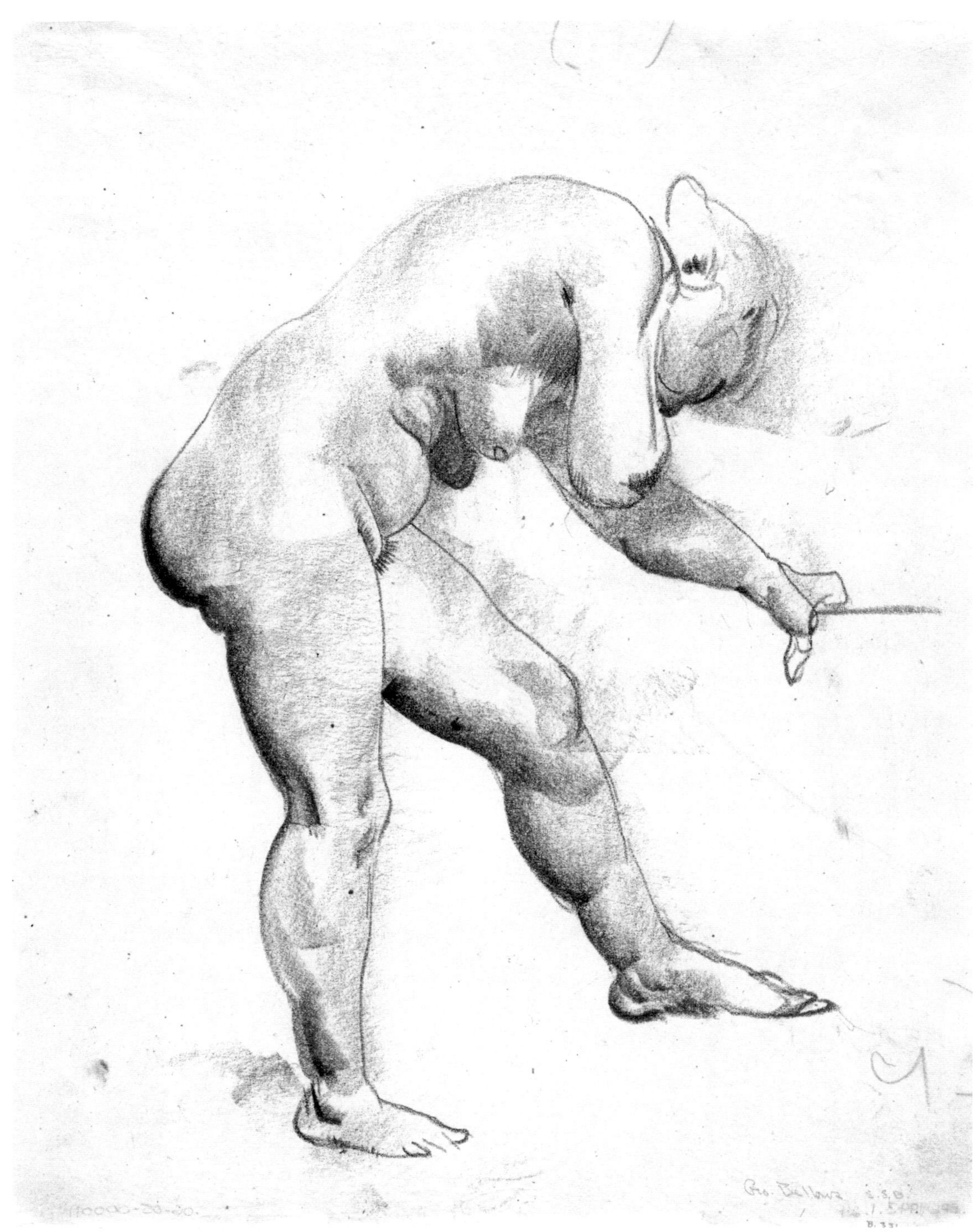

12. THE OLD RASCAL

Winter 1916. Crayon, pen and ink, and scratchwork on cream heavyweight wove paper, 9 3/16 x 7 1/2 in., 234 x 191 mm (image); 10 1/8 x 7 3/4 in., 256 x 195 mm (sheet). Initialed in ink in the lower right corner of the image: *GB*.

W.29, BPL 1943.1.16.

SOURCE FOR: *The Old Rascal*, 1916. Lithograph, 10 1/8 x 9 in., 257 x 229 mm; B.167, M.11, M.&A.10. Described by the artist as *A Rabelaisian Study*.

Sold by H. V. Allison Galleries to A. H. Wiggin, June 1943.

Bellows began making lithographs during the winter of 1916. After a few relatively unsuccessful attempts on his own, he hired George Miller, a young commercial lithographer, to print for him. That first season, they produced about thirty-five editions.[27]

For the next nine years, Bellows took his lithographic images from drawings done either at the time he thought of making a print or often years earlier. Forty-six of the forty-eight sheets in the Wiggin Collection document how easily the artist recalled and recycled imagery from one medium and time to another.

Without evidence connecting it to another project, *The Old Rascal* appears to have been created at about the same time as the print, most likely in preparation for it. Like several other early pairs of drawings and prints, these two are in the same orientation, raising the possibility that Bellows either employed transfer paper in getting his image onto the litho stone or deliberately reversed his drawing on stone so that the printed image would read in the same direction as his original drawing.

As indicated by Bellows' reference to François Rabelais, *The Old Rascal* is a precursor to the illustrations for novels he made on commission in 1922 (see cat. nos. 32–34 and 36–37). Like them, it lacks the spontaneity, vitality and wit of his urban scenes.

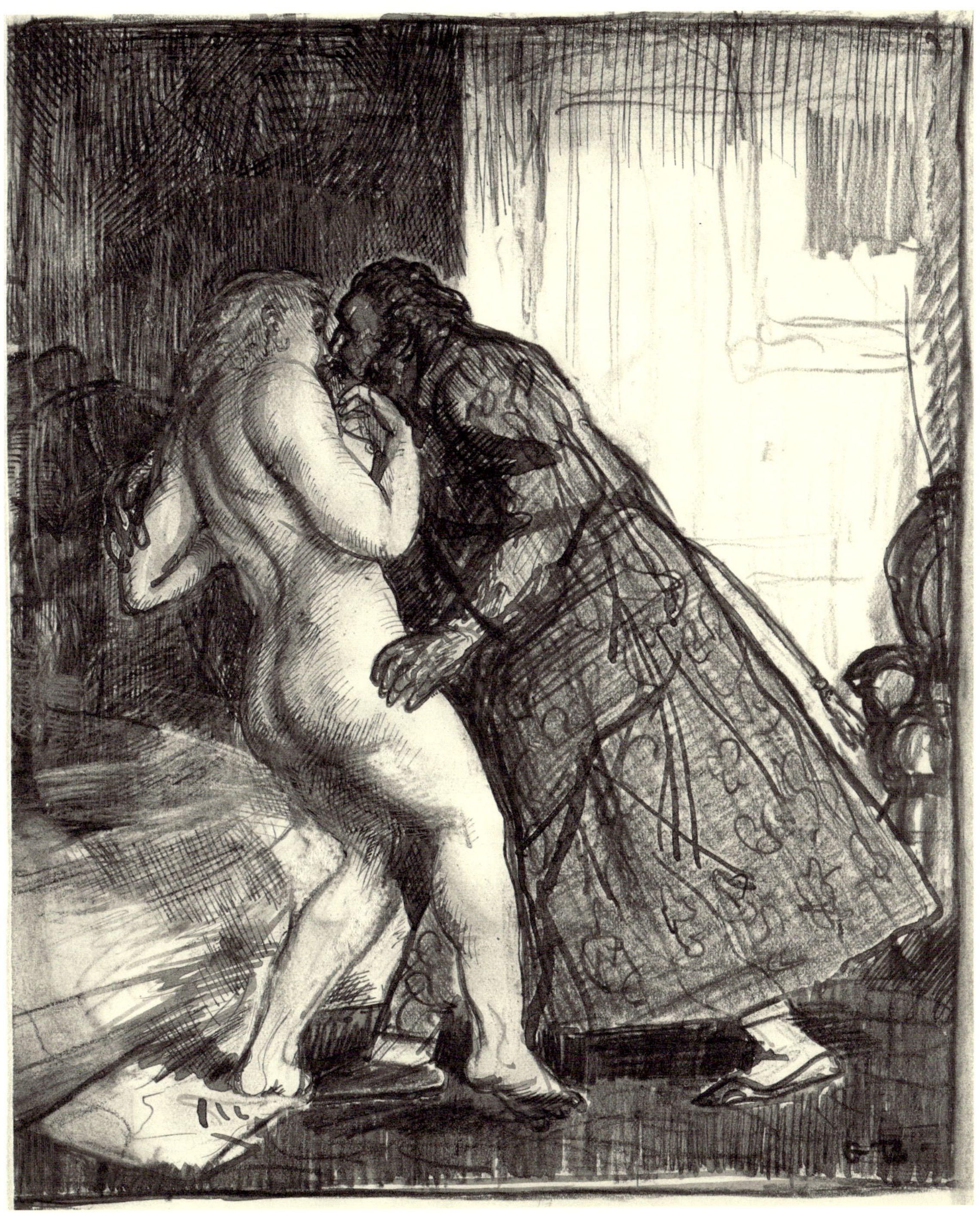

13. PRELIMINARIES (Preliminaries to the Big Bout)

Spring 1916. Crayon and black ink and brush on lightweight, smooth, cream-colored wove paper (watermark: Natoma), 17 x 22¾ in., 430 x 580 mm (image); 21⅛ x 25¾ in., 537 x 655 mm (sheet). Unsigned. Collector's marks: Wiggin Collection black ink stamp in lower left corner, BPL/MB black ink stamp in lower right corner.

W.32, BPL 1942.1.2.

SOURCE FOR: *Preliminaries*, 1916.[28] Lithograph, 15¾ x 19½ in. B.21 as *Preliminaries to the Big Bout*, M.24, M.&A. 13. Described by the artist as: *Society attends a big fight at Madison Square Garden, New York.*

Sold by H. V. Allison Galleries to A. H. Wiggin, October 1942, as *Preliminaries to the Big Bout*.[29]

On March 25th, 1916, Madison Square Garden held the first prize fight which ladies were allowed to attend—a perfect opportunity for an artist who knew his way around both sporting events and elegant New Yorkers. The result is one of Bellows' most atmospheric and evocative drawings, quick, fluid, yet in perfect control.[30] Although he hadn't yet drawn the ostensible subject of the picture, the boxing ring and the match within it, he had defined his real subject, the women and their men in evening dress.

Reworking the image with crayon on stone, Bellows modified his composition. In the lithograph, he pulled back a bit from the fashionable group, lessening their concentrated mass and impact in favor of the fight going on behind them. As a counterpoint, he turned the brunette's head slightly so that she looks directly, and provocatively, at us. The resulting image is more accessible as an illustration, but less expressive as a work of art.

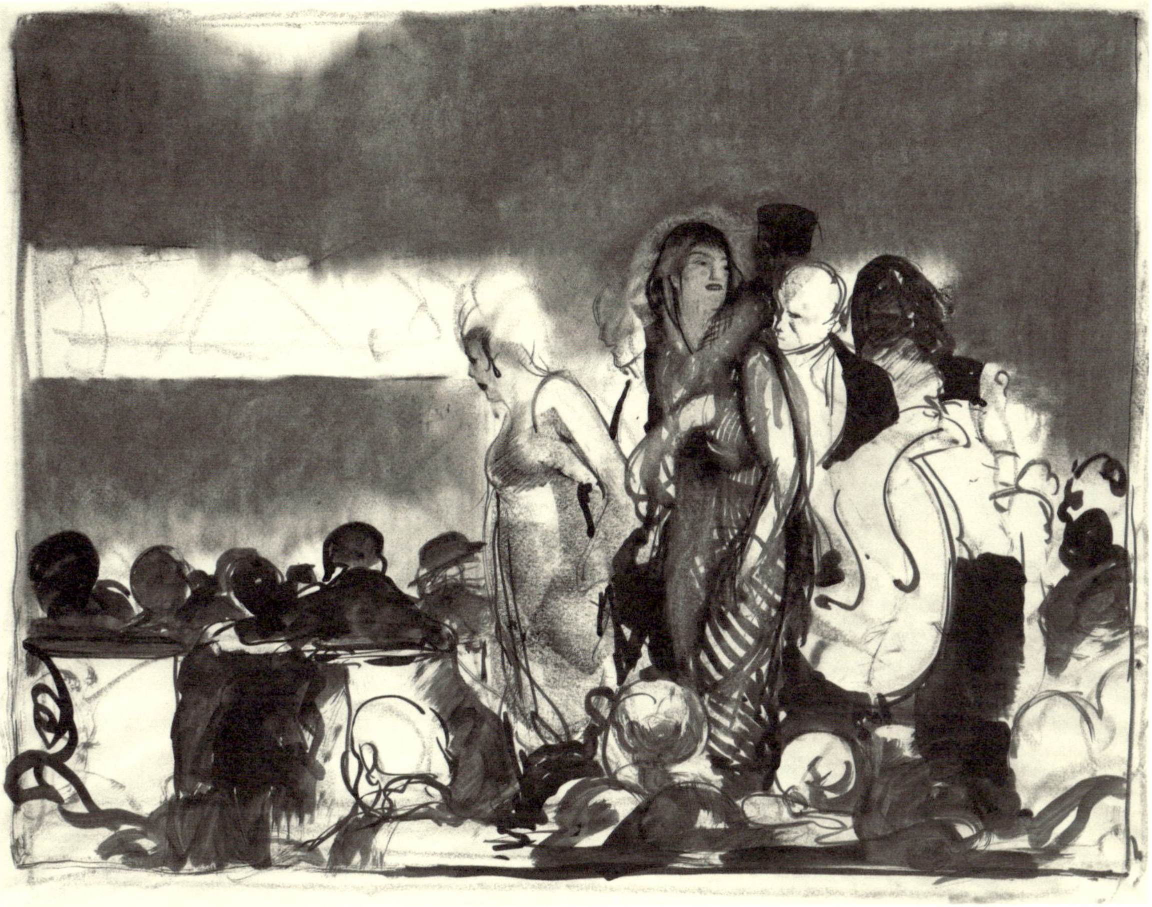

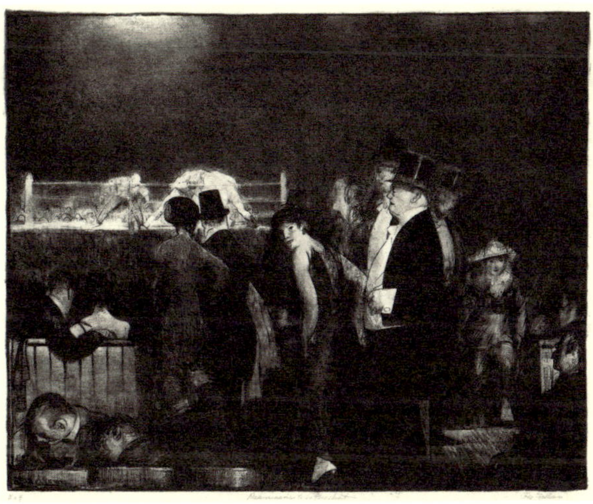

Preliminaries to the Big Bout,
1916, lithograph.

14. WELL AT QUEVADO[31]

Fall 1917. Graphite, crayon, pen and ink, ink wash and brush, and scratchwork on a paper-faced, wood pulp board 10 x 15⅝ in., 255 x 397 mm (image); 12⅜ x 18⅛ in., 315 x 460 mm (sheet). Signed in graphite on the lower right bottom edge of the image: *Geo. Bellows E.S.B.* Collector's mark: Wiggin black stamp in lower right corner.

W.50, BPL 1943.1.29.

STUDY FOR: *Well at Quevado*, October 1917. Oil on canvas, 38½ x 52½ in., 978 x 1334 mm. Minnesota Museum of Art, St. Paul.

SOURCE FOR: *Well at Quevado*, 1917–19. Lithograph, 9½ x 13½ in., 241 x 342 mm. B.187, M.70.

Sold by H. V. Allison Galleries to A. H. Wiggin, June 1943.

This image of a southwestern *ranchero* comes from a trip Bellows and his family took to visit friends in northern New Mexico in October 1917, while on their way back east after spending the summer in California.

Bellows enjoyed the West. His paintings from his months there, especially one of this same subject and title, are intensely colored. The related lithograph, produced most likely in one of his winter work sessions at the press back in New York, was, however, a failure. We know of only two surviving impressions. The likely reasons for his rejecting the print are suggested by the drawing, especially in the difficult passage from the valley in the middle ground to the dark mesas in the background to the very active sky above. In the painting, he kept this composition from collapsing with brilliant color. In the drawing, he varied his ink washes enough to suggest the same space, although the transition from valley to mesa is somewhat muddled. In the print, his command of litho washes did not meet the challenge posed by his composition, and he stopped the project before printing a full edition.[32]

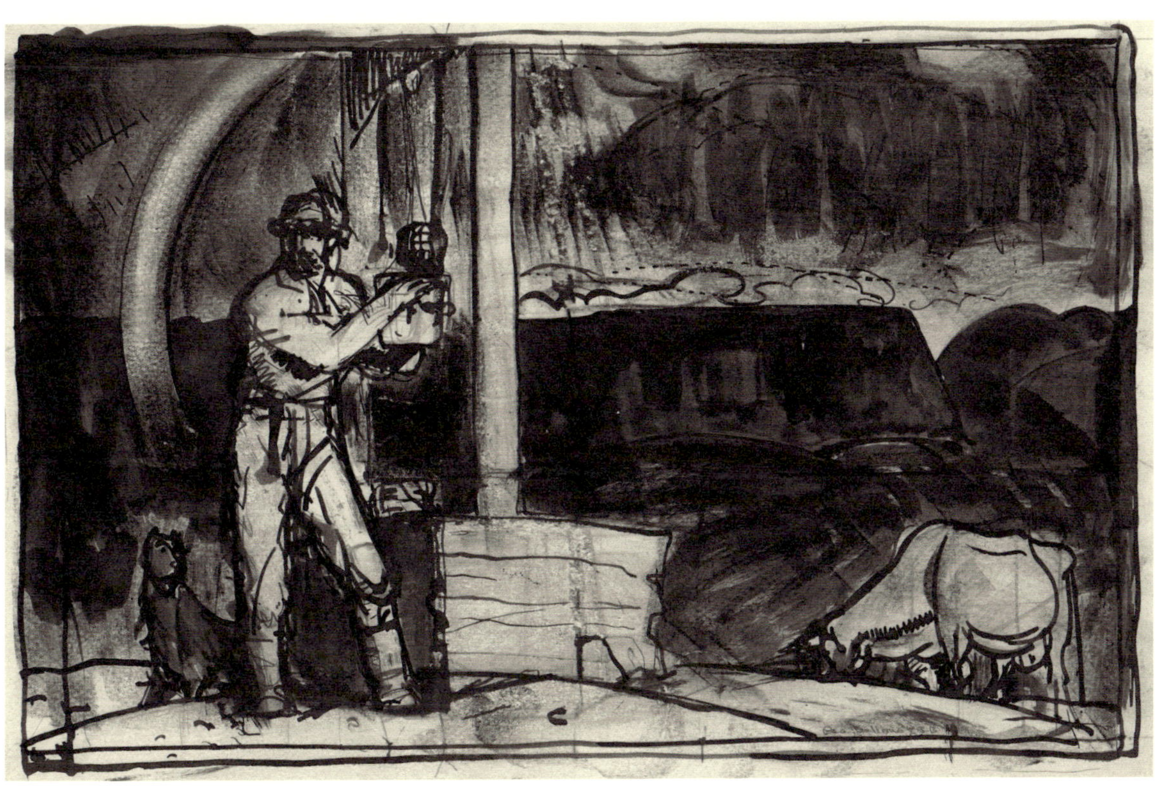

15. FOUR FIGURES IN A ROOM (Two Girls)

Winter 1917. Graphite on lightweight wove paper, 4 15/16 x 6 1/8 in., 125 x 155 mm (image); 5 1/2 x 7 in., 139 x 177 mm (sheet). Signed in graphite in lower right corner of image: *Geo Bellows ESB.*

W.49, BPL 1943.2.9.

SOURCE FOR: *Two Girls*, 1917. Lithograph, 7 5/8 x 8 7/8 in., 193 x 226 mm. B.85, M.41. Described by the artist as *Just a drawing*.

Given by Emma S. Bellows to the Boston Public Library, June 1943 as *Two Girls*.

Although it was also made in preparation for a lithograph, this image of four women in a bedroom differs from the academic life studies Bellows drew the previous year as part of his learning lithography (see cat. no. 11). As Lauris Mason observed about the print, "The girls are animated, rather than adopting the usual static pose of the other nude compositions."[33]

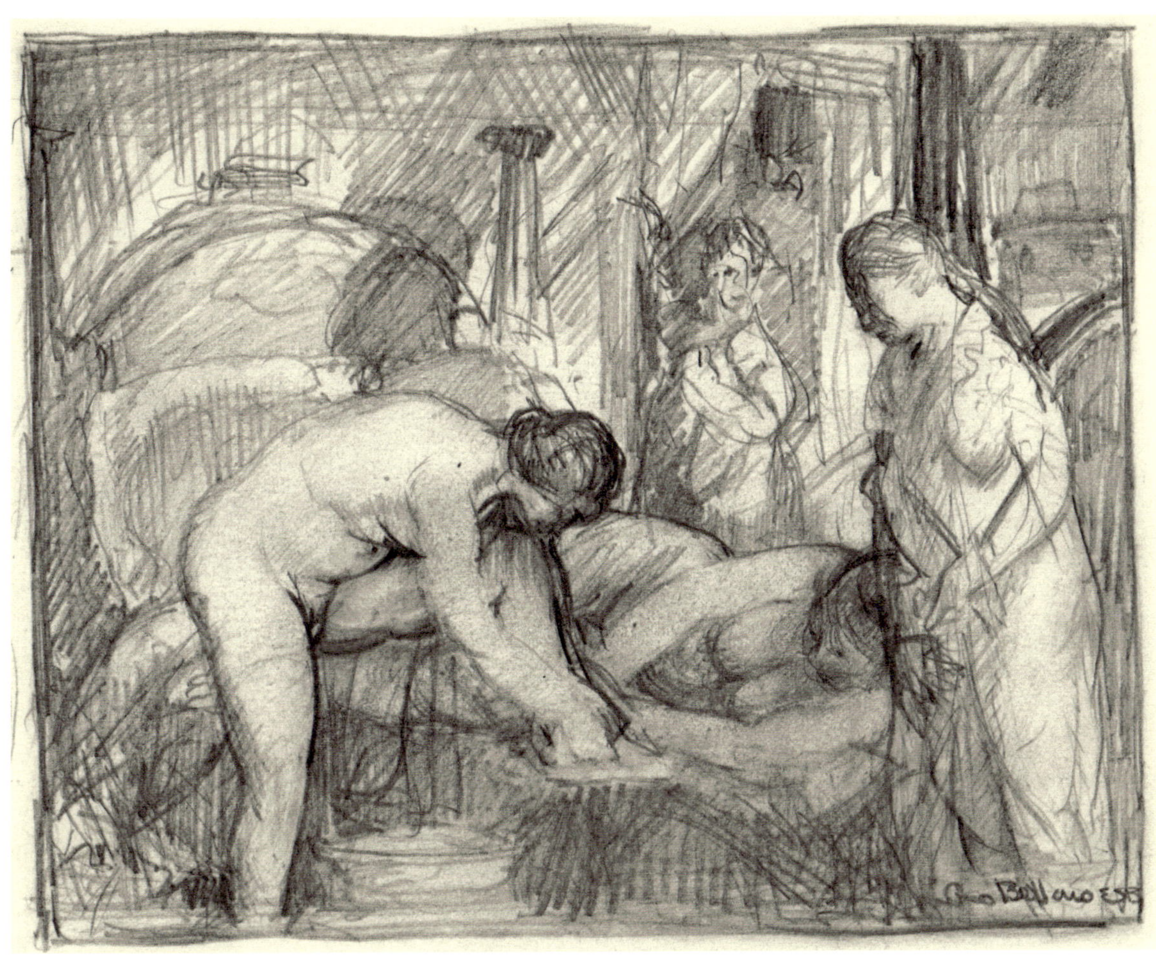

16. A KNOCK DOWN

1917–21. Crayon on light weight, cream colored, wove paper (watermark: Natoma), with a pale orange wash, applied by brush, covering the image and spilling over into the margins, 15 x 19 3/16 in., 380 x 488 mm (image); 21⅝x 27⅜ in., 549 x 696 mm (sheet). Signed in crayon in the lower right corner of the image: *Geo Bellows*, titled *A Knock Down* lower center. Collector's mark: BPL/MB black ink stamp in lower right corner.

W.21, BPL 1943.1.12.

SOURCE FOR: *The White Hope*, 1921. Lithograph, 14½ x 18¾ in., 372 x 476 mm. B.44, M.96, M.&A.56.

Sold by H. V. Allison Galleries to the Boston Public Library, June 1943.

For an artist whose early notoriety arose from his energetic boxing paintings of 1907–09, this drawing is curiously static. The event depicted, the title match between Jack Johnson and Jim Jeffries, occurred in Reno on July 4, 1910. Nearly one hundred postcard photographs of the Johnson/Jeffries fight were published and sold by Dana Photo, San Francisco, CA. The artificial appearance of the drawing most likely arises from its being a composite image of figures derived from photographs and arranged according to a geometrical system.[34]

Bellows drew Jeffries slumped on the canvas and Johnson standing powerfully above him, at the moment of a knockdown. Knockdowns occurred three times during the fight and each was recorded by photographers. The positioning of the two fighters and the

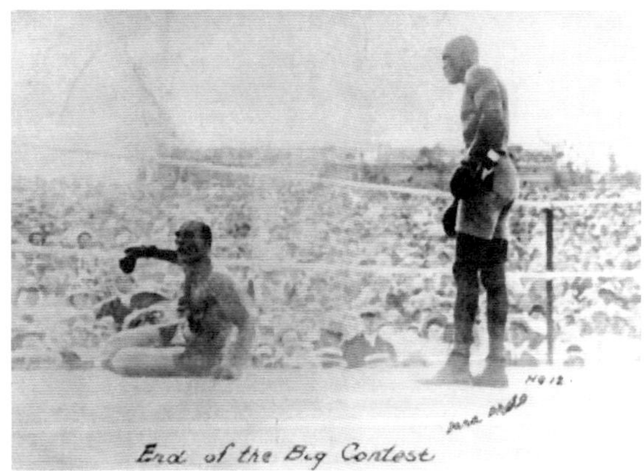

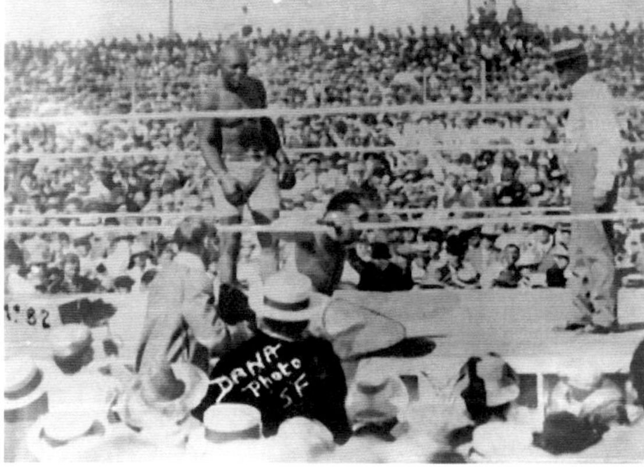

Johnson/Jeffries Fight: *End of the Big Bout*, Dana Photo No. 12 (L), Dana Photo No. 82 (R), photo postcard, 3½ x 5½ inches.

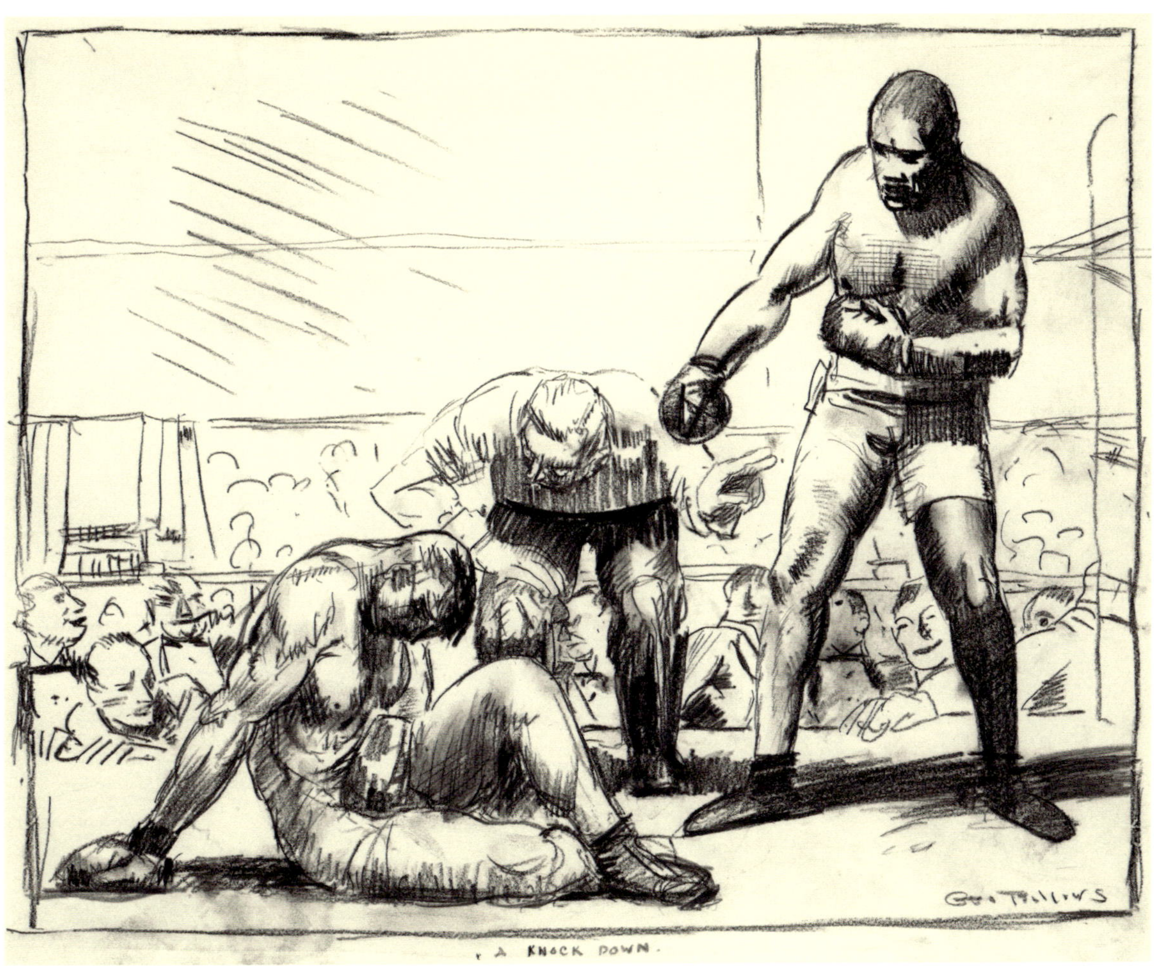
Geo Bellows
A KNOCK DOWN.

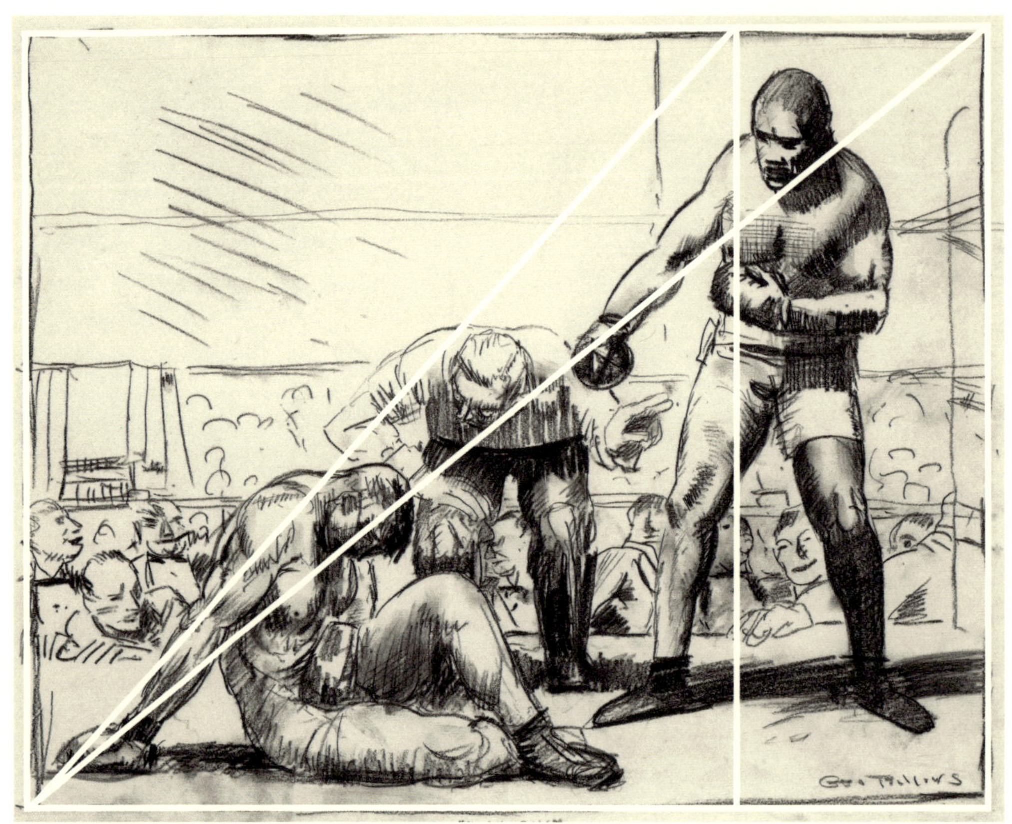

A Knock Down.

referee between them aligns closely to a subdivision of the drawing's surface according to the principles of rebatement, in which the shorter side of the rectangle is used to generate a square inside the rectangle and diagonal lines are drawn across both the rectangle and the square. Bellows began using rebatement in paintings as early as 1909, well before the fight in Reno.[35]

The use of both photography and compositional systems are elements that run through Bellows' work, and it would be tempting to identify *A Knock Down* as a very early instance in which he employed both. There are, however, several factors that suggest a much later date. One is the resemblance between the slumped figure of Jeffries and *Male Torso*, a lithograph of 1916. Another is the stiffness of the poses, which we normally associate with drawings done after the fall of 1917, when Bellows first encountered Jay Hambidge and his theory of Dynamic Symmetry. Dynamic Symmetry is a complicated compositional system whose simplest form recapitulates rebatement as applied to rectangles of specified proportions. *A Knock Down* conforms to one of these proportional ratios, approximately 1:1.3.[36] If this drawing were done as early as 1910, it and its sibling lithograph would be eleven years apart, the longest gap between a drawing and a print derived from it. There is precedent for Bellows recycling ideas from drawings after many years—*Hungry Dogs*, 1907, became a print in 1916—but the time span is usually less than four. Dating it after 1917 reduces the time between the drawing and lithograph to a maximum of four years.[37]

THE TRAGEDIES OF THE WAR IN BELGIUM (*Cat. nos. 17–19*)

Spring–Winter 1918

The War Series consists of twenty lithographs, thirty related drawings and five paintings produced by the artist in response to published reports of the atrocities inflicted on civilians during Germany's invasion of Belgium in August 1914. Bellows used as source material *The Bryce Report*, published in abridged form in the *New York Times*, May 13, 1915, and Brand Whitlock's "Belgium: The Crowning Crime," published in eleven installments in *Everybody's Magazine*, February–December 1918. James Bryce, a member of the International Court at The Hague in 1914 when war broke out, was chairman of the committee investigating Germany's treatment of civilians in Belgium and France. Whitlock was United States Ambassador to Belgium. A number of the images, in their final lithographic versions, were published in *Vanity Fair* and *Everybody's Magazine* between August and December 1918.[38]

17. THE LAST VICTIM

Graphite, crayon, and brush and ink wash, spray and brush varnished on Strathmore Drawing Board, with an overlay of grayish/white pigment, applied by brush irregularly and unevenly over the surface of the image, 19 x 23 11/16 in., 482 x 602 mm (image); 22 7/8 x 29 in., 582 x 737 mm (sheet). Signed in crayon in the lower right corner of the image: *Geo Bellows—* and titled *The Last Victim* lower center and inscribed on the reverse in crayon *Property of / Geo Bellows / 16 E 19 ST / New York City.*

W.22, BPL 1943.1.13.

SOURCE FOR: *The Last Victim*, 1918. Lithograph, 18 7/8 x 23 3/8 in., 480 x 597 mm. B.25, M.56, M.&A.27. Published in *Vanity Fair*, November 1918, 36. Described by the artist as: *German soldiers enter a peasant home during the first passage through Belgium. They kill mother, father, brother and have a further inspiration about the girl. Incidents of this nature were wholesale according to the official evidence.*

Sold by H. V. Allison Galleries to A. H. Wiggin, June 1943.

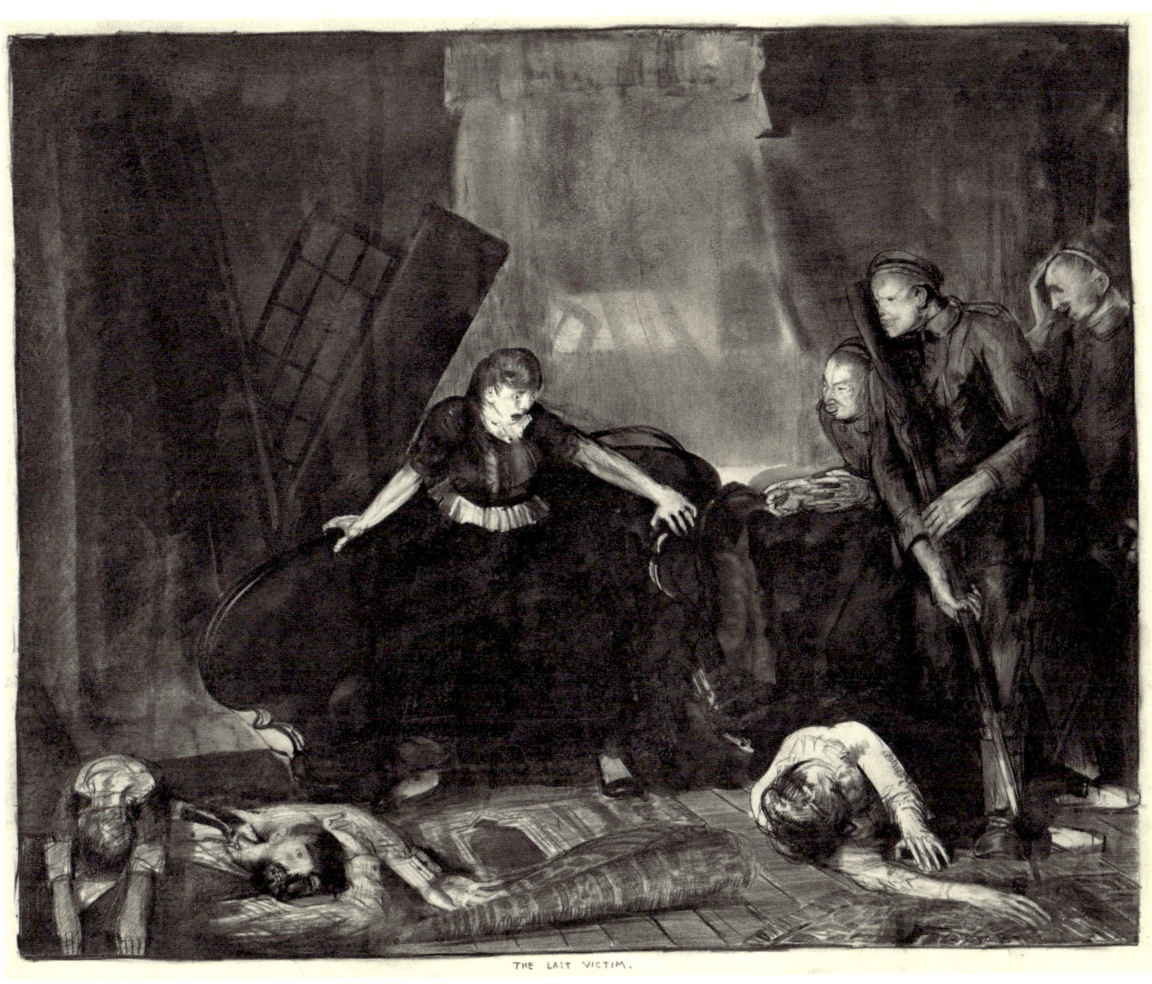

THE LAST VICTIM.

18. RETURN OF THE USELESS

Graphite, crayon and black ink on cream colored thin card, most likely Strathmore Drawing Board, spray and brush varnished, $19\frac{3}{4}$ x $12\frac{11}{16}$ in., 503 x 552 mm (image); $22\frac{15}{16}$ x $25\frac{1}{2}$ in., 583 x 649 mm (sheet). Signed in crayon within the image, on the lower crate used as a step: *Geo. Bellows—*, titled in ink lower center *Return of the Useless* and annotated in another hand in graphite lower right *for Belgium Dec* and upper center *–6 $\frac{7}{8}$– with care do not rub!* Collector's mark: BPL/MB black ink stamp in lower right corner of sheet.

W.35, BPL 1943.1.19. Published in *Everybody's Magazine*, December 1918, 13 to illustrate the eleventh installment of "Belgium: The Crowning Crime" by Brand Whitlock.[39]

SOURCE FOR: *Return of the Useless*, 1918. Lithograph, $18\frac{7}{8}$ x $23\frac{3}{8}$ in., 503 x 546 mm. B.149, M.67. Described by the artist as: *Belgian slaves being shipped back and dumped, broken in health and useless for further exploitation by their German masters. A man has fallen exhausted and is being kicked by a guard.*

STUDY FOR: *Return of the Useless*, November 1918. Oil on canvas, 59 x 66 in., 1499 x 1676 mm. Record Book B, p. 154. Private collection.

Sold by H. V. Allison Galleries to A. H. Wiggin, June 1943.

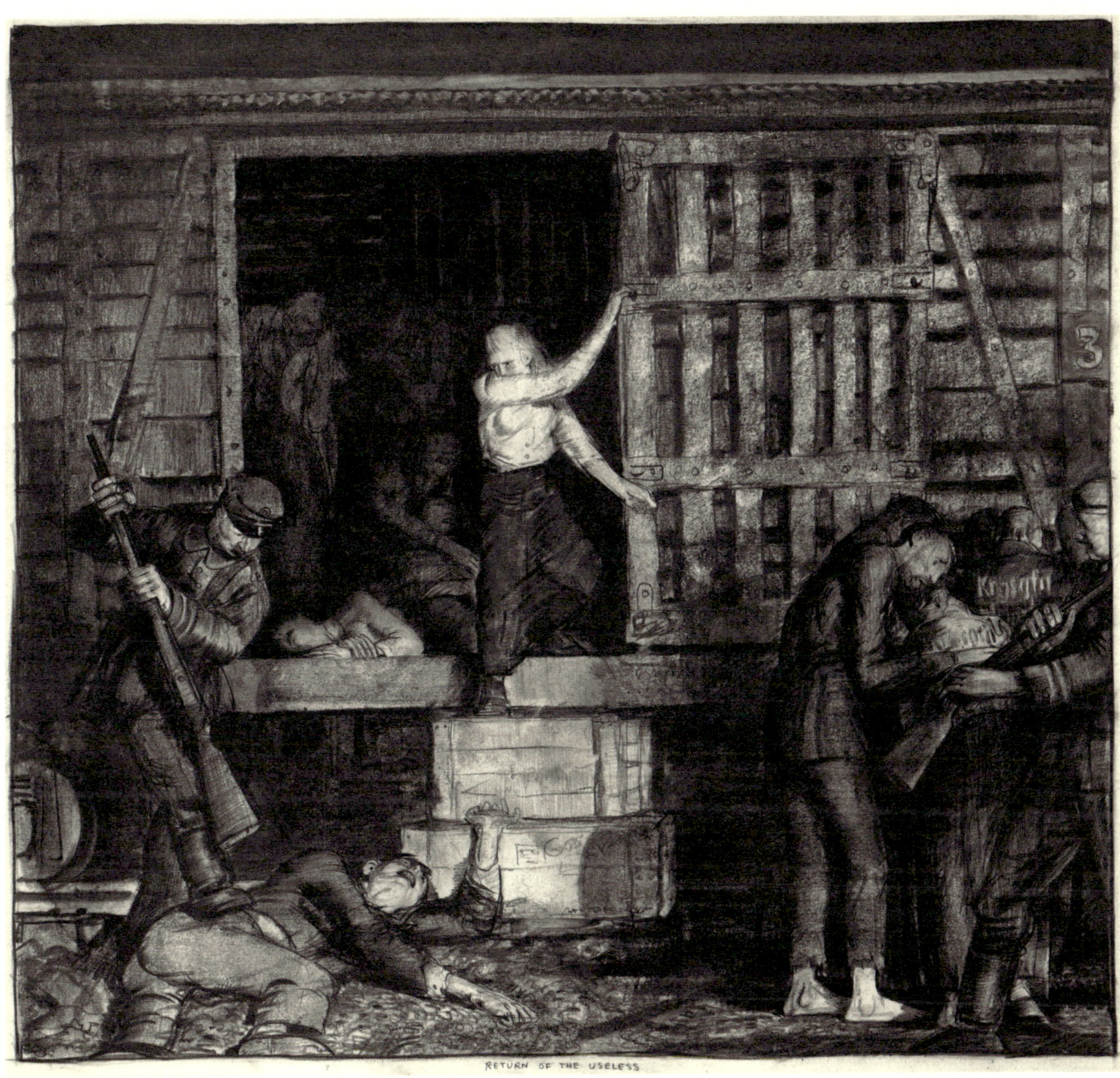

RETURN OF THE USELESS

19. THE BARRICADE

Crayon, varnished, on Strathmore Drawing Board, with a panel of the same paper attached at either side of the central sheet, 17 3/16 x 28 7/8 in., 437 x 735 mm (image); 22 7/8 x 28 7/8 inches, 582 x 735 mm (sheet). Signed in crayon at the bottom edge of the image, just to the right of center: *Geo Bellows—* and titled *THE BARRICADE* in crayon lower center.

W.3, BPL 1943.1.3.

SOURCE FOR: *The Barricade*, 1918. Lithograph, 17 1/8 x 21 1/2 in., 436 x 724 mm. B.41, M.61. Described by the artist as: *Belgian civilians in at least one instance were stripped and marched in front of the troops as a shield.*

STUDY FOR: *The Barricade*, 1918. Oil on canvas, 49 1/8 x 83 1/4 in., 1248 x 2115 mm. Record Book B, p. 143. Birmingham Museum of Art, AL.

Sold by H. V. Allison Galleries to A. H. Wiggin, June 1943.

In November 1918, Bellows exhibited his War Series at Keppel Galleries in New York. In the preface to the show's checklist, he wrote:

> *In presenting these pictures of the tragedies of war, I wish to disclaim any intention of attacking a race or a people. Guilt is personal, not racial. Against that guilty clique and all its tools, who organized and let loose upon innocence every diabolical device and insane instinct, my hatred goes forth, together with my profound reverence for the victims.*[40]

Hatred and reverence are the powerful combination that sustained the artist through all twenty searing, explicit depictions of the documented brutality inflicted by soldiers on civilians.

The War Series has been compared favorably to Francisco Goya y Lucientes' *Disasters of War*, 1810–20, one of the monuments in the histories of both political art and printmaking.[41] A source of praise much closer to home came from Charles Dana Gibson, the premier illustrator in America. Gibson previewed the work as it was collected at Keppel Galleries in the spring prior to the fall exhibition, and wrote later that summer to Bellows:

> *These war things of yours are tremendous. . . . I saw the five powerful lithographs and was again deeply impressed by them and I hope they hang in the room when they discuss peace terms. . . . It is a pity these pictures were not made when the war started.*[42]

Gibson's praise cannot be underestimated. As an aspiring artist in high school and college, Bellows closely imitated Gibson's elegant style. In 1904, when Bellows first arrived at the New York School of Art and presented his portfolio of Gibsonesque drawings to Robert Henri, Henri noted their derivative nature and set out to change the younger man's aesthetic.[43] Bellows, enthusiastic and enormously talented, embraced Henri's teachings and became the most critically and commercially successful member of his circle of New York realists. Now, fourteen years later, Gibson, the stylish inspiration of his youth, championed the most inelegant, unstylish work of his maturity.[44]

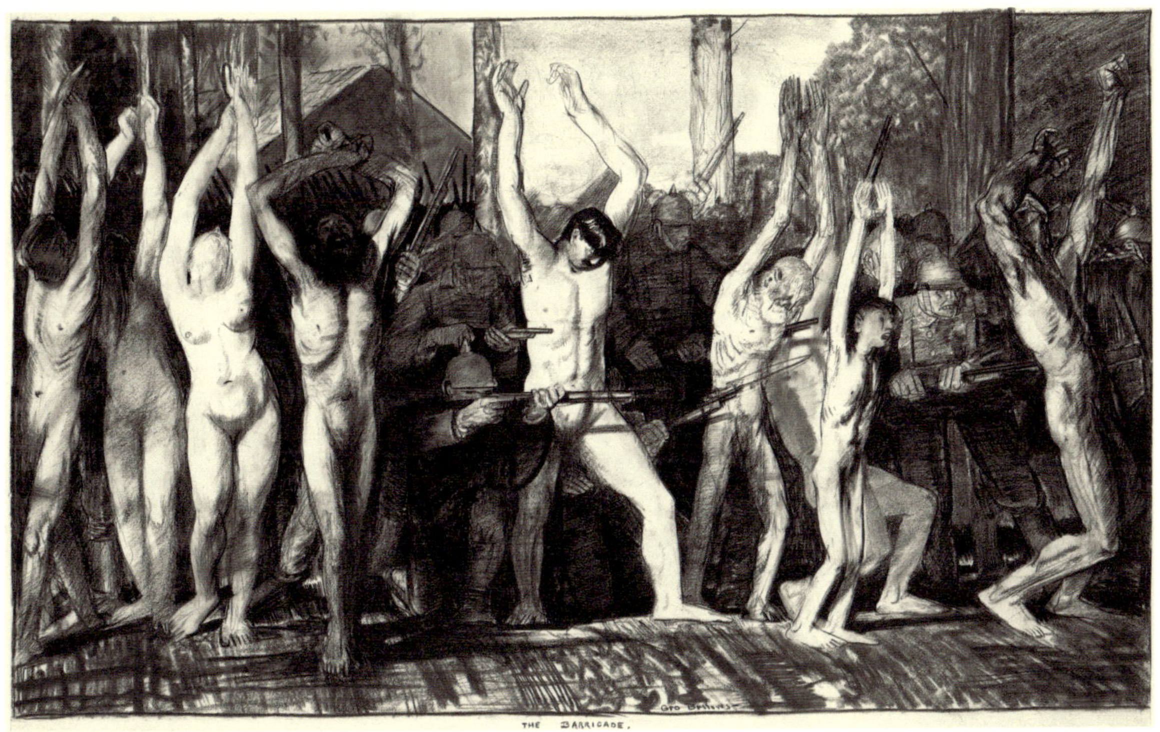
Geo Bellows
THE BARRICADE.

20. BASE HOSPITAL

1916–1918. Crayon and graphite on newsprint, mounted on paper faced, two ply woodpulp board, 11½ x 9¼ in., 292 x 235 mm (image and sheet); 17⅝ x 14 1/16 in., 449 x 357 mm (mount). Signed in graphite at the center of the bottom edge of the image: *Geo Bellows ESB.*

W.4, BPL 1943.1.4.

SOURCE FOR: *Base Hospital*, 1918. Lithograph, 17¼ x 13½ in., 445 x 340 mm. B.145, M.52, M.&A.53.[45] Described by the artist as: *Study of a doctor's clinic at a dressing station in a cathedral. An effort to see what could be done with photographs as material.*

Sold by H. V. Allison Galleries to A. H. Wiggin, June 1943.

As he acknowledges in his comment regarding the lithograph, Bellows based his drawing upon a photograph, *Church Field Hospital*, reproduced in *Collier's New Photographic History of the European War*, New York, 1916, 137, with the caption: "One of the many beautiful French churches close to the battle fronts. This one is being utilized as a first-aid field hospital."

Comparison of the drawing with the photograph shows how easily Bellows constructed an effective illustration. Although he followed the photograph relatively faithfully in the group of figures standing around the doctor and patient, he brings them closer into the foreground while pushing the background of the building farther away from them. In the intervening space, he invents a tall crossing or apse from which dramatic sunlight streams onto a wall behind the medical team.

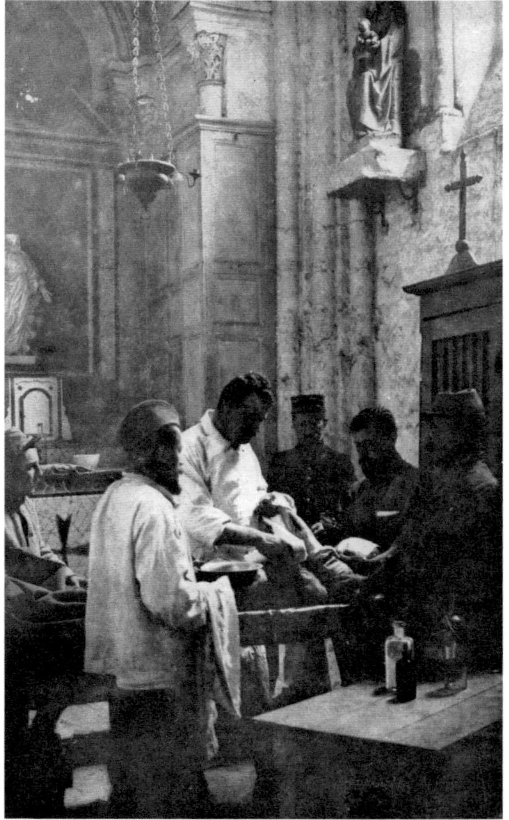

Church Field Hospital, 1916, photograph.

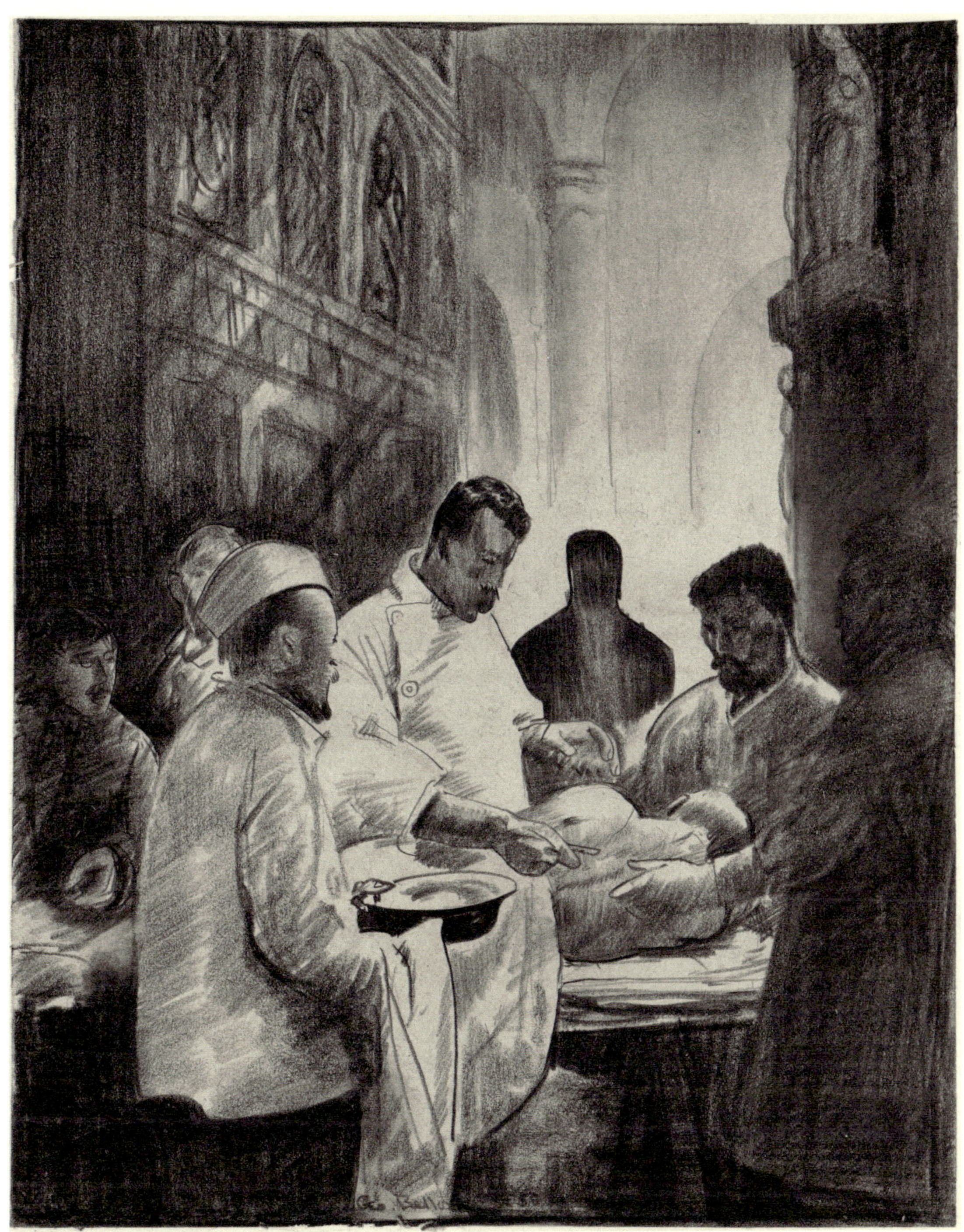

21. DOVES AND FIGURES

Fall 1918. Crayon on lightweight, wove newsprint mounted on 4-ply ragboard, 17¼ x 13 5/16 in., 440 x 339 mm (sheet); 19 9/16 x 15½ in., 497 x 394 mm (mount). Signed in graphite in the lower right corner of the sheet: *Geo. Bellows for red cross (symbol)*. Collector's mark: BPL/MB black ink stamp in lower left corner.

W.13, BPL 1957.1.1.

STUDY FOR: *Dawn of Peace*, November 1918. Oil on canvas, 104 x 79 in., 2642 x 2007 mm. Record Book B, p. 155. Allentown Art Museum, PA.

STUDY FOR: *Hail to Peace, Christmas 1918*, 1919. Lithograph, 4½ x 3¼ in., 114 x 83 mm. B.178, M.68.

Lebowich Gift to Boston Public Library, July 1957.

In November 1918, shortly after Armistice was declared, the prestigious art dealer Joseph Duveen, acting on behalf of his client Helen Clay Frick, commissioned Bellows to make two large paintings celebrating the end of the war.[46] This sheet is a very preliminary study for one of them, *Dawn of Peace*. In two rectangles in the upper half of the sheet, the artist roughed out his basic composition, and in the lower half he drew several doves in flight.

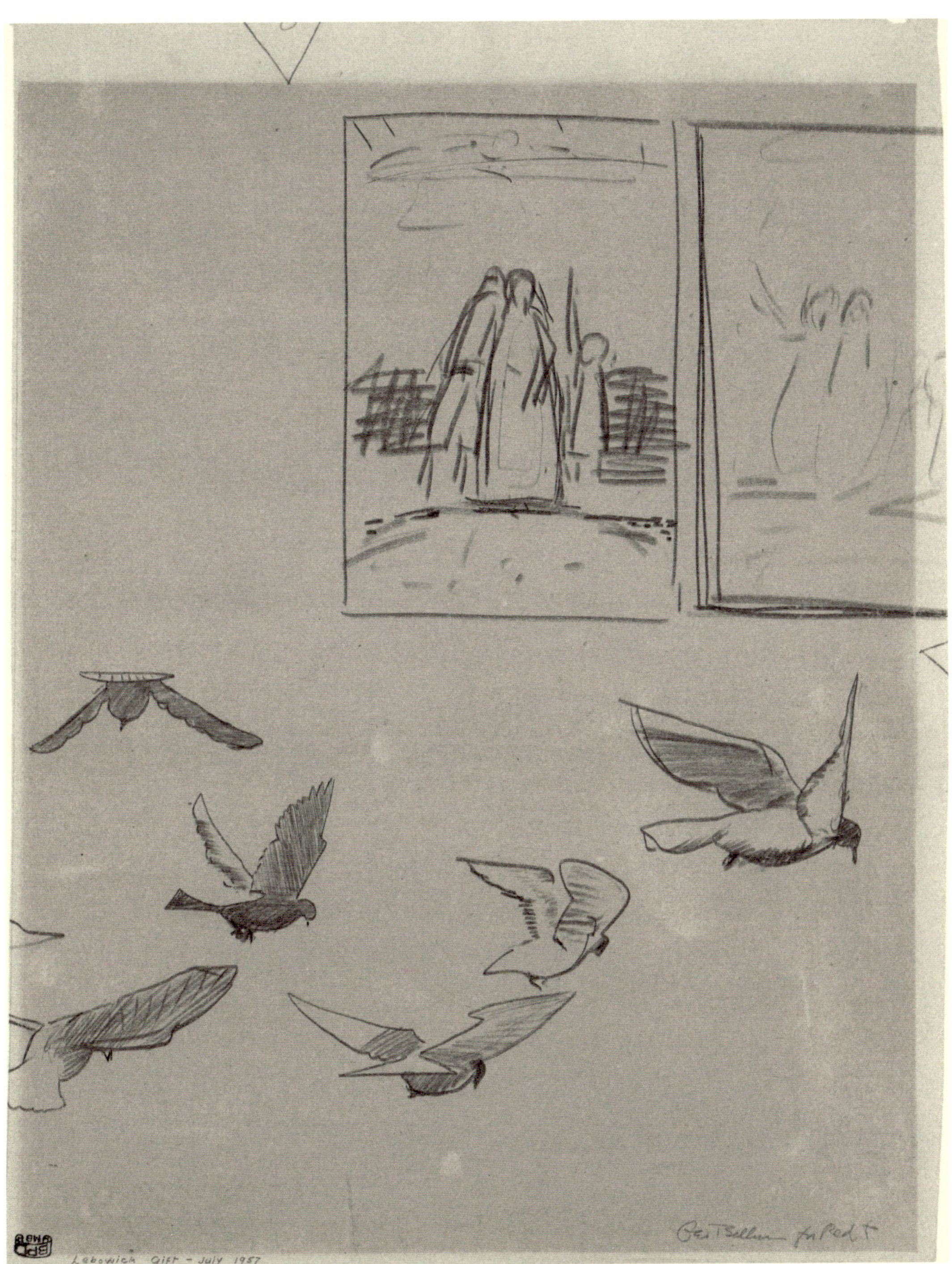

22. THE BEACH and GIRL ON BEACH (on the reverse) (Study for Legs of the Sea)

June 1919. Graphite on cream wove paper (partial watermark: . . . CHESS with D in a diamond above), 6⅝ x 8⅛ in., 168 x 206 mm (sheet). Signed in graphite right of center on bottom edge of sheet: *Geo. Bellows E.S.B.*

W.24 and 25, BPL 1943.2.6.

PRELIMINARY STUDIES FOR: *The Beach*, June 1919. Oil on canvas, 26 x 32 in., 660 x 813 mm. Record Book B, p. 163. Private Collection.

Given by Emma S. Bellows to the Boston Public Library, June 1943, as *Study for Legs of the Sea*.

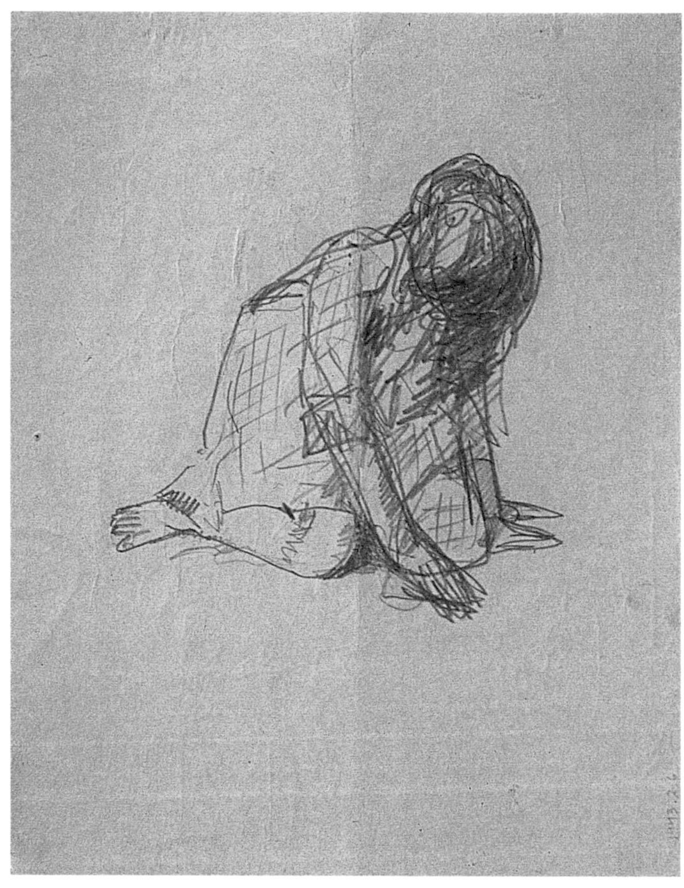

Cat. no. 22, Girl on Beach (reverse)

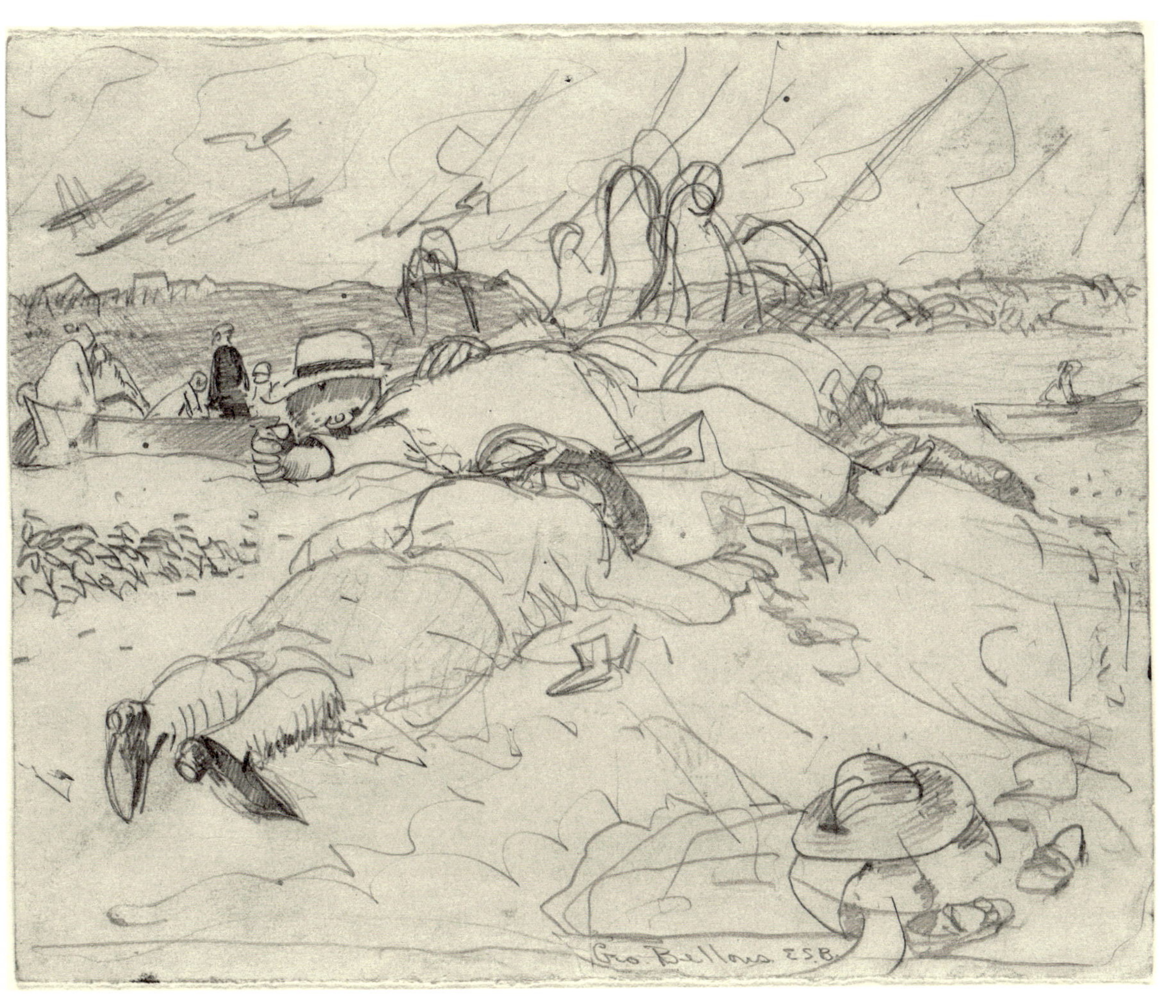
Geo. Bellows E.S.B.

23. THE BEACH (Legs of the Sea)

June 1919. Crayon on smooth, lightweight, cream-colored, wove paper (watermark: Natoma), 14¼ x 20¹¹⁄₁₆ in., 363 x 525 mm (image); 15⅝ x 21¹⁵⁄₁₆ in., 397 x 559 mm (sheet). Signed in crayon in the lower right corner of the image: *Geo Bellows—*. Collector's mark: BPL/MB black ink stamp lower right corner.

W.26, BPL 1943.1.14.

STUDY FOR: *The Beach*, June 1919. Oil on canvas, 26 x 32 in., 660 x 813 mm. Record Book B, p.163. Private Collection.

SOURCE FOR: *Legs of the Sea*, 1921. Lithograph, 8½ x 10⅝ in., 216 x 271 mm. B.131, M.85, M.&A.42.

Sold by H. V. Allison Galleries to A. H. Wiggin, June 1943, as *Legs of the Sea*.

Starting after their marriage in September 1910, George and Emma Bellows, and eventually their two daughters and sometimes a grandparent or aunt, left New York each summer for vacation. The first few seasons were spent in Emma's hometown, Montclair, New Jersey. Beginning in 1913, the family traveled farther afield, to Monhegan Island and other parts of Maine, to Carmel, California and Middletown, Rhode Island. From 1920 to 1925, the family summered in Woodstock, New York, where George built a house and studio. Vacations in mostly rural surroundings were important sources of inspiration for the artist.

These three sketches come from a visit to Third Beach, Newport, Rhode Island. Bellows' humorous take on the fully dressed couple collapsed on the sand documents his return from the savage images of his War Series to a pre-war mood of gentle satire.[47]

The existence of two very similar drawings, one a quick sketch in graphite on light paper (cat. no. 22) and the other a much more finished crayon drawing on heavier paper, indicates that the first was made on-site and the second back in the studio, intended to be used as a reference point for a painting. The normal procedure for most artists, such a development of the image is relatively rare for Bellows. He was known for having a powerful memory that made field sketches unnecessary.[48]

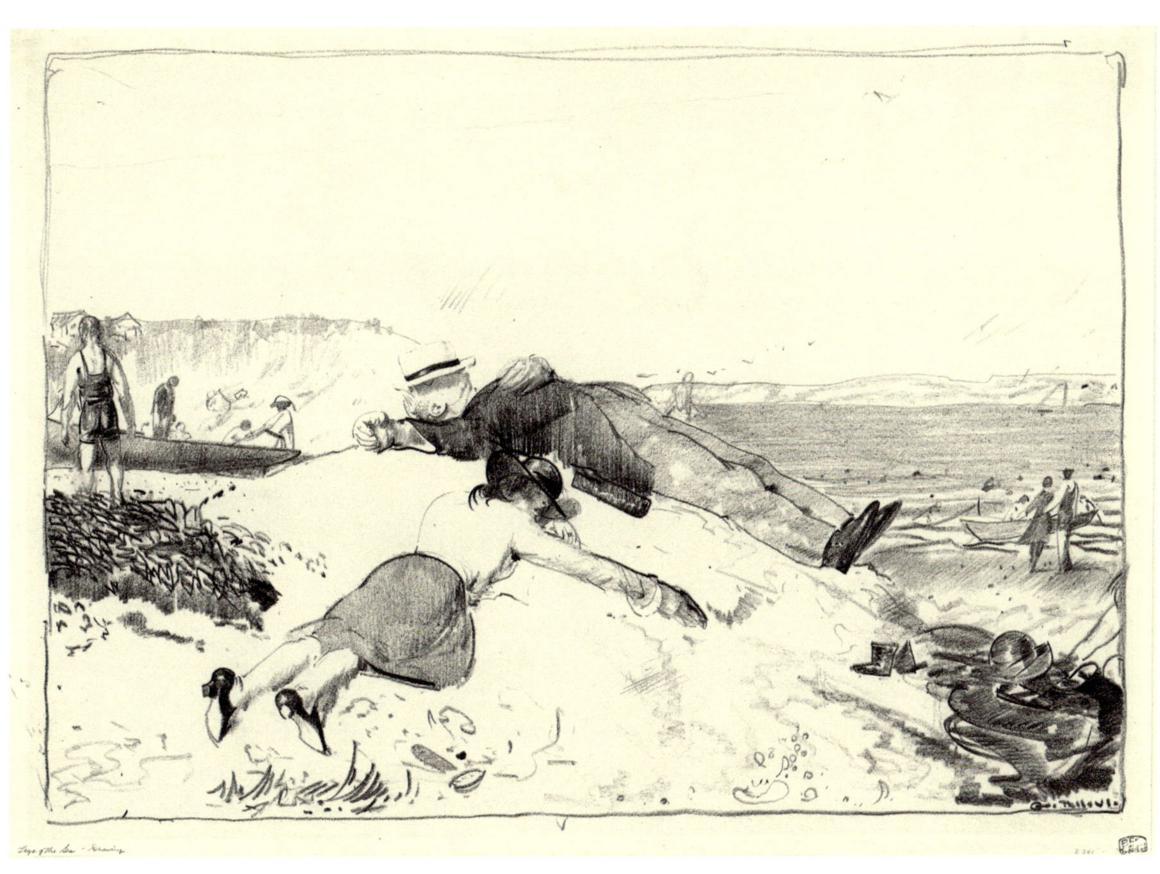

24. STUDY FOR BATHING BEACH

Summer 1918 or 1919. Crayon on cream lightweight wove paper (watermark: IMPERIAL), 10⅜ x 7⅞ in., 263 x 200 mm (sheet). Signed in graphite in lower right corner of sheet: *Geo Bellows E.S.B.*

W.5, BPL 1943.2.1.

STUDY FOR: *Bathing Beach*, 1921. Lithograph, 8⅜ x 7 in. B.18, M.86, M.&A.30.

Given by Emma S. Bellows to the Boston Public Library, June 1943.

25. STUDY FOR BATHING BEACH (Girl on Sand)

Summer 1918 or 1919. Crayon on lightweight cream wove paper, 8 x 10⅝ in., 203 x 270 mm (sheet). Signed in graphite in lower right corner of the sheet: *Geo. Bellows ESB.*

W.16 as *Girl on Sand*, BPL 1943.2.4.

STUDY FOR: *Bathing Beach*, 1921. Lithograph, 8⅜ x 7 in., 215 x 179 mm. B.18, M.86.

Given by Emma S. Bellows to the Boston Public Library, June 1943.

A pair of preparatory drawings for another scene at Third Beach, Newport suggests that Bellows relied more on the convention of sketching on-site than the legend of his photographic memory admits. These two sheets look like visual notes recorded for use at another time and place, in this case several years later in New York, when their figures appeared in a lithograph.

The similarities between the second sheet of the girl lying on the sand and a photo of Emma Bellows swimming in the surf with water wings raise the question of the artist's involvement with photography. Several other drawings in the Wiggin Collection are connected to photographs, and further investigation may reveal the extent to which Bellows used the medium as a source for his art.[49]

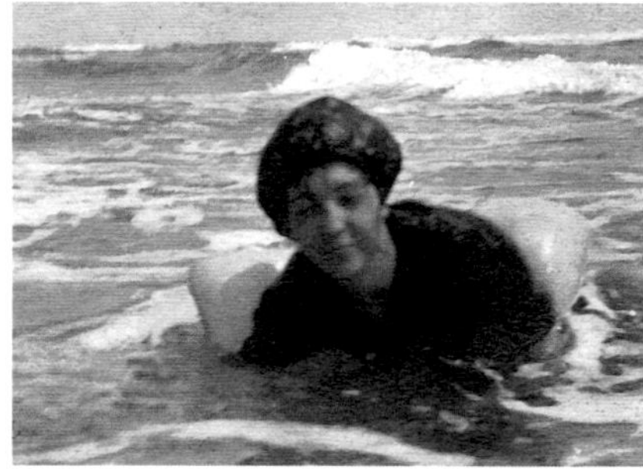

Emma Bellows Swimming, Rhode Island, 1918–19, photograph, approx. 1½ x 3 inches.

Cat. no. 24.

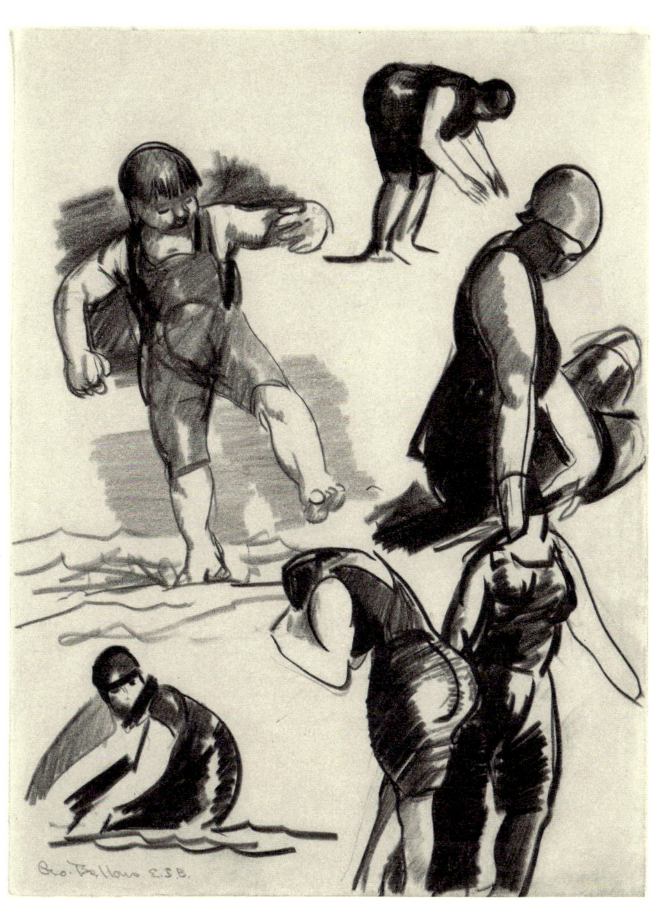

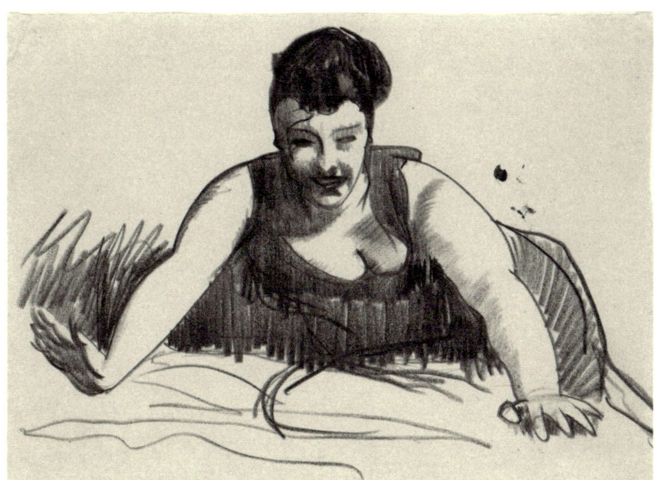

Cat. no. 25.

26. STUDY FOR INDOOR ATHLETE NO. 1

Winter 1917–Winter 1921. Graphite on heavy weight cream wove paper, with a less-developed sketch of a similar subject on the reverse, 7⅞ x 7¹⁄₁₆ in., 200 x 179 mm (sheet). Initialed in graphite in the lower right below the figure: *G.B. E.S.B*; signed in graphite in the lower left corner of the sheet: *Geo. Bellows, E.S.B.*

W.7 and 8, BPL 1941.1.1.

STUDY FOR: *Indoor Athlete No. 1*, 1921. Lithograph, 6½ x 9¾ in., 164 x 251 mm. B.62, M.81 as *Indoor Athlete, First Stone*, M.&A.37.

Sold by Frederick Keppel Galleries to A. H. Wiggin, October 1936.

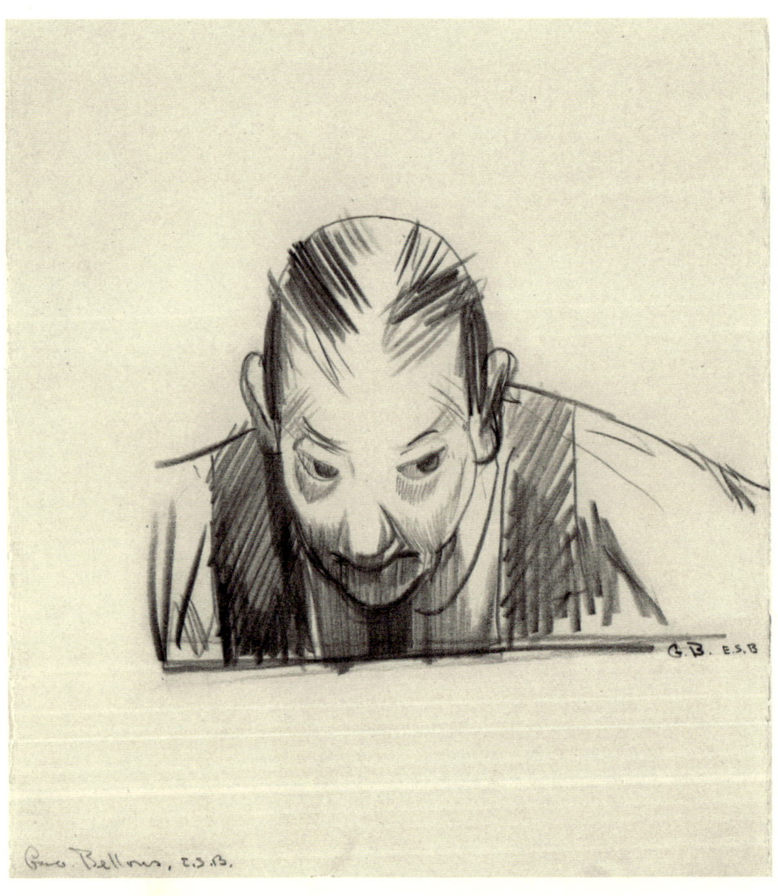

27. STUDY FOR INDOOR ATHLETE NO. 2

Winter 1917–Winter 1921. Most likely crayon, possibly graphite, on cream wove heavy weight paper, with a partial sketch of geometric shapes with numerical notations on the reverse, 6⁵⁄₁₆ x 5¾ in., 164 x 145 mm (sheet). Signed in graphite in lower left corner of sheet: *Geo. Bellows E.S.B.*

W.9, BPL 1941.1.2.

STUDY FOR: *Indoor Athlete No. 2*, 1921. Lithograph, 5¼ x 9 in., 130 x 228 mm. B.77, M.82 as *Indoor Athlete, Second Stone*, M.&A.38.

Sold by Frederick Keppel Galleries to A. H. Wiggin, October 1936.

George and Emma Bellows formed a billiards club in 1917 with their friends Randall Davey, Robert Henri, John Sloan and their wives. By 1920, he and his friends were also playing at the National Arts Club in Gramercy Park, which is most likely the setting for these studies.[50] Comparison to the related pair of lithographs shows that these are preliminary sketches rather than preparatory drawings for the complete images and probably done on-site.

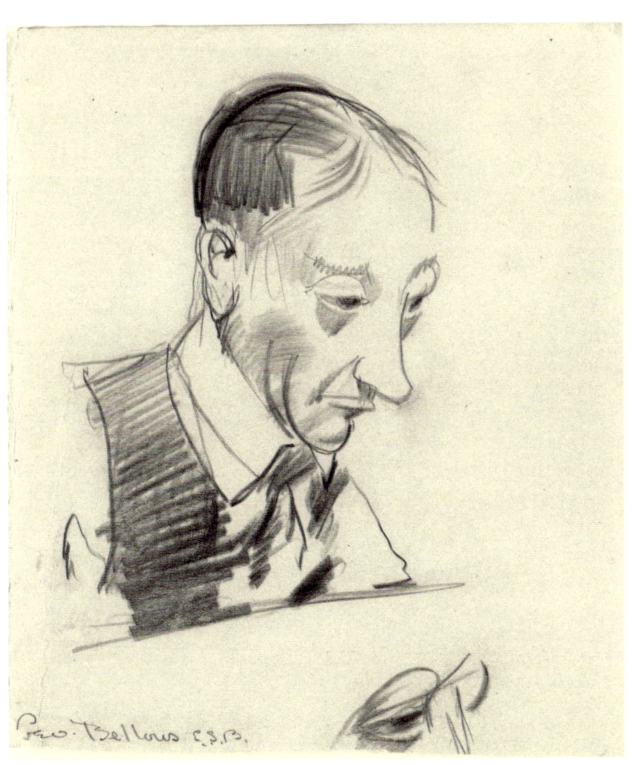

28. PARADE FORMS ON THE RIGHT (Spring, Central Park)

1921. Crayon on medium, cream-colored wove paper, 13½ x 10¾ in., 342 x 273 mm (image); 18⅜ x 16 11/16 in., 467 x 425 mm (sheet). Signed in crayon in the lower right corner of the image: *Geo. Bellows* and titled *Parade Forms on the Right* lower center.

W.42, BPL 1943.1.23.

SOURCE FOR: *Spring, Central Park*, 1921. Lithograph, 8½ x 7 in., 215 x 178 mm. ESB.72, M.90, M.&A.53.

Sold by H. V. Allison Galleries to A. H. Wiggin, June 1943 as *Spring, Central Park.*

George Bellows knew exactly what it took to make a winning illustration: clear presentation, keenly observed detail, and an effective "hook."[51] *Parade Forms on the Right*, a fully realized but relatively minor example of his drawing style, contains all of these ingredients. Bellows puts his main subject, two stylish young women, front and center. Details such as the women's fur muffs and lightweight shoes, the tree limbs and the angle of the cast shadows establish an atmosphere: a sunny but still chilly morning or afternoon in early spring, after the snow is gone but before the leaves are fully out. The suggestion of a group of women and girls in the left background adds a subtle note of safety, while the group of men in the right middle ground contributes a fantasy of romantic intrigue that the artist dispels with his gently sarcastic title.

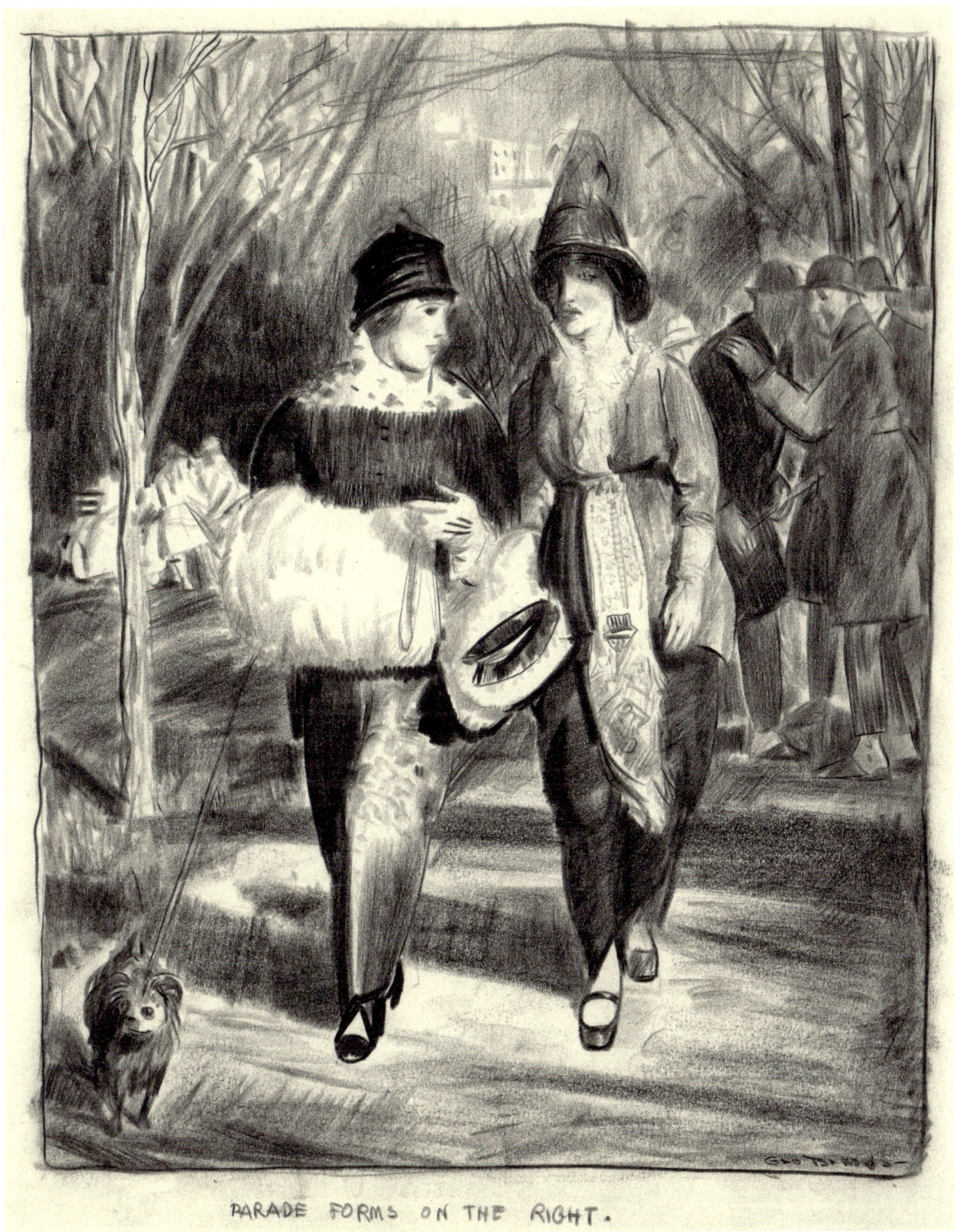

PARADE FORMS ON THE RIGHT.

29. INTRODUCING GEORGES CARPENTIER

July 1921. Crayon with touches of pale brown wash on smooth, dark cream, wove one ply card stock, 19 x 25¼ in. Signed in graphite in the lower right corner of the image: *Geo Bellows*; an erased title in graphite center, below the image: CHOCK FULL O NUTS. Collectors' marks: Wiggin Collection black ink stamp in lower right recto corner, BPL/MB black ink stamp in lower left recto corner.

W.19, BPL 1943.1.11.

A closely related crayon and wash drawing, formerly in the Chester Dale collection, was published in *New York World*, July 1921. It is the SOURCE FOR: *Introducing Georges Carpentier*, 1921. Lithograph, 14½ x 20⅞ in., 368 x 530 mm. ESB.116, M.98.

Sold by H. V. Allison Galleries to A. H. Wiggin, June 1943.

On July 2, 1921, eighty thousand spectators gathered at Boyle's Thirty Acres in Jersey City to watch the heavyweight champion Jack Dempsey defeat the French light-heavyweight George Carpentier. With the First World War fresh in memory, the crowd strongly favored Carpentier, a decorated veteran in the French army, over Dempsey, whom they considered a draft dodger.[52]

Bellows, on assignment for *New York World*, sat in the press section, seen here in the foreground.[53] By expertly controlling his sense of space and scale and picking his exact moment, he offers much more than a ringside seat. From the humorous detail of a man eating in the extreme right foreground to the elevated platform of the film crews holding the middle ground to the vast expanse of the crowd in the background, Bellows conveys the experience of attending the first million-dollar gate in prizefighting history. It began with a roar of applause for Carpentier and quickly ended with a knockout by Dempsey in the fourth round. Bellows chose the defeated Frenchman's only moment of acclaim, before the fight actually started.[54]

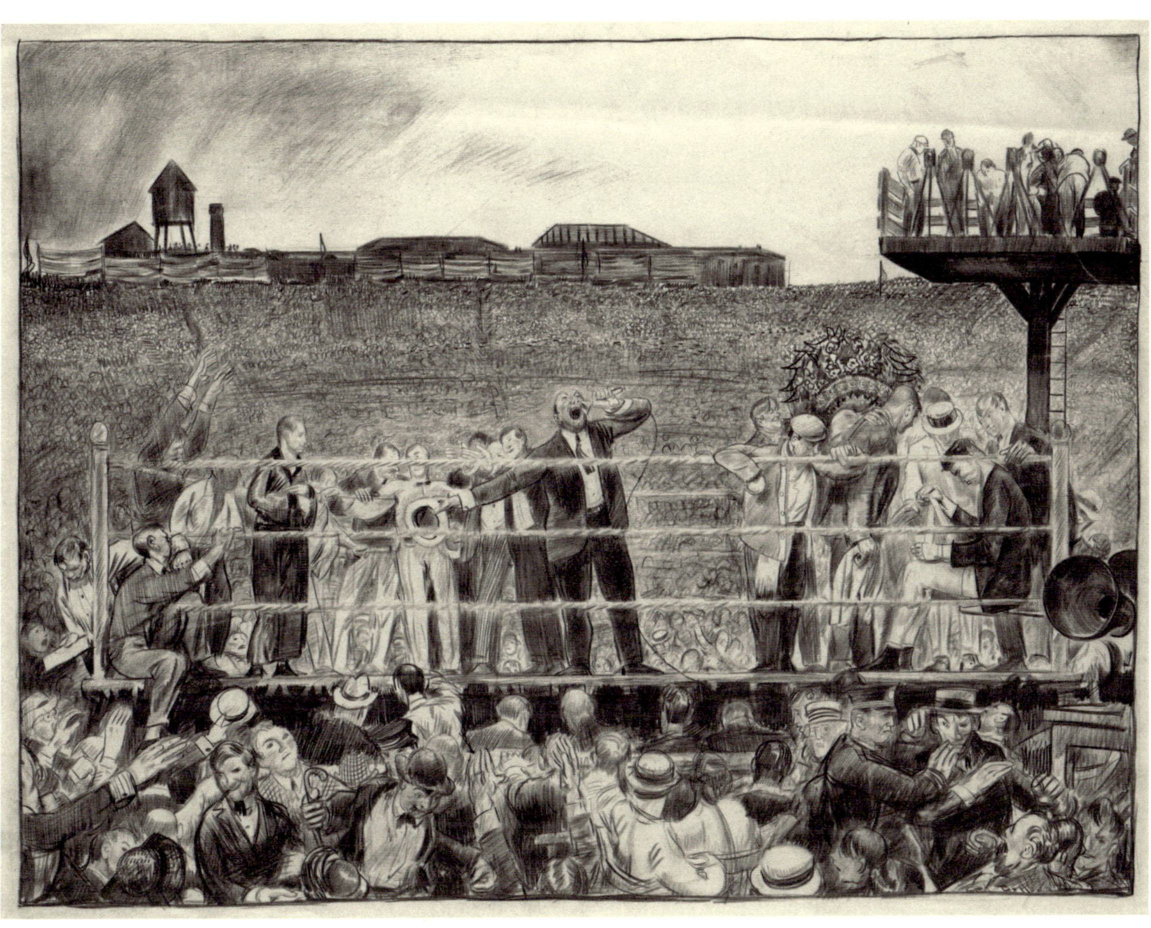

30. ELSIE, FIGURE

1921. Crayon on brown newsprint paper, 11 11/16 x 5 7/8 in., 297 x 150 mm (sheet). Signed in graphite in lower right below image: *Geo Bellows E.S.B.*

W.14, BPL 1943.2.3.

STUDY FOR: *Study (Three Women Visiting)*, 1921. Crayon, 11 3/4 x 14 in., 298 x 356 mm. Art Institute of Chicago.

SOURCE FOR: *Elsie, Figure*, 1921. Lithograph, 10 1/2 x 8 in., 274 x 202 mm. B.59, M.109.

Given by Emma S. Bellows to the Boston Public Library, June 1943.

31. ELSIE

1921. Crayon on off-white, medium weight, wove paper, 14 1/8 x 10 1/2 in, 360 x 267 mm (sheet). Signed in graphite in lower right corner of the sheet: *Geo. Bellows—E.S.B.*

W.15, BPL 1943.2.2.

STUDY FOR: *Elsie, Emma and Marjorie, No. 1*, 1921. Lithograph, 9 5/8 x 12 1/4 in., 243 x 311 mm. B.144, M.103 as *Elsie, Emma and Marjorie, First Stone.*

Given by Emma S. Bellows to the Boston Public Library, June 1943.

In 1921, Bellows produced a group of twelve lithographs showing him and Emma socializing with their closest friends Robert and Marjorie Henri, Elsie and Eugene Speicher, and Leon Kroll. Of these, four deal with a single gathering of the three couples, with the women seated in the foreground and the men standing in the background. Both drawings of Elsie Speicher were steps in the artist's development of the four prints.

Two decades later, Kroll described their evenings together:

> *(Bellows) and Speicher and Henri and Kroll used to meet regularly in the evenings, about three times a week. The meetings usually took place in Bellows' 19th Street studio, but they frequently met in the home of one of the others. The artists' wives were almost always included. The ladies would occasionally join the men in a game of poker, but more often they retired to another room to gossip and knit while the men talked about art.*[55]

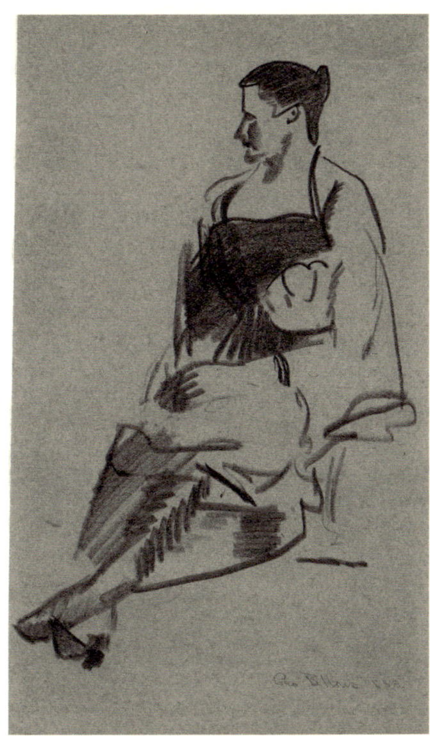

Cat. no. 30.

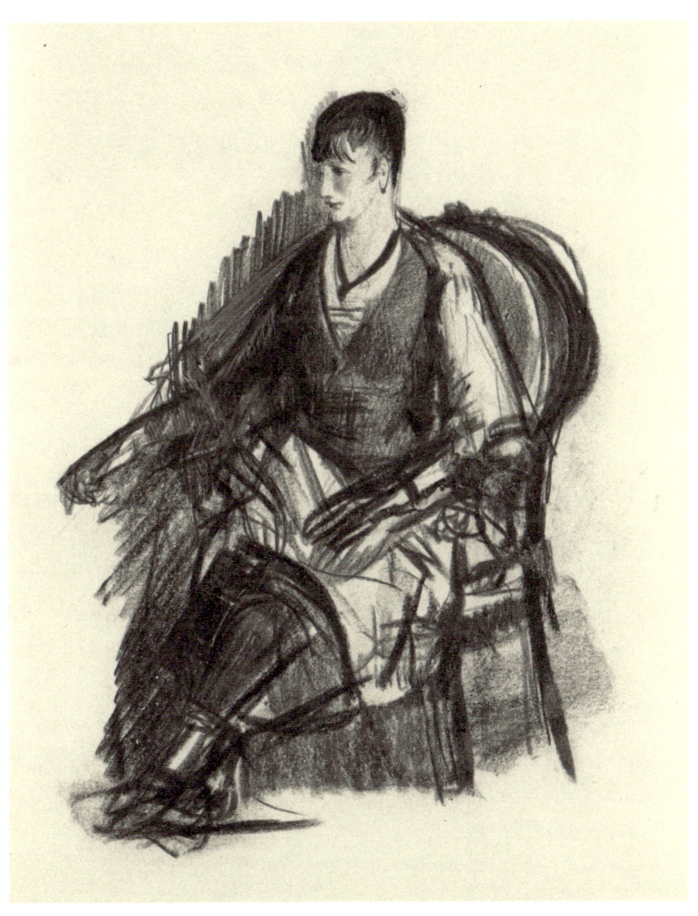

Cat. no. 31.

Illustrations for THE WIND BLOWETH (*Cat. nos. 32–34*)

January and February 1922.

Record Book B, p. 267.

Catalogue numbers 32–34 are two preparatory sketches and one finished drawing from a group of fifteen illustrations and one portrait of the author commissioned by *Century* magazine to accompany its serialized publication of Donne Byrne's novel, *The Wind Bloweth*, April to September 1922.[56] For this job, Bellows prepared, as he noted in his Record Book, "some 60 studies of periods and places in crayon." Two of these studies and one finished composition are in the Wiggin Collection. Eight of the fifteen finished images were reproduced in the hardcover edition of the book, also published by Century in 1922. During 1923–24, the artist reworked four of them into lithographs.

32. STUDY FOR THE IRISH FAIR

Crayon on cream, medium weight wove paper, spray varnished, 9 ¾ x 5 7/16 in., 248 x 138 mm (image); 12 7/16 x 10 1/8 in., 316 x 256 mm (sheet). Initialed in graphite in the lower right corner of the image: *GB*.

W.20, BPL 1943.2.5.

A preparatory study for the finished drawing *The Irish Fair*, which illustrated "The Bold Fenian Men," the last of six parts serialized in *Century* magazine, September 1922. Robert Henri is the likely model for this figure.[57] This drawing is the SOURCE FOR: *The Irish Fair*, 1923. Lithograph, 18 7/8 x 21 3/8 in., 477 x 528 mm. ESB.68, M.153.

Given by Emma S. Bellows to the Boston Public Library, June 1943.

Century magazine paid Bellows $100 each for the sixteen drawings. He produced them during the winter, and they appeared with the serialized text of the novel over six months from the spring through the fall. *The Wind Bloweth* relates the adventures of a Scots-Irish boy, "Shane Campbell of the sea and the Antrim Glens." For his source material, Bellows used the text, which he admired, recent sketches of Ireland by his friend Robert Henri, and the recollections of elderly Irish painter and brilliant conversationalist, John Butler Yeats.[58] The same year, he sold his difficult boxing painting, *Club Night*, 1909, to the Cleveland Museum of Art for $1500. The combined income gave him the capital to buy his own property in Woodstock, New York, where he designed and built his house that spring and summer.[59]

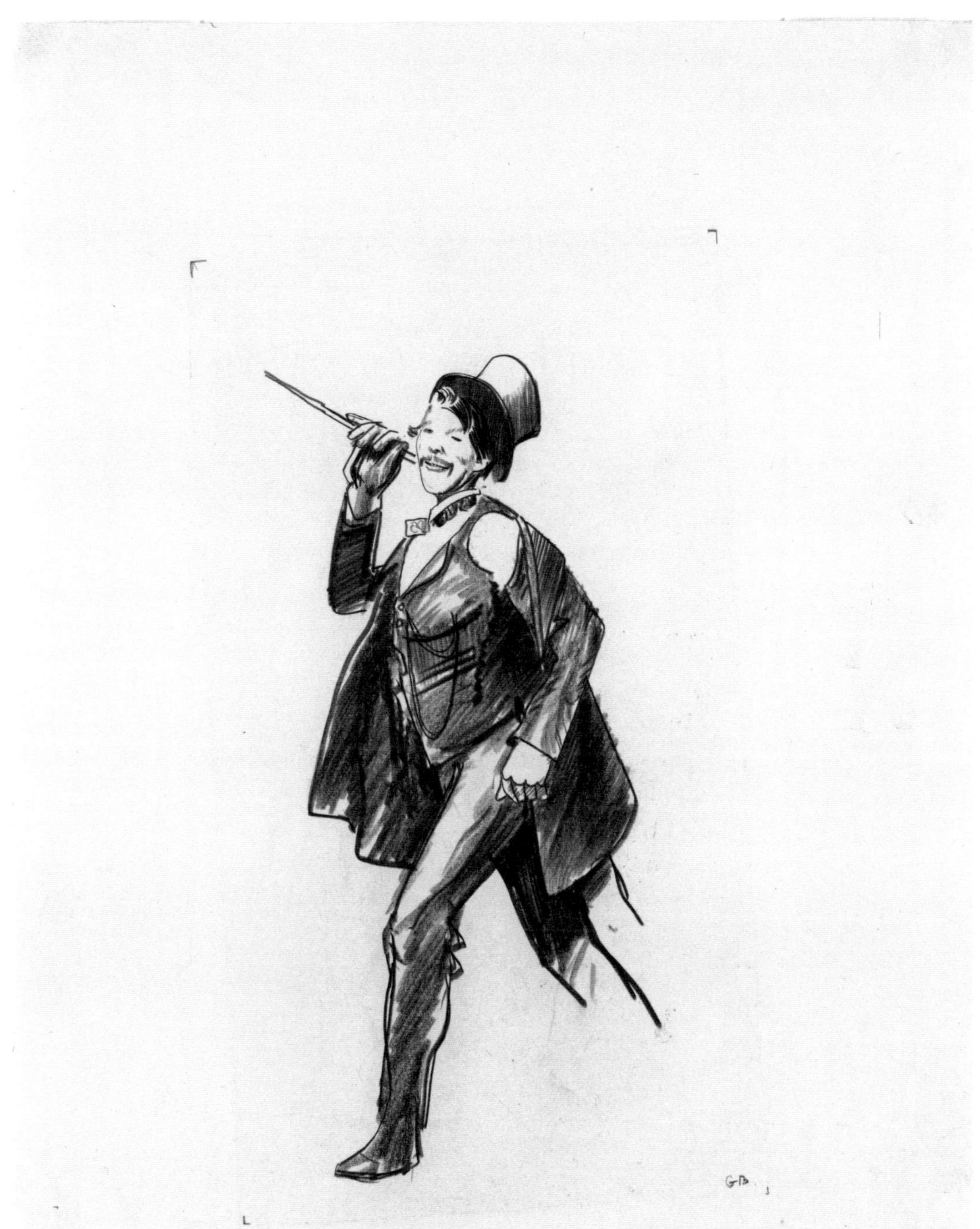
GB

33. PUNCHINELLO

Crayon on tan, one-ply card, 9 11/16 x 6 in., 247 x 153 mm (image); 11 7/8 x 8 7/16 in., 301 x 213 mm (sheet). Signed in graphite in lower right below image: *Geo Bellows.*

W.33, BPL 1943.2.8.

A preparatory study for the finished drawing described in cat. no. 34.

Given by Emma S. Bellows to the Boston Public Library, June 1943.

34. PUNCHINELLO IN THE HOUSE OF DEATH

Crayon, black ink and brush, and graphite on smooth, cream-colored Strathmore Drawing Board, 16 1/4 x 19 5/8 in., 415 x 499 mm (image); 21 3/4 x 26 1/8 in., 554 x 666 mm (sheet). Signed in crayon on the bottom edge of the image, to right of center: *Geo Bellows—*, annotated in the lower margin *The Wake at Ardee, the house of death became a booth of Punchinello.* Collector's mark: BPL/MB black ink stamp in lower right corner.

W.34, BPL 1943.1.18.

Published in *Century* magazine, May 1922, 101 to illustrate "The Wake at Ardee," the second of six serial parts, and also in the hardcover edition of *The Wind Bloweth* published by the Century Company the same year.

SOURCE FOR: *Punchinello in the House of Death*, 1923. Lithograph, 16 x 19 3/8 in., 409 x 494 mm. ESB.109, M.151, M.&A.65.

Sold by H. V. Allison Galleries to A. H. Wiggin, June 1943.

> *A great paraffin lamp threw broad, opaque shadows, making the whole a strange blur in the kitchen, while in the bedroom opening off it, where the tense, dead woman lay, was a glare of candles as from footlights, and there gathered the old women of the neighborhood . . . But in the kitchen they would be laughing, chatting . . . and now, to the muted sound of a melodeon, a man would dance a hornpipe.*
>
> Donn Byrne, *The Wind Bloweth*, 100–102

Cat. no. 33.

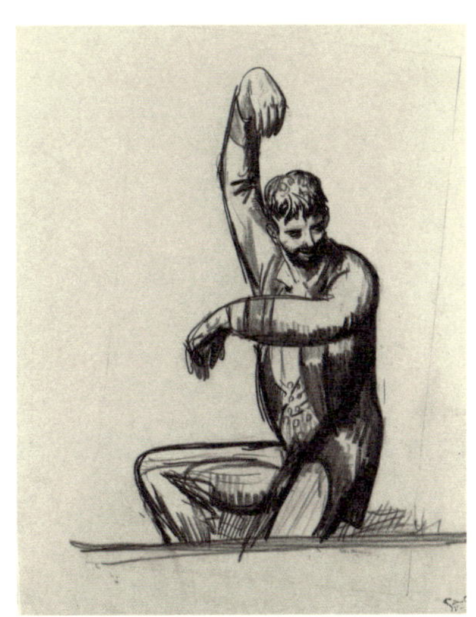

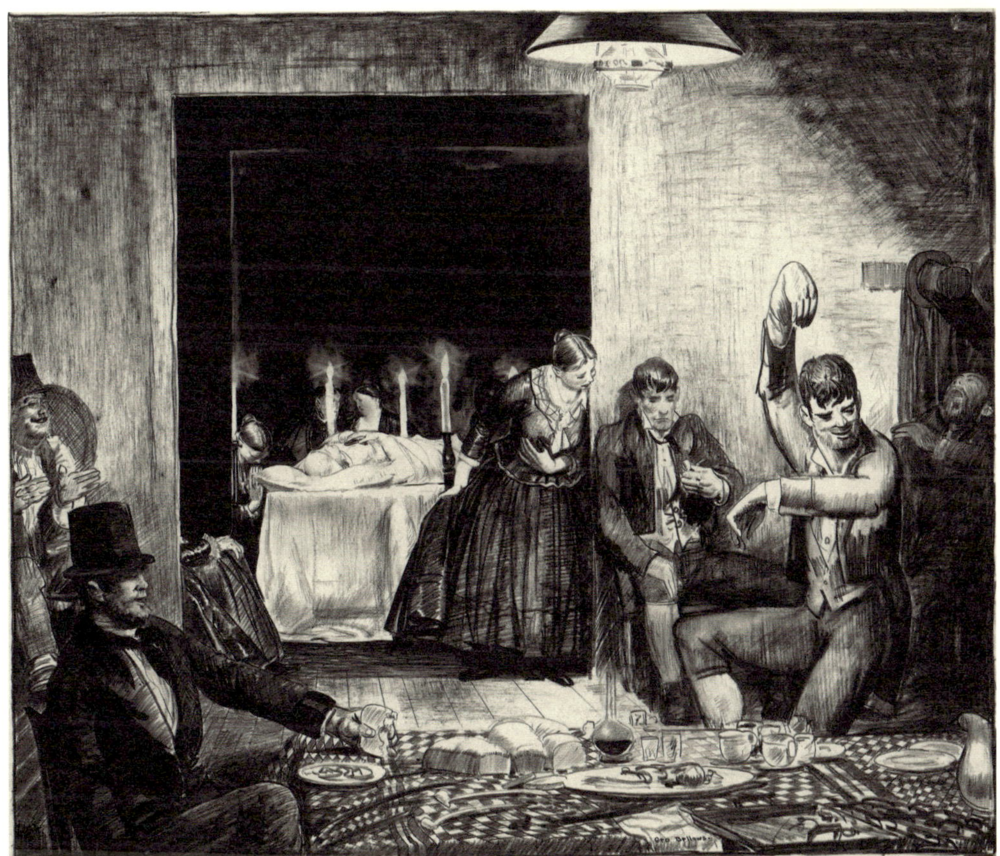

Cat. no. 34.

35. BUILDERS

Winter 1922. Crayon on cream lightweight wove paper, spray varnished, 12⅜ x 10⅛ in., 315 x 255 mm (image and sheet). Initialed in crayon in the lower right corner of the sheet: *GB*.

W.10, BPL 1956.1.1.

Sold by Childs Galleries to The Boston Public Library, July 1956.

The presumably Irish setting of this drawing suggests that it is related to the illustrations produced for *The Wind Bloweth*. Bellows made a number of sketches of the Irish and their land that were not used as illustrations for the novel.[60]

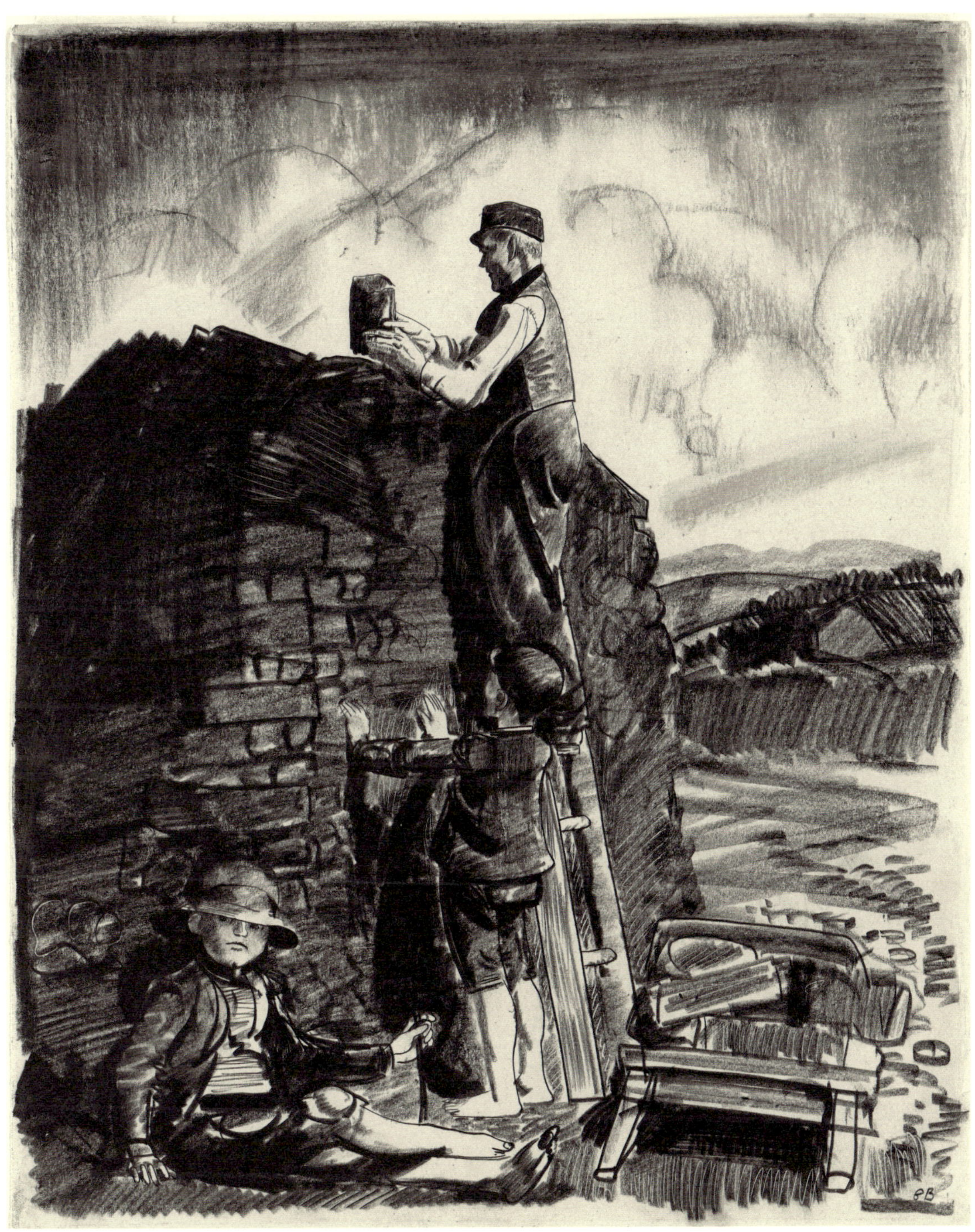

Illustrations for MEN LIKE GODS (*Cat. nos. 36–37*)

Winter 1922–Spring 1923.

Record Book B, pp. 292–293.

Catalogue numbers 36–37 are two finished drawings from a group of twenty-six illustrations commissioned by *Hearst's International Magazine* to accompany the serialized publication of H. G. Wells' novel, *Men Like Gods*, December 1922 to June 1923.[61] Twenty-two of these, all drawings except for one lithograph, were published. The remaining four, all lithographs, were not. None appeared in the hardcover version of the novel published by Knopf in 1924.[62]

36. THE BATTLE

Black crayon with orange/red underdrawing on smooth, cream-colored Strathmore Drawing Board with blind stamp, 24⅛ x 20 in., 613 x 509 mm (image); 28⅜ x 23¹⁄₁₆ inches, 722 x 586 mm (sheet). Signed in crayon at top edge in top right corner of the image: *Geo Bellows*—, and titled *The Battle* in graphite lower center. Collector's mark: BPL/MB black ink stamp in lower right corner.

W.6, BPL 1943.1.5. Published in *Hearst's International Magazine*, March 1923.

SOURCE FOR: *The Battle*, 1923–24. Lithograph, 15¾ x 13 in., 399 x 330 mm. B.192, M.159.

Sold by H. V. Allison Galleries to A. H. Wiggin, June 1943.

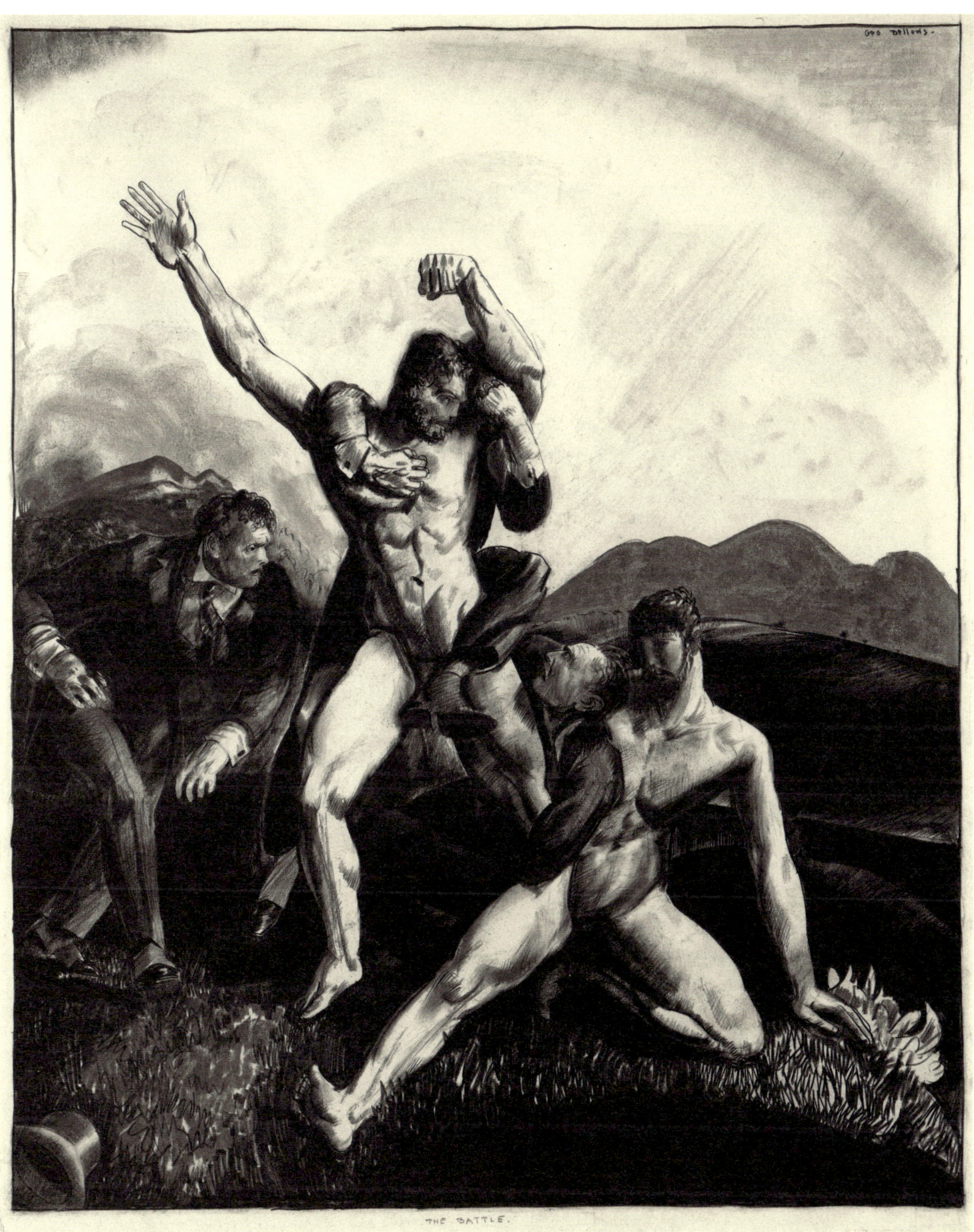
Geo Bellows.
THE BATTLE.

37. THE RETURN TO LIFE

Crayon, ink wash and brush, and chalk on smooth, cream-colored, one ply card, 18¹⁄₁₆ x 14½ in., 460 x 370 mm (image); 12¾ x 10¹⁄₁₆ in., 324 x 256 mm (sheet). Signed in crayon in the lower right corner of the image: *Geo Bellows—*, titled *The Return to Life* lower center.

W.36, BPL 1943.1.20. Published in *Hearst's International Magazine*, April 1923.

SOURCE FOR: *The Return to Life*, 1923. Lithograph, 18 x 14½ in., 460 x 368 mm. B.17, M.160.

Sold by H. V. Allison Galleries to A. H. Wiggin, June 1943.

The success of the Donn Byrne project earlier in the year led to a $3,800 contract to illustrate a utopian fantasy novel by H. G. Wells in which a group of people travel three thousand years into the future to a society of cooperation, enlightenment and peace.

At this point in his development, Bellows was actively using the compositional system of Dynamic Symmetry, a complicated theory of geometric interrelationships devised by the classical archaeologist Jay Hambidge. He met Hambidge late in the fall of 1917, and had integrated the basic principles of the theory into his War Series images produced the following spring.[63]

Bellows used Dynamic Symmetry as an underlying structure for many, but by no means all of his compositions during the rest of his brief career. While one might expect that, after six years, he could integrate the system more subtly into his work, the stiff, jarring angularity of an image like *The Battle* (cat. no. 36) indicate that theory and practice were not always compatible.[64]

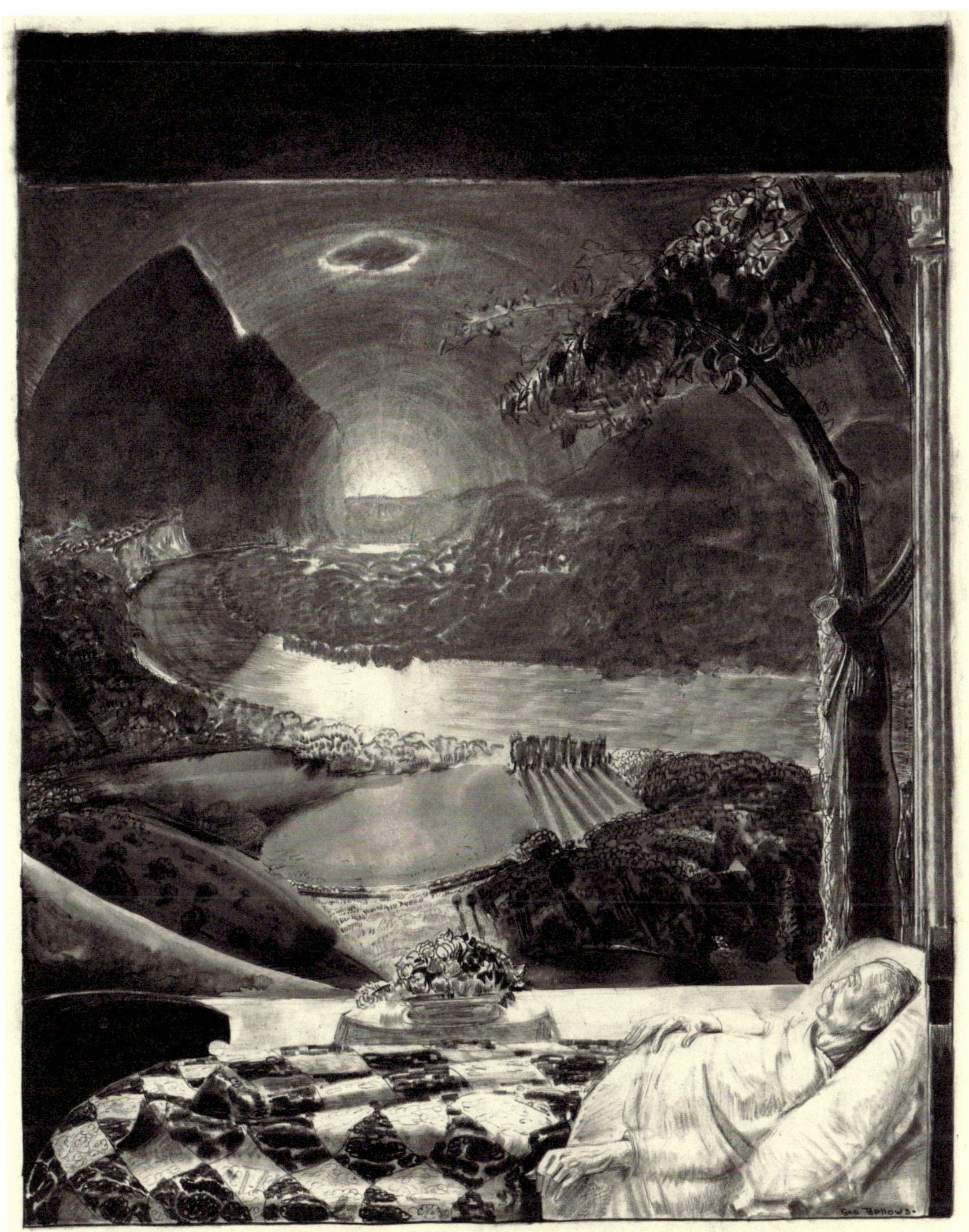
Geo Bellows

38. NUDE CHILD *(not in exhibition)*

c. 1923. Crayon on smooth surfaced, cream colored, lightweight wove paper, 12¾ x 10¹⁄₁₆ in., 324 x 256 mm (sheet). Signed in graphite on the bottom edge to the right of the child: *Geo. Bellows*. Collector's mark: BPL/MB black ink stamp in lower right recto corner.

W.28, BPL 1956.1.2.

Sold by Childs Galleries to the Boston Public Library in 1956.

Although it does not have an exact match, this flaxen haired, cherubic child resembles closely the children playing in the foreground of the *Garden of Growth*, one of the illustrations Bellows made for Wells' novel.

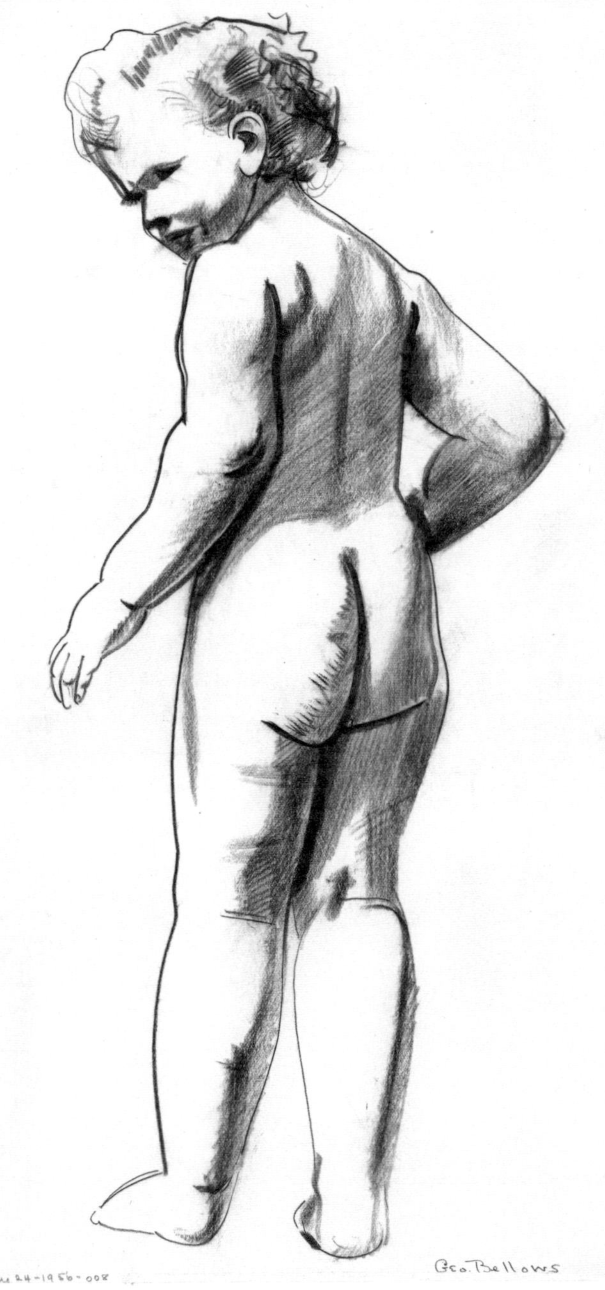

39. THE LAW IS TOO SLOW

Winter 1922–23. Crayon on smooth, cream-colored, thick, wove paper, most likely Strathmore Drawing Board, 21⅛ x 16^{15}/16 in., 537 x 431 mm (image); 27^{11}/16 x 23 in., 704 x 585 mm (sheet). Signed in crayon in the lower right corner of the image: *Geo Bellows—*, and titled *The Law Is Too Slow* in graphite lower center. Collectors' marks: Wiggin Collection black ink stamp in lower right corner, BPL/MB black ink stamp in lower left corner.

Record Book B, p. 11, no. 341. W.23, BPL 1941.1.4. Commissioned by the *Century* magazine in December 1922.

SOURCE FOR: *The Law Is Too Slow*, 1923. Lithograph, 17⅞ x 14½ in., 455 x 370 mm. B.73, M.147, M.&A.63. Published in the *Century* magazine to illustrate "Nemesis" by Mary Johnston, May 1923, 2.

Sold by Frederick Keppel Galleries to A. H. Wiggin, October, 1936.

> *They said that the man, a black man, had done the crime. Perhaps he had, perhaps he had not. The probabilities seem to indicate that he had, but it is not certain, was not certain then and is not certain now. Those who conducted the lynching proceeded, of course, upon the assumption that he was guilty.*[65]

In the summer of 1903, when Bellows turned twenty-one, the southern United States suffered a notable increase in lynching. One involving the abduction and burning of an African American man was reported in his local newspaper, the Columbus *Dispatch*. The reporter's description was so graphic that Bellows never forgot the story, and he returned to the memory when he received this commission from the *Century* at the end of 1922. Along with his images of World War I, *The Law Is Too Slow* demonstrates that, despite his normally good-natured approach to social satire, Bellows could channel his righteous anger into powerful images of human brutality.[66]

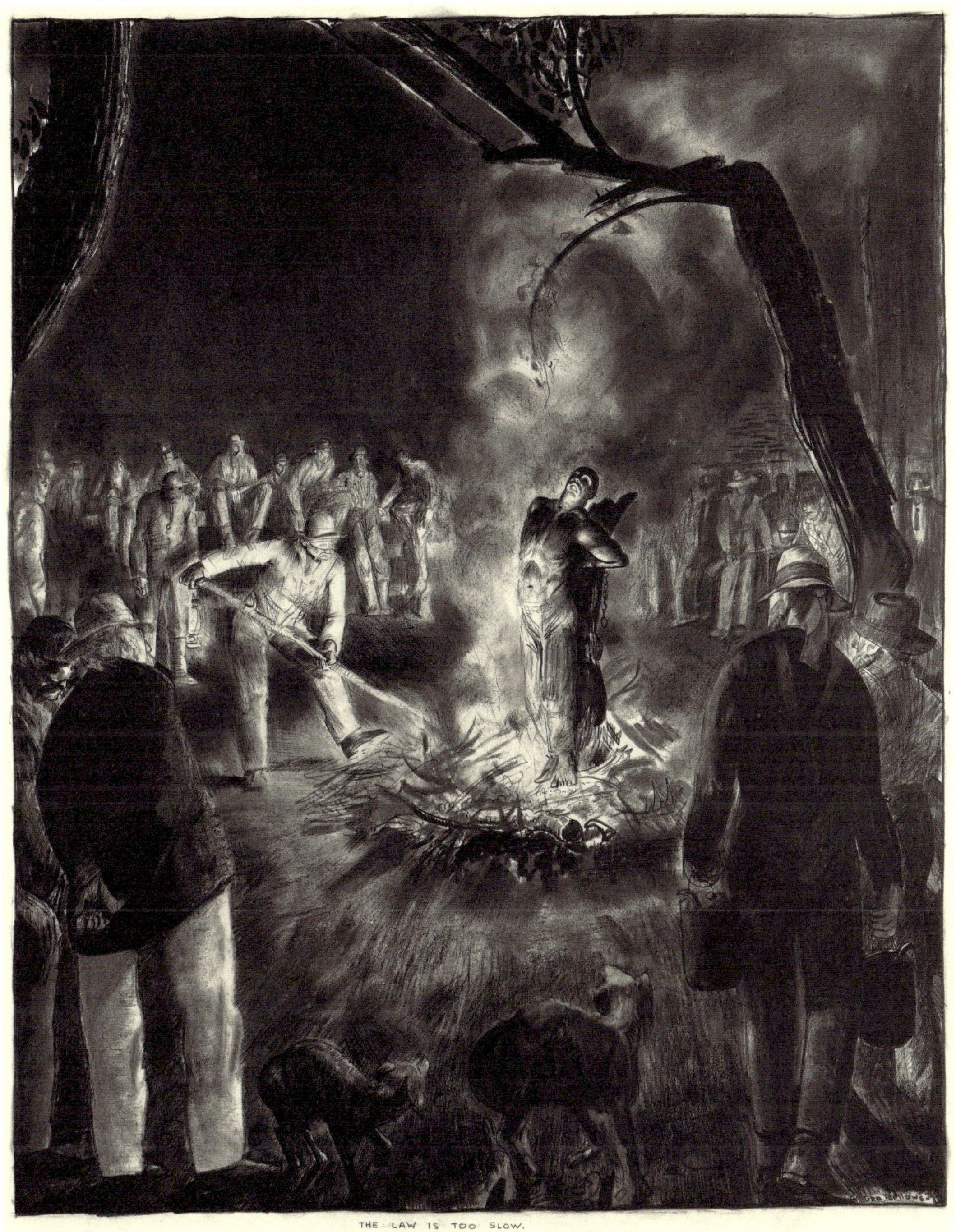

THE LAW IS TOO SLOW.

40. GIRL SEWING

c. Winter 1923. Crayon on lightweight cream wove paper, 12½ x 10⅛ in., 318 x 257 mm (sheet). Signed in graphite, lower left corner of sheet: *Geo. Bellows E.S.B.*

W.17, BPL 1943.1.9.

SOURCE FOR: *Girl Sewing*, 1923. Lithograph, 11 ⅝ x 6 ¾ in., 297 x 172 mm. B.180, M.139.

Sold by H. V. Allison Galleries to A. H. Wiggin, June 1943.

Between 1921 and 1924, Bellows produced fifty-two lithographs portraying family and friends. This drawing is the model for one of them, a portrait of his wife Emma. Bellows' gentle images of his wife and daughters are among his most affecting works. As his close friend and fellow artist, Eugene Speicher related:

> *You would not call him very affectionate, but he had a great deal of affection bottled up in him. He was a sentimentalist at heart and could not conceal it in his portraits of children. He would weep at a children's concert or at a touching moment in a play or movie. After all, an artist without a responsive emotional nature has only the dry intellect left.*[67]

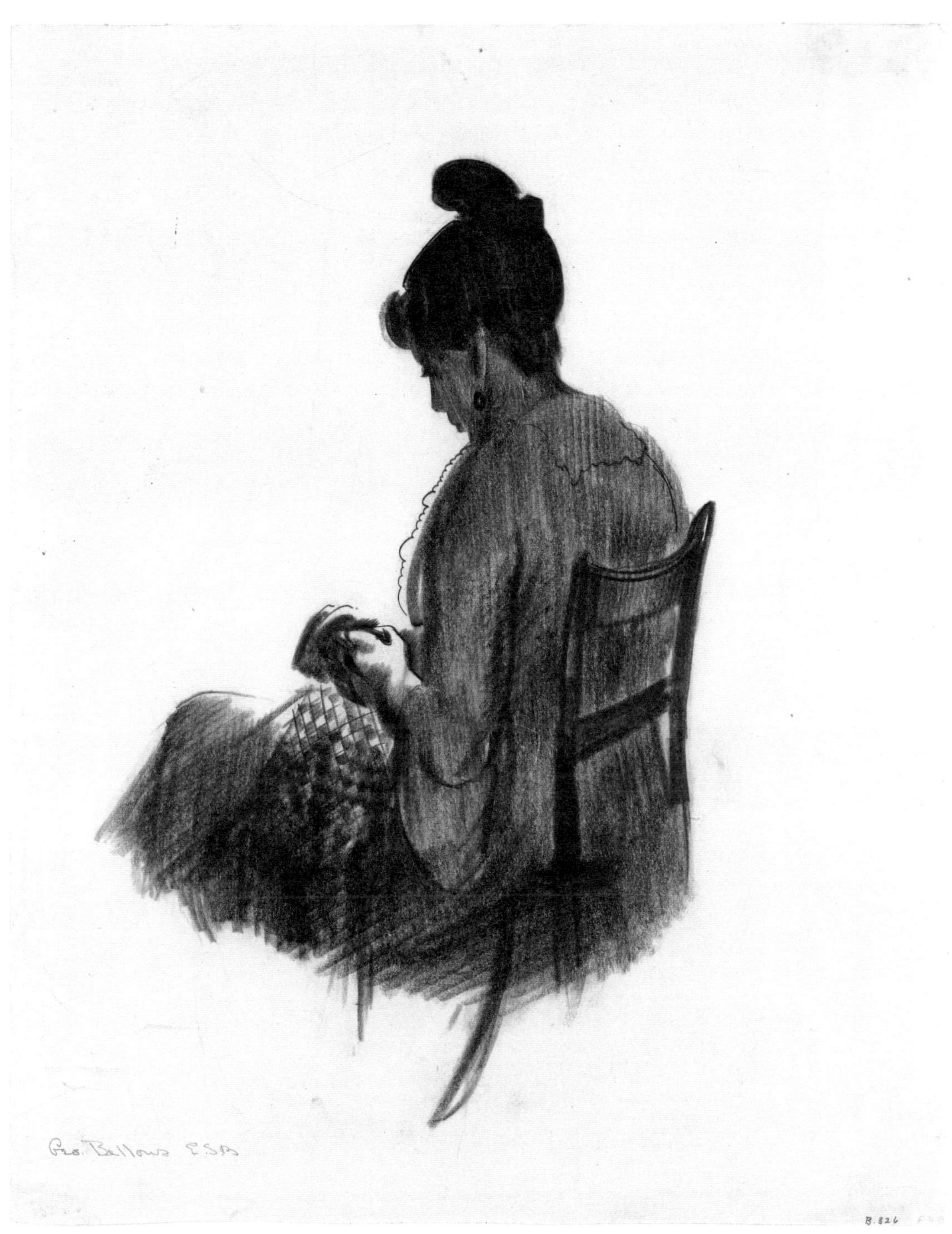

41. SIXTEEN EAST GAY STREET

Summer 1923. Crayon on off-white, two-ply Strathmore drawing paper, 9⅝ x 11⅞ in., 244 x 302 mm (image); 11½ x 14⅝ in., 290 x 372 mm (sheet). Signed in crayon at the lower left edge of the image: *Geo Bellows.*

W.39, BPL 1943.1.22.

SOURCE FOR: *Sixteen East Gay Street*, 1923–24. Lithograph, 9 ¼ x 11 ¾ in., 237 x 297 mm. B.84, M.183, M.&A.74.

Sold by H. V. Allison Galleries to A. H. Wiggin, June 1943.

In August 1923, George and Emma Bellows traveled to Columbus to be with his mother, Anna, as she neared the end of her life. Such an emotional visit may have stimulated this nostalgic image of his childhood neighborhood.

Some months later, in March 1924, he suggested that a reproduction of the nearly identical lithograph be published in Columbus' Central High School Memorial Book, noting parenthetically that the address was "not correct."[68]

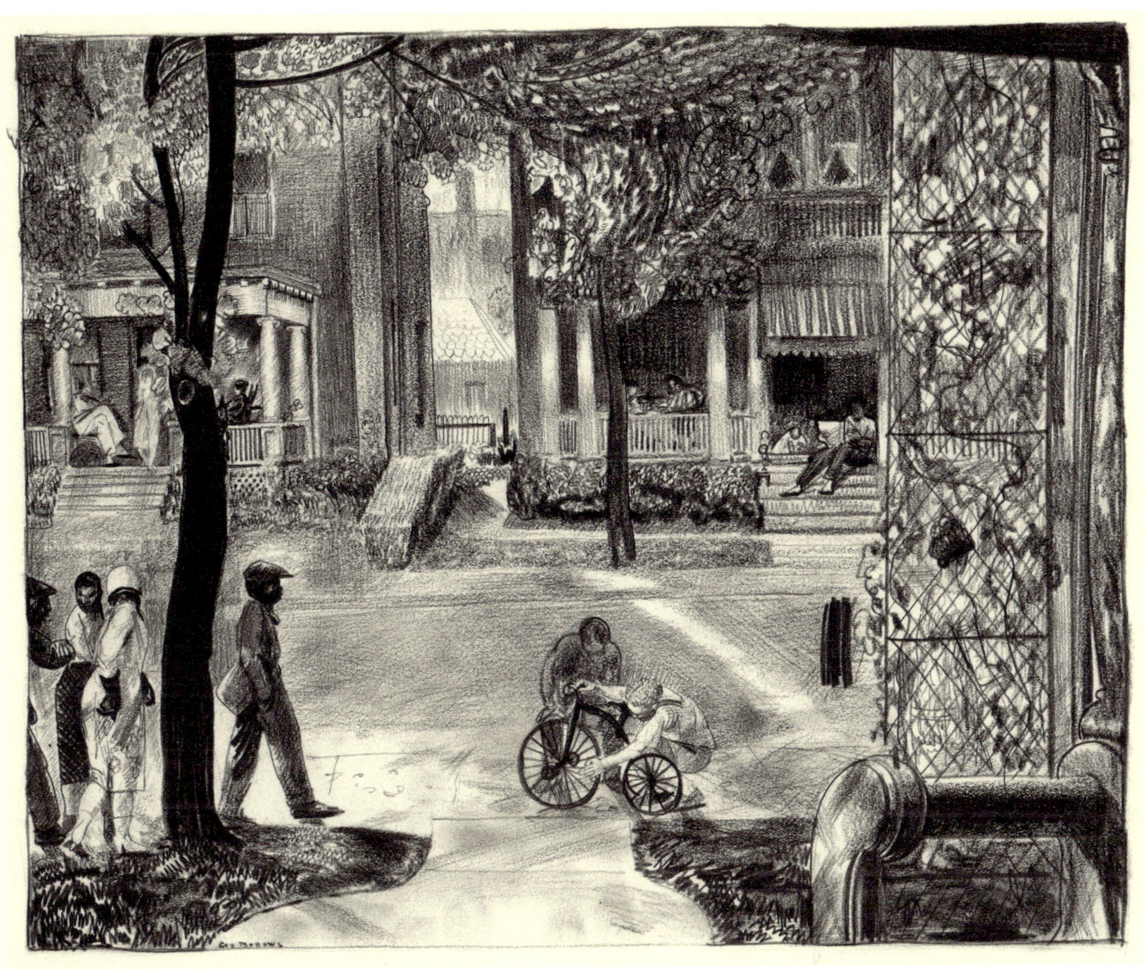

42. AUNTIE MASON AND HER HUSBAND *(not in exhibition)*

c. Summer 1923. Crayon, with touches of either black ink or, more likely, moistened chalk, 10⅛ x 9⅛ in., 258 x 232 mm (image); 14⅜ x 11³⁄₁₆ in., 366 x 285 mm (sheet). Signed in crayon at the bottom of the image near the lower left corner: *Geo Bellows—*.

W.2, BPL 1943.1.2.

SOURCE FOR: *Auntie Mason and her Husband*, 1923. Lithograph, 11 ¼ x 10 in., 253 x 229 mm. B.50, M.180.

Sold by H. V. Allison Galleries to A. H. Wiggin, June 1943.

The young couple in late-nineteenth-century dress is apparently related to the artist's father.[69] This double portrait is one of a small group of images depicting his youth in Columbus that Bellows made in 1923/24, perhaps in response to the death of his mother in August 1923. It is also part of a much larger group of images of family and friends that became of increasing interest to him in the 1920s. The details of the period clothing suggest that he may have used an old family photograph as his source.

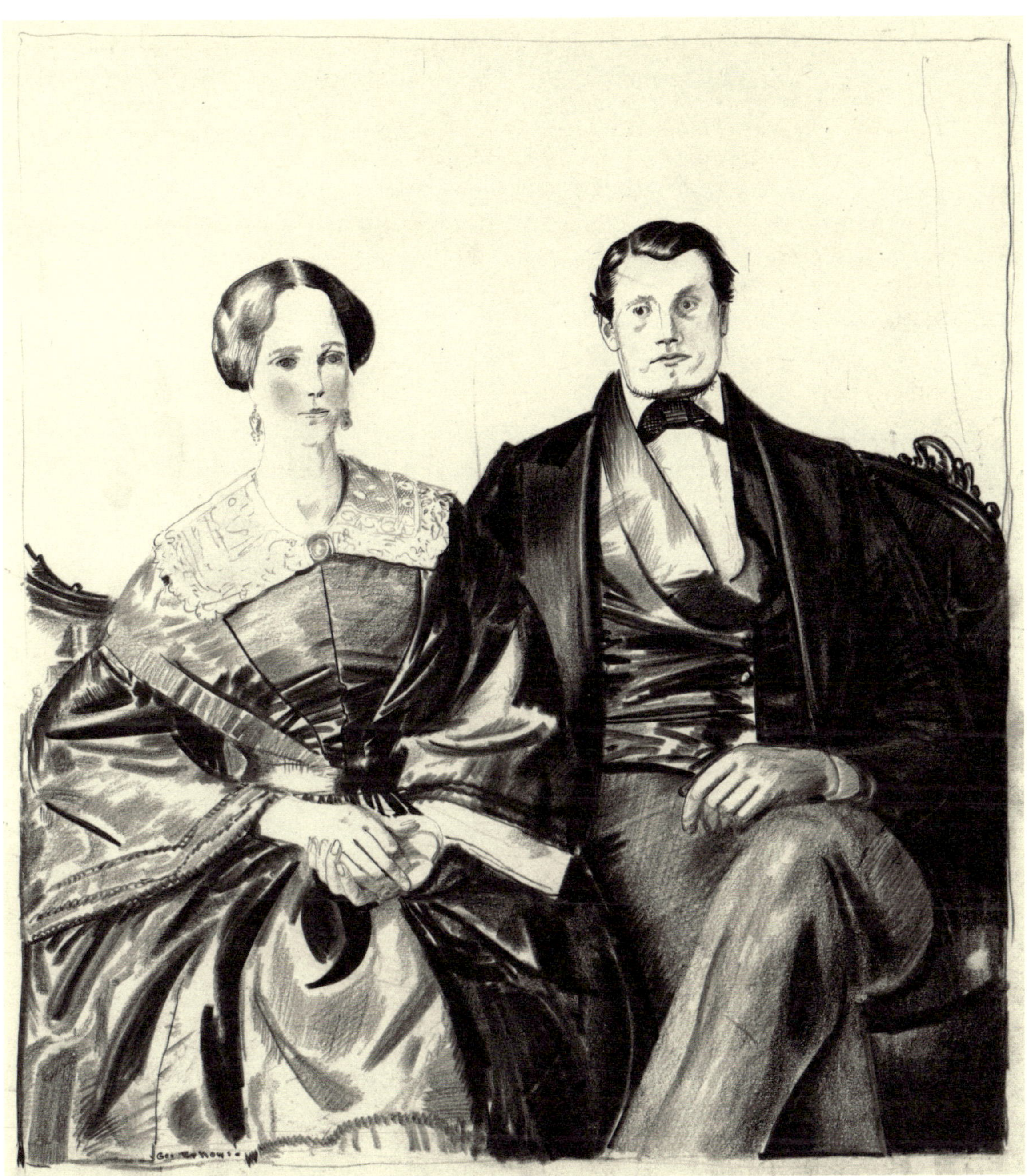

43. STUDY OF MARY *(not in exhibition)*

1923. Crayon and touches of black ink or moistened chalk, with graphite squaring, ruling, notations and design modifications on image on cream colored, smooth surfaced wove paper, 12 7/16 x 10 in., 316 x 255 mm (image and sheet). Signed in graphite on bottom edge in the lower left corner: *Geo. Bellows ESB.* and annotated *chair in center—I stand to right, ⅔ front.*

W.46, BPL 1943.1.27.

Preliminary study for the following drawing.

Sold by H. V. Allison Galleries to A. H. Wiggin, June 1943.

44. STUDY OF MARY *(not in exhibition)*

1923. Crayon on lightweight cream-colored wove paper (watermark: Natoma), 14¼ x 11½ in., 360 x 292 mm (image); 19 13/16 x 14 13/16 in., 504 x 378 mm (sheet). Signed in graphite in the lower right corner of the image: *Geo. Bellows E.S.B.* Collector's mark: Wiggin Collection black ink stamp just outside the lower right corner of the image.

W.47, BPL 1943.1.28.

SOURCE FOR: *Study of Mary*, 1923. Lithograph, 11¼ x 10 in., 289 x 255 mm. B.14, M.132.

Sold by H. V. Allison Galleries to A. H. Wiggin, June 1943.

Mary McKinnon, a fellow artist and friend of Bellows, was a fashion illustrator. Her husband, John De Vries, was a vice-president at the J. Walter Thompson Agency, which handled many of the advertising accounts for magazines to which both Bellows and McKinnon submitted illustrations. She is the subject of an oil portrait made the previous year, now in a private collection.[70]

The earlier of the two drawings is squared, with the left-hand column of squares numbered, a technique normally used in preparation for enlarging an image. In the lower margin, Bellows noted his position in relation to his subject. Such careful preparation of a sketch was hardly necessary for making either the second drawing or the lithograph, since all three are roughly the same size, and it is likely that Bellows anticipated painting another formal portrait of his friend.

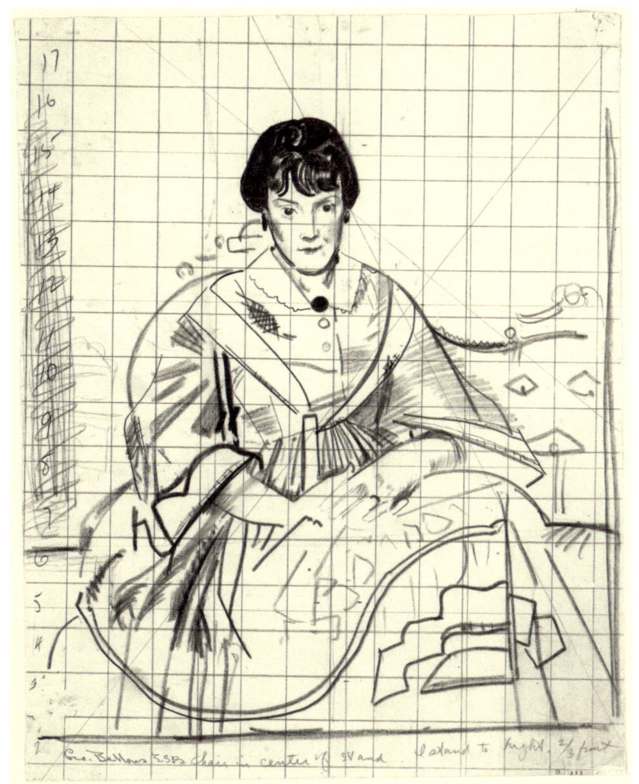

Cat. no. 43.

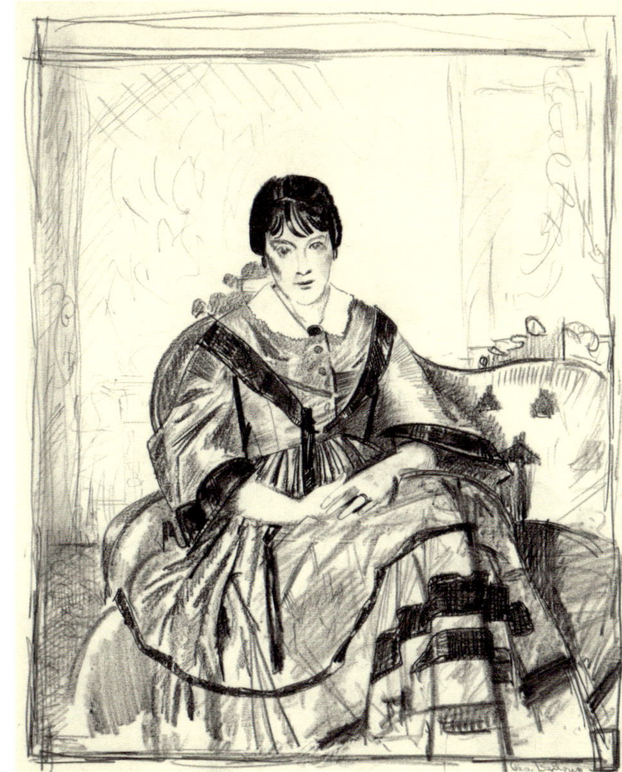

Cat. no. 44.

45. THE APPEAL TO THE PEOPLE

Summer–Fall 1923. Graphite, crayon, and blue-grey chalk on smooth, cream-colored one-ply wove card stock, 14⅛ x 18⅜ in., 359 x 468 mm (image); 21⅜ x 26⅞ in., 545 x 685 mm (sheet). Signed in crayon on the lower fence rail in image to the left of center: *Geo Bellows—* and signed in crayon in lower left corner of the image: *GB*. Collector's mark: BPL/MB black ink stamp lower right corner.

W.1, BPL 1943.1.1.

SOURCE FOR: *The Appeal to the People*, 1923–24. Lithograph, 14 x 18⅛ in., 356 x 463 mm. B.115, M.167.

Sold by H. V. Allison Galleries to A. H. Wiggin, June 1943.

The Appeal to the People is based closely on a photograph from an unidentified newspaper or magazine captioned *Eamon De Valera speaks in County Clare, 1923*. De Valera (1882–1975), an Irish patriot and politician for sixty years, spent the spring and summer of 1923 campaigning for the upcoming national elections on behalf of his party, Sinn Fein. On August 15, while he was making a speech in Ennis, County Clare, British forces seized and imprisoned him.[71]

While its Irish subject relates tangentially to Bellows' illustrations from the previous year for novelist Donne Byrne's *The Wind Bloweth*, this drawing is of a very different nature. Unlike the great majority of his drawings, which come from either the artist's observation or his imagination, it derives quite literally from a photograph. As such, it documents Bellows' receptivity towards other people's work as a source for his own. Ironically, journalistic photography had in the previous two decades made obsolete the journalistic illustration practiced as a profession by his older Ash Can colleagues.[72]

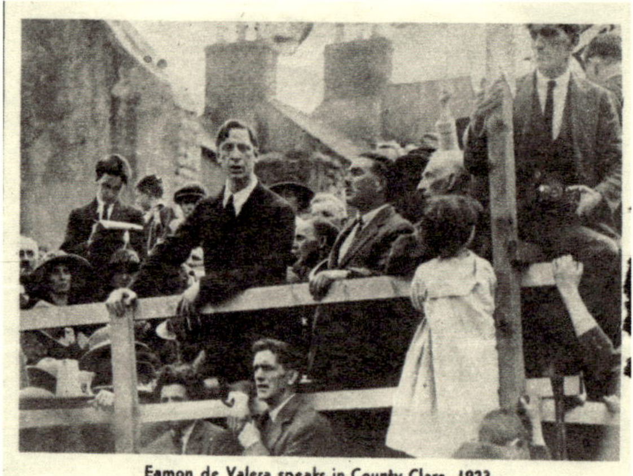

Eamon De Valera speaks in County Clare, 1923.

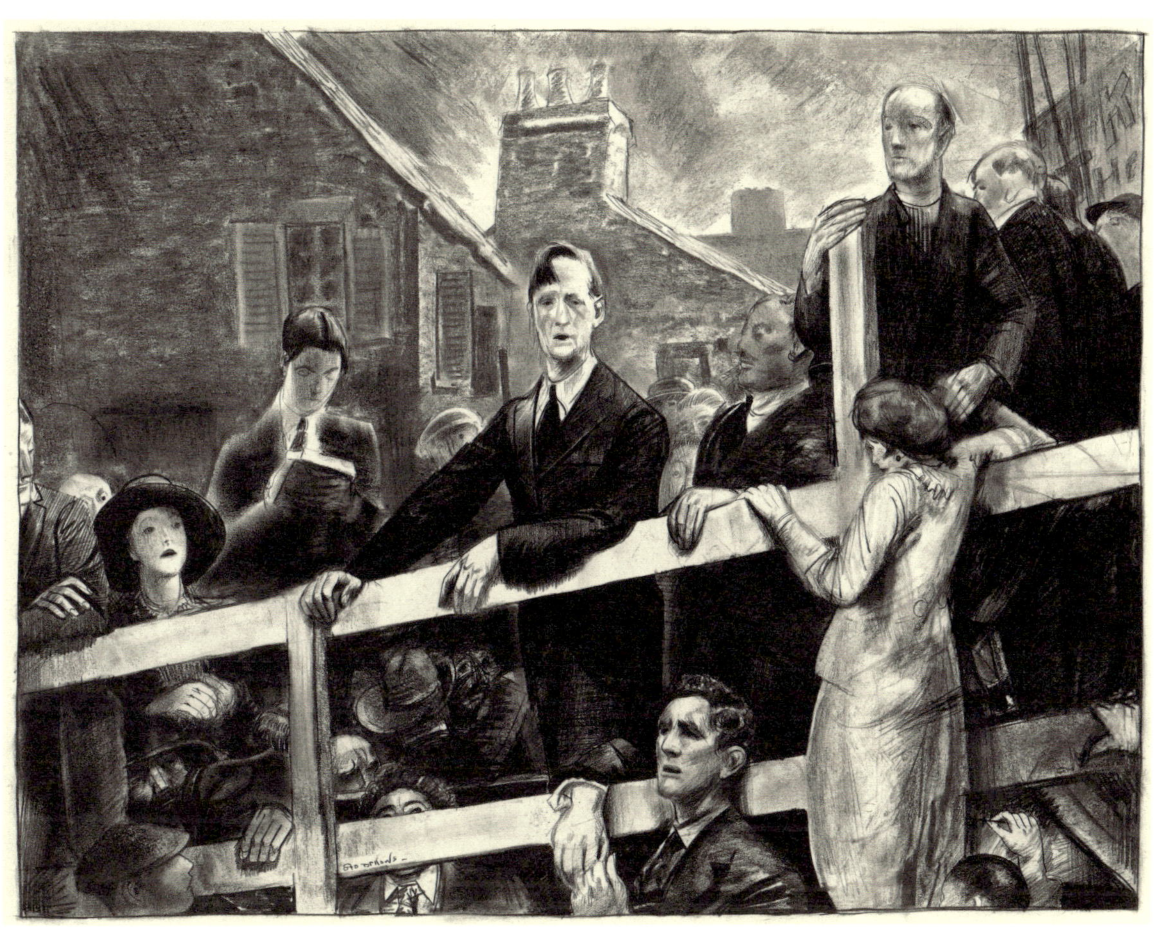

46. THE DEAD LINE

c. 1923. Crayon and pen and ink on cream, lightweight wove paper, spray varnished, 12 x 10⅞ in., 304 x 275 mm (image); 13¹³⁄₁₆ x 12⁹⁄₁₆ in., 350 x 319 mm (sheet). Signed in graphite in the lower right corner of the image: *Geo Bellows*.

W.12, BPL 1943.1.8.

SOURCE FOR: *The Deadline*, 1923. Lithograph, 12 x 10⅞ in., 307 x 277 mm. B.15, M.148.

Sold by H. V. Allison Galleries to A. H. Wiggin, June 1943.

Bellows based this drawing on a photograph of the April 28, 1913 mining disaster in Courtney/Finleyville, Pennsylvania which left ninety-seven miners dead.[73] He cropped the composition, rearranged some of the foreground characters, and placed the group in front of a dark tunnel entrance instead of against the receding hillside at the actual site. All these changes tighten the composition and make it more dramatic.

Like *The Appeal to the People* (cat. no. 45), which is also based on a photograph, this image has the characteristically stilted feel of work derived from an external source, despite Bellows' extraordinarily facile and skillful hand. It is instructive to compare these two socially conscious subjects from 1923 with his 1918 series about World War I atrocities. The earlier images were the artist's inventions based on eyewitness accounts and composed according to the principles of Dynamic Symmetry. The later ones derive their general proportions and composition from the work of other people. Compared to his best efforts, the former are awkward, and the latter wooden, at least to the degree that someone as talented as Bellows could make them.

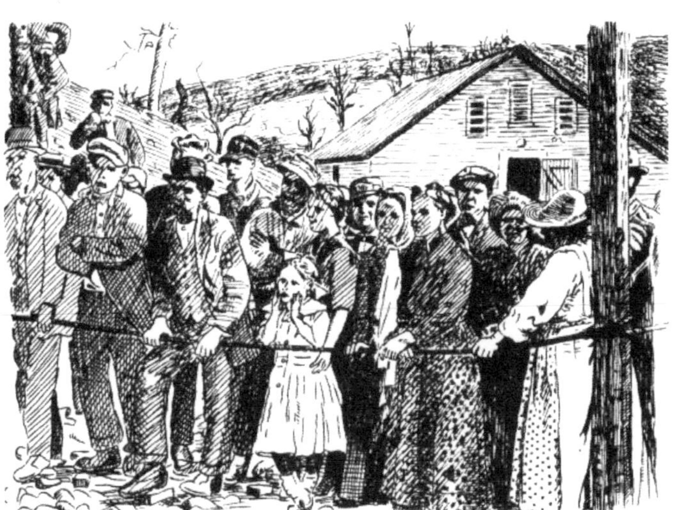

Miner's Families at the Cincinnati Mine Entrance, after the April 28, 1913, Explosion, after 1913, line drawing after photograph, dimensions unknown.

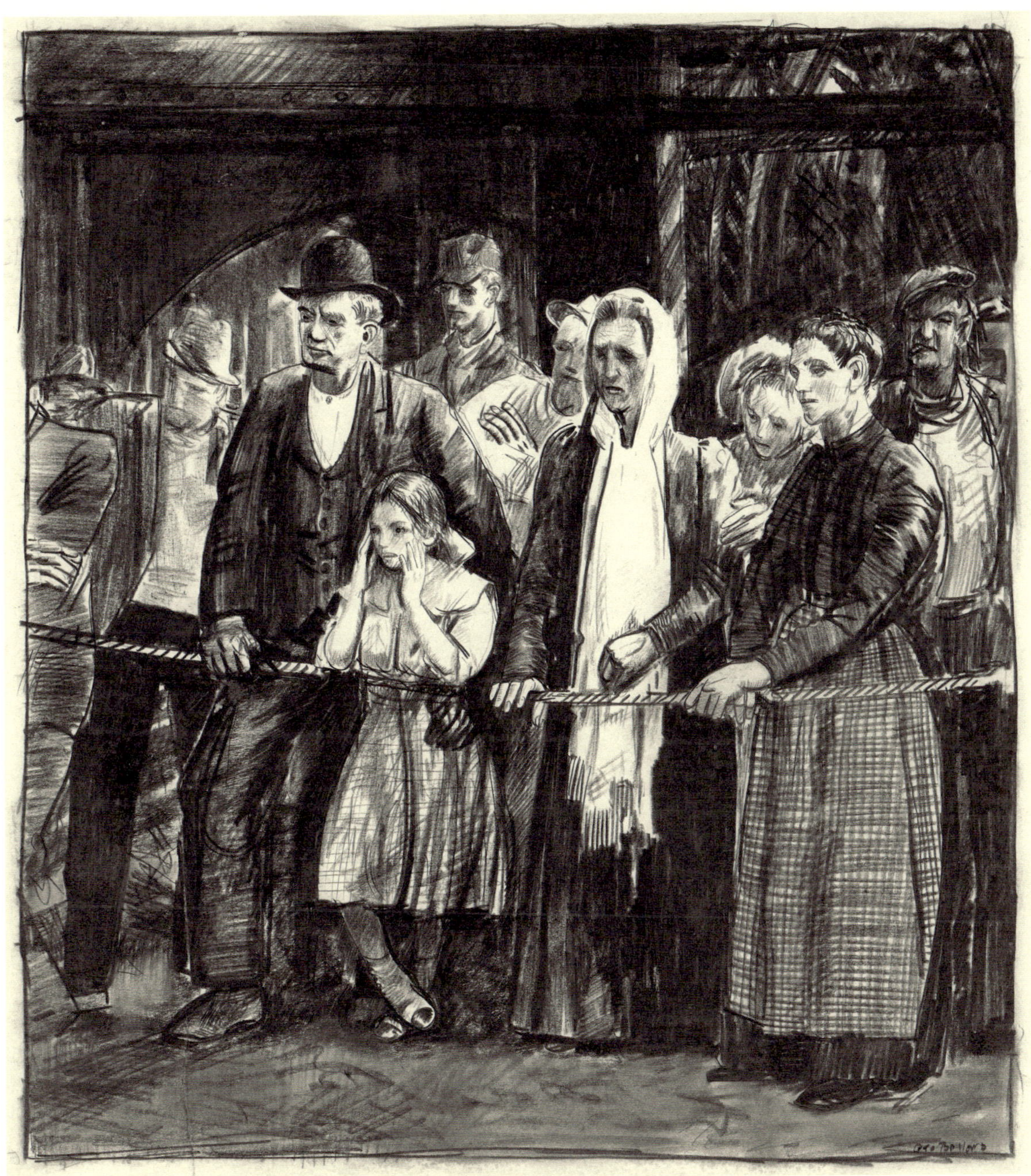

47. ENERGIZING THE BROKEN (Salvation Army)

June 1924. Crayon, graphite ruled lines and drawing lines, ink wash and brush, opaque watercolor and brush on smooth, cream colored, thick, wove paper, most likely Strathmore Drawing Board, 17 15/16 x 17 7/8 in., 457 x 454 mm (image); 23 x 21 7/8 in., 586 x 556 mm (sheet). Signed in crayon in the center of the bottom edge of the drawing: *Geo Bellows*, titled and dated *6-9-24* on the reverse. Collector's marks: Wiggin Collection black ink stamp and BPL/MB black ink stamp in lower right corner.

Record Book C, p. 14, as a note in ESB's hand. W.37, BPL 1941.1.3. Commissioned to illustrate "With God's Help" by H. Addington Bruce, *Good Housekeeping Magazine*, October 1924, 51.

Sold by Frederick Keppel Galleries to A. H. Wiggin, October 1936.

The setting and characters of this illustration are very similar to his earlier drawings of life on New York's lower East Side. In the Wiggin sheets *Splinter Beach*, 1912, and *Pinched*, 1914 (cat. nos. 2 and 7), and in many others drawn as early as 1907, Bellows followed Robert Henri's fundamental principle of taking one's material directly from real life.[74]

But by the summer of 1924, Bellows was no longer a young art student mining the city for subject matter. He was critically and commercially successful, with a family and a house in the country. About to leave New York for another summer in Woodstock and without the time to find a Salvation Army model, he requested photos of their "accoutrements" from *Good Housekeeping* in order to complete the assignment. The result suffers in comparison to his earlier work, a somewhat artificially staged diorama instead of a lively source of genuine compassion and humor.[75]

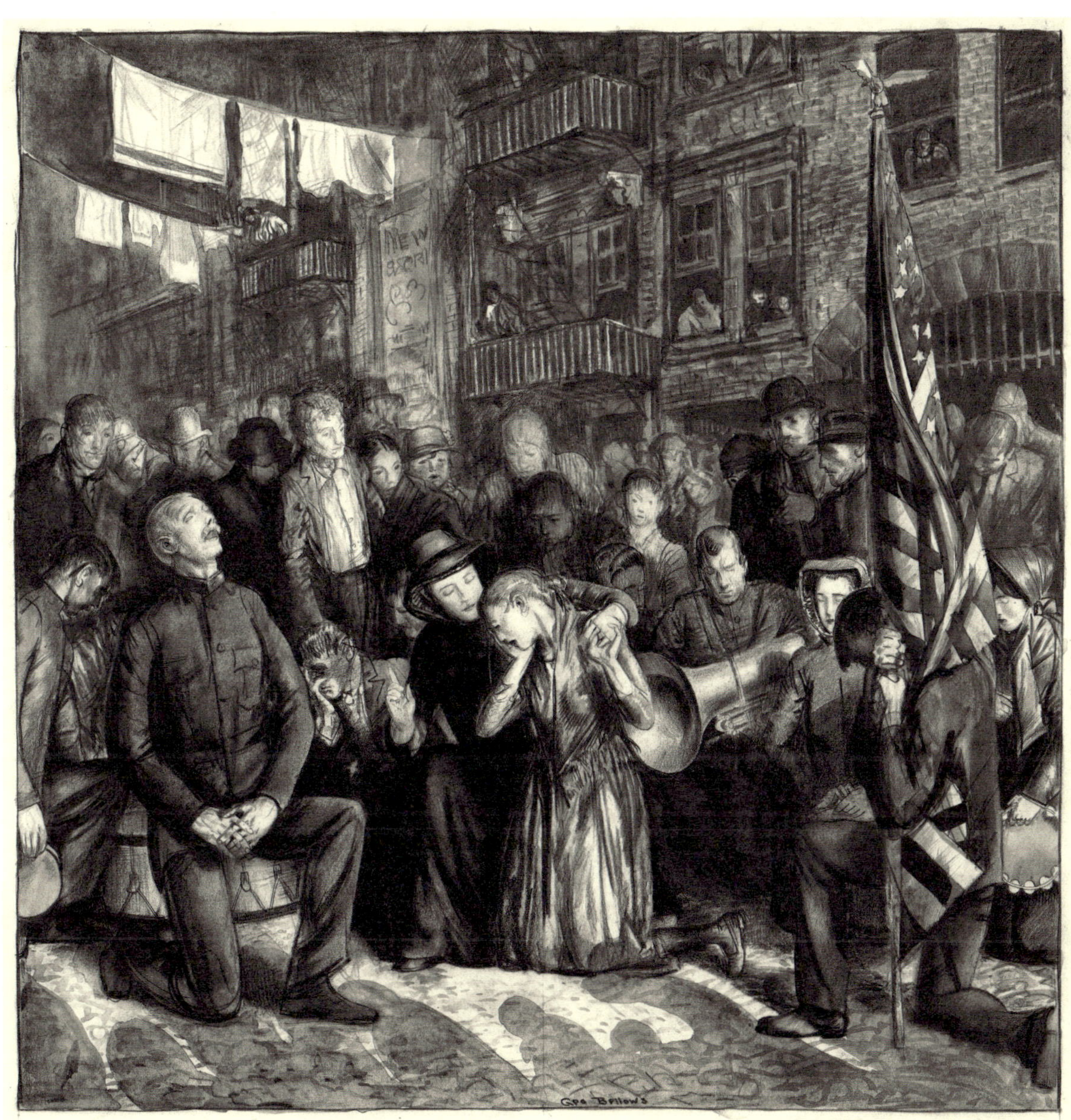
NEW
Geo Bellows

48. STUDY OF A GIRL (Miss Tate) *(not in exhibition)*

Summer, 1924. Crayon on smooth surfaced, cream colored wove paper mounted on 8-ply woodpulp board, 9⅝ x 9 7/16 in., 245 x 239 mm (image and sheet); 12⅛ x 12¾ in., 308 x 324 mm (mount). Signed in crayon in the lower left corner of the image: *G.B.*; annotated in graphite *Study of a Girl* at the bottom edge, lower left corner.

W.45, BPL 1943.1.26.

SOURCE FOR: *Miss Tate*, 1921 or 24. Lithograph, 10⅝ x 8½ in., 270 x 207 mm. B.141, M.129.

Sold by H. V. Allison Galleries to A. H. Wiggin, June 1943.

In letters written to Emma Bellows in March 1943, Agnes Tait identified herself as the model for two portraits Bellows painted in Woodstock. They are, most likely, *Roumanian Girl*, 1921, now in the Samuel Dorsky Museum of Art, State University of New York at New Paltz, and *Lady in a Green Dress*, 1924, now in a private collection. The young woman depicted in this drawing is clearly the subject of the second painting. This connection between drawing and painting adds evidence to the dating of the related lithograph to this same year.[76]

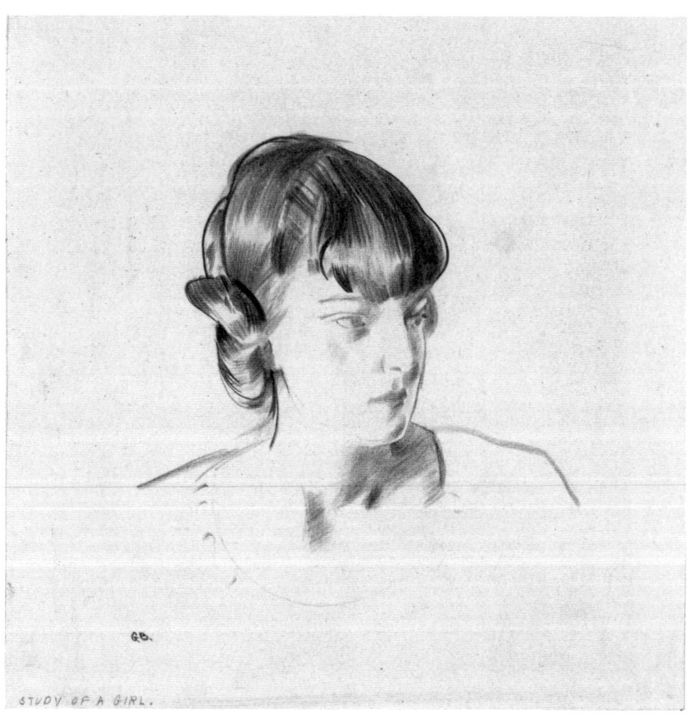

CATALOGUE NOTES

1. The artist's descriptions of his lithographs cited throughout this catalogue come from Albert Roullier Art Galleries, *Catalogue of an Exhibition of Original Lithographs by George Bellows N.A.*, Chicago, January 6–20, 1919.

2. F.J.M., "The Independent Artists," *The Nation* (April 7, 1910): 360.

3. Art Young, a political cartoonist on the board of *The Masses*, commented on the artists in Henri's circle opposing political captions being added to their images by the magazine's editors:

> *The dissenting five artists were opposed to "a policy." They want to run pictures of ash cans and girls hitching up their skirts in Horatio Street—regardless of ideas—and without title. On the other hand a group of us believe that such pictures belong better in exclusive art magazines. Therefore we put an emphasis on the value of constructive cartoons for a publication like* The Masses.
>
> Young, Art, "Clash of Classes Stirs 'The Masses'," *New York Sun*, April 8, 1916, 6.

Young had specifically in mind a Bellows drawing of three bums picking food from garbage published in the February 1914 issue of the magazine with the title *Real Tragedy* and the caption *Dey's woims in it*. It reappeared in the *Philadelphia Record* fourteen months later, on April 25, 1915, with the same caption but a different title: *Disappoints of the Ash Can*. The Wiggin drawing, *Dogs Early Morning*, published in *Harper's Weekly* a few months before the earlier of the two appearances of the *Woims/Ash Can* cartoon, was the first Henri-school drawing to feature ash cans prominently. A newspaper review of contemporary American magazine illustration mentioned this aspect of it: "Bellows essays a New York subject with an elaborate use of his imagination . . . , showing dogs preying on ash cans and gutter heaps." (James Britton, "Art: Illustration a la Mode," *The Hartford Daily Courant*, September 19, 1913, cited in Robert Hunter, "The Rewards and Disappointments of the Ashcan School: The Early Career of Stuart Davis" in Lowery Stokes Sims, *Stuart Davis American Painter*, exhibition catalogue, Metropolitan Museum of Art, New York, 1992, 36–41.)

Eighteen years after Young's association of the artists with ash cans, "Ash Can School" was first used as a formal title in Holger Cahill and Alfred Barr, *Art in America: A Complete Survey*, New York: Reynal & Hitchcock, 1934, 31. Whether or not the label was intended to be pejorative, Emma Bellows took it as such. In a letter to the editors of *Life* magazine regarding their caption for a reproduction of Bellows' famous painting *Stag at Sharkey's*, she wrote:

> *In the descriptive note . . . it reads "George Bellows, last of the Ashcan school." To classify George Bellows thus is news to me because the title "Ashcan school" has in the past been applied specifically to a group of eight men who revolted against the unprogressive spirit of the National Academy in the early nineteen hundreds and George Bellows was not one of them.*
>
> *I have always considered it highly insulting to designate as the Ashcan school such distinguished artists as compose "The Eight" and feel it is about time someone spoke in a loud strong voice against highlighting this "Ashcan" tag wherever these important men are mentioned.*
>
> *Until George Bellows was mistakenly included in this group it did not seem proper for me to express myself so emphatically but given this opportunity I now ask in whose opinion could George Bellows who painted "Forty two Kids, Polo at Lakewood, Edith Cavell, Elinor Jean and Anne and the Crucifixion" merit the classification "Ashcan"?* Emma S. Bellows to *Life* magazine, February 22, 1949, in George Bellows Papers (Box 3, Folder 1), Archives and Special Collections, Amherst College Library.

4. For reasons not readily apparent, Charles Morgan, *Drawings of George Bellows*, Alhambra, CA: Borden Publishing Company, 1973, gave this drawing the title *On a Raft*.

5. A note in the artist's Record Book in Emma Bellows' hand incorrectly cites *Masses Aug 1913* in the artist's entry for this drawing, formerly in the Harold Rifkin collection and now in another private collection. Comparison of the Wiggin and Rifkin drawings demonstrate Bellows' considerable facility as a draughtsman. While they are identical in subject and similar in their larger compositional elements, they differ in almost every detail. Although drawn in reverse to one another, one is clearly not a copy of the other. If we wonder why he would go to such trouble just to see what the tugboat looked like going the other way, we have to remember that redrawing the image in reverse was not much trouble for a natural talent like Bellows. This point becomes important when considering the complicated relationships between his drawings and his lithographs, a topic we can hardly avoid when dealing with the Wiggin Collection. Since it was formed as a deliberate adjunct to Wiggin's already complete collection of the lithographs, it is by far our most extensive source for understanding how the artist used his drawings as sources for his prints.

6. Considered as a group, these five works comprise a response to the challenges to the Ash Can style of realism presented by avant-garde European art at the International Exhibition of Modern Art, better known as the Armory show, held in New York from February 15 to March 15, 1913. Preceded by two successful paintings, the Wiggin drawing, from the winter of 1912, exudes the confidence of an artist at the top of his game. The ex-Rifkin drawing, finished just after the Armory show in June 1913 for publication in *The Masses*, is one of five large, ambitious drawings Bellows made for the magazine that spring and early summer before he left the city for vacation. All five contain his winning but now slightly dated combination of the humorous, sympathetic, energetic, and all-American. The lithograph, printed in 1916, is part of what we might now consider a sampling of past work in a new medium, a restatement of the style for which he had become rich and famous, without any apparent recognition of the momentous changes in the art world going on around him over the last several years.

See Marianne Doezma, *George Bellows and Urban America*, New Haven: Yale University Press, 1992, 187.

7. Identification of the unusual mixture of media used in this drawing was settled in 1987, when Marjorie Cohn, then Head Conservator at the Harvard University Art Museums, and her two interns inspected it at the Boston Public Library:

> *It seems to us that the only technique, which fits all observable characteristics, and the simplest solution to this technical conundrum, is that the design is based on a monoprint, which has been heavily worked over in ink, crayon, graphite and collage. The monoprint was done by turning the paper face down on a flat surface rolled up with a heavy, viscous ink, probably either printer's ink or oil paint. The design was drawn through from the back and the resulting design, the reverse of the drawing, is thus seen on what is now the front of the sheet as a heavy black line drawing surrounded by a sort of halo of black-dotted printed texture, where the paper texture's peaks stuck to the inked surface.*
>
> Marjorie Cohn to Jane Myers, November 3, 1987

Since the drawing was intended to be photographically reproduced and printed in the magazine at reduced scale, the variations within the image caused by the different media were not visible in its published form. That he would go to the trouble to trace an image by this method, then cut it up, paste it onto board, add other pieces of paper on top and alongside it, and work the whole thing over in graphite and pen is a testament to his energetic, exploratory approach to his work, an approach which made his later foray into lithography so significant to the development of that medium in the United States.

8. Much of the background biographical data in the catalogue entries are taken from Charles H. Morgan, *George Bellows Painter of America*, New York: Reynal and Company 1965.

9. Besides the drawing and lithograph of *Business Men's Class*, 1913 and 1916, Bellows produced two

other Y.M.C.A. lithographs, *The Shower-Bath*, 1917, and *Business-Men's Bath*, 1923. He described *The Shower-Bath* as *Humoresque of the Business men's class at the Y.M.C.A.* A comment to his former professor and friend Joe Taylor indicates that, as one might expect, he enjoyed making this sort of drawing: "It is great fun to make black and whites with some sense of humor. . . . " George Bellows to Joseph Taylor, June 15, 1914, in George Bellows Papers (Box 1, Folder 12), Archives and Special Collections, Amherst College Library.

Honoré Daumier (1808–1879) was the master of French social and political cartoons for almost forty years, during which he produced over four thousand lithographs. Published in popular newspapers, his images would have been easily accessible to New York artists visiting Paris, notably Bellows' teacher Robert Henri, who lived in Paris between 1888–91 and 1895–97 and encouraged his students to study European masters: "It will do well for your to look at Daumier's lithographs. His fancy is fine. His statement is assured." Robert Henri, *The Art Spirit*, Philadelphia: J. P. Lippincott, 1923, 183.

Bellows admired Daumier. In 1908 he made a crayon copy of Daumier's important lithograph *Rue Transnonain*, 1834, and signed it *Bellows/From Daumier* (Record Book A, p. 50). For more on Daumier, start with the website, *Daumier and His Lithographs* (http://www.daumier.org/8.0.html).

While Doezma, 187, refers to the style of *Business Men's Class* as Bellows' "own creative conflation of stereotype and individual characterization," Rebecca Zurier takes a sharper look at his approach to social satire, contrasting his "mixture of concern and condescension" in his images of tenement life with his "unadulterated aesthetic admiration of the rich . . . " (Rebecca Zurier, Robert W. Snyder and Virginia Mecklenburg, *Metropolitan Lives The Ashcan Artists and Their New York*, National Museum of American Art, Washington D.C., November 17, 1995–March 17, 1996, 110). A third perspective comes from Robert Haywood, "George Bellows's Stag at Sharkey's: Boxing, Violence and Male Identity," *Smithsonian Studies in American Art*, 2, 2 (Spring 1988): 5, who noticed that Bellows' images of sport played with contemporary assumptions. The YMCA, whose reputation as a bastion of moral rectitude was commonly accepted, becomes the object of good-natured ridicule. Sharkey's boxing club, illegal, sordid and dangerous, becomes an arena of epic struggle.

All three opinions have merit, and serve to delineate the limits of Bellows' graphic art as social commentary. Daumier's expression of both outrage and compassion far outstripped Bellows'. Talented, successful and perceptive, Bellows, unlike Daumier, did not choose to dedicate himself and his career to exposing social pretension, cruelty and injustice.

10. *The Masses*, October 1913, 3. See also Rebecca Zurier, *Art for the Masses (1911–1917): A Radical Magazine and its Graphics*, exhibition catalogue, Yale University Art Gallery, New Haven, 1985, 27. Her catalogue, a model of its kind, provided valuable contextual perspective for this project. For the particulars of Bellows' contributions to the magazine, see also Charlene Stuart Engel, "George Wesley Bellows' Illustrations for the Masses and Other Magazines and the sources of His Lithographs of 1916–17." Ph.D. dissertation, University of Wisconsin, Madison, 1976.

Three of the five drawings published in *The Masses* in 1913 are in the Wiggin Collection: *Splinter Beach*, *Business Men's Class* and *Solitude*, which appeared in the April, July and September issues. The other two, *Philosopher on a Rock*, now in a private collection, and *Why don't they go to the Country for a Vacation?*, Los Angeles County Museum of Art, were published in June and August. Bellows continued to contribute four or five images annually to the magazine until 1917.

11. Winslow Homer (1836–1910) produced illustrations for *Harper's Weekly* between 1857 and 1875. He was one of Bellows' favorite artists, and contemporary critics commented on the connections between the two. See Bruce Robertson, *Reckoning with Winslow Homer: His Late Paintings and their Influence*, exhi-

bition catalogue, Cleveland Museum of Art, 1990, 113 ff. For an overview on Bellows' place in the tradition of American Realism, see John Wilmerding's introduction to Quick, Myers, Doezema and Kelly. For the affinity between the two artists, see Franklin Kelly's essay "'So Clean and Cold': Bellows and the Sea" in the same catalogue.

12. Thomas Beer in his notes in Beer and Emma S. Bellows, *George W. Bellows: His Lithographs*, New York: Alfred A. Knopf, 1927, 29, tells us that "these night scenes in Central Park are fruits of his curiosity about plebian love. He went peering and poking along the paths with an embarrassed wife on his arm, wondering about these people."

13. Morgan, 1965, 171. Bellows first went to Monhegan at the urging, and in the company of Robert Henri. According to Roberton, 89, Henri was directly responsible for inspiring his students " . . . to go there and confront the heritage of Homer on his own turf . . ."

14. Eugene Speicher, a close friend and fellow artist, wrote: "I was always astonished at his vivid memory. . . . He seldom, if ever, used models or even made drawings for [his] pictures." See Art Institute of Chicago, *George Bellows / Paintings, Drawings and Prints*, exhibition catalogue, 1946, 5.

15. Donald Braider, *George Bellows and the Ashcan School of Painting*, New York: Doubleday and Company, 1971, 121.

In a letter to his former college professor and good friend Joe Taylor, on the occasion of Taylor's visiting New York in the summer of 1919, Bellows advised Taylor to go to Petitpas and make Yeats' acquaintance.

> *When you go there you will probably see an old man with a white beard surrounded usually by several people engaged in talk. . . . He in his prime was a great portrait painter. Geo Moore says he's the greatest conversationalist he ever met. I think so. Go up and introduce yourself to him and tell him I told you to. You'll probably have a fine evening with the old man if he's feeling fit.*
>
> George Bellows to Joseph Taylor, August 13, 1919, in George Wesley Bellows Papers (Box I, Folder 14), Archives and Special Collections, Amherst College Library.

16. American journalistic illustration flourished in the first decades of the twentieth century. In a 1913 editorial Norman Hapgood, the new editor of *Harper's Weekly*, described the magazine's reason for recruiting artists as illustrators:

> *What we want is not what we do because there is a widespread demand for it, but what they* (the artists) *do because it expresses them as intelligent, gifted men.* Norman Hapgood, "To Artists," *Harper's Weekly* (August 16, 1913): 3.

17. The two women are most likely prostitutes. Their inclusion in the street scene has been taken as an example of the artist's characteristically ambiguous handling of controversial social issues, because we cannot be certain that they are streetwalkers. The image itself, however, suggests otherwise, especially their deliberate positioning in the foreground patch of sunlight, which sets them so obviously apart from the rest of the crowd. See Sean Wilentz, "Low Life, High Art," *The New Republic* (September 28, 1992): 41–44.

18. Bellows placed a very similar arrangement of a woman scolding a boy within a crowd several years earlier in the drawing *Why don't they go to the Country for a Vacation* and related painting *Cliff Dwellers*, both from 1913 and both now in the Los Angeles County Museum of Art. These figures are also the central event in another closely related and most likely contemporary drawing, *The Cliff Dwellers*, now in the Art Institute of Chicago.

19. John Reed (1887–1920) was a successful reporter, author, poet and adventurer whose eyewitness

account of the October 1917 Russian Revolution, *Ten Days that Shook the World*, capped a career of organizing and reporting on behalf of radical political and social causes in the United States. He and Bellows would have met at board meetings of *The Masses*, which they both joined in 1913. According to Deborah Fairman, "The Landscape of Display: the Ashcan School, Spectacle, and the Staging of Everyday Life," *Prospects*, 18 (1993), 209, Bellows asked for the assignment to cover Sunday's rally.

20. William Ashley Sunday (1862–1935) ended his successful first career as a major-league baseball player in 1894 by turning down lucrative offers from the Phillies, Redstockings and Pirates in favor of working for the evangelist J. Wilbur Chapman. Two years later, Chapman left his evangelical ministry and the next year Sunday held his first revival meeting. By 1917, he was calling forward nearly 100,000 people a year to accept Christ. A main part of his preaching was directed against drinking alcohol, and he was instrumental in the temperance movement's successful sponsorship of the Twenty-first Amendment in 1919. The rally in Philadelphia attended by Bellows and Reed was reported in the *New York Times* on January 11, 1915. The quote from one of Sunday's sermons comes from a copy of handwritten notes by Charlene Engel in the Charles Morgan Papers (Box 13, Folder 36), Archives and Special Collections, Amherst College Library.

21. Joyce Carol Oates, *George Bellows*, New York: The Ecco Press, 1995, 12, makes the interesting comparison between the composition of *The Sawdust Trail* and El Greco's *The Burial of Count Orgaz* (1586, Santo Tomé, Toledo), which is divided horizontally into two zones, the heavenly above and the earthly below, connected by an angel reaching through the celestial clouds. If her parallel is accurate—Bellows could have known the Spanish painting through Robert Henri, who encouraged his pupils to study the European Old Masters—we should credit Bellows with a more cunning type of satire than is usually associated with his rollicking, good-natured American humor.

22. George Bellows, "The Big Idea: George Bellows Talks About Patriotism for Beauty," *Touchstone* 1 (July 1917), 270.

Bellows took one more swipe at evangelism in a drawing published in *The Masses* (February 1916, 4), which shows a drunk "Y.M.C.A. Sport" haranguing a young man in a crowd of people listening to an energetic preacher of the "American Fundamentalist Party."

In a short memoir written for Frank Seiberling, Jr., "George Bellows, 1882–1925 / His Life and Development as an Artist," Ph.D. dissertation, The University of Chicago, 1948, 230, Emma Bellows played down her husband's strong feelings about the evangelist:

> *George had both a keen mind and a zest and feeling for living experience. He attracted to himself and was himself attracted to sudden and dramatic events and actions. They typified his life. For all his theorizing, his true place was never in the ivory tower but out in the living contemporary stream.*
>
> *Yet his ability to analyze gave him a certain detachment. In a few of his lithographs, as* The Law Is Too Slow, *he reflected a direct emotional reaction, but more often he was the detached observer. Even the* Dance in a Mad House *was no more than what he saw and is not an emotional commentary. Likewise, his attitude towards Billy Sunday. He was simply a reporter with a sense of humor and of the dramatic.*

23. George Bellows to Joseph Taylor, January 15, 1914, in George Bellows Papers (Box I, Folder 12), Archives and Special Collections, Amherst College Library,. The "prayer meeting" to which he refers is the two-page reproduction of *Deponent Testifies That He Is No Longer a Sinner*, *Harper's Weekly*, January 3, 1914, 16–17. See cat. no. 5 for a sketch on which the published drawing is based.

24. There is a wealth of material about Billy Sunday on-line. For photos of his preaching poses, see http://billysunday.org/images.html.

25. I am grateful to Glenn Peck, author of the on-line catalogue raisonné of Bellows paintings

(http://hvallison.com/home.aspx), for reminding me of Bellows' capability of reversing his drawings on the fly.

26. See Jane Myers and Linda Ayres, *George Bellows, The Artist and His Lithographs 1916–1924*, Amon Carter Museum, 1988, 11.

27. When he was fifteen, George Miller (1894–1965) began his career as an apprentice at the American Lithographic Company. Six years later, in 1915, he became foreman of their proving department. Bellows' colleague Albert Sterner, who had a litho press in his studio, was a friend of the company's co-owner. Sterner was the first artist to invite Miller to print original "fine art" lithographs. The following year Joseph Pennell and Bellows, who also owned presses, hired him. Miller retained his day job with the company while working evenings with these artists. In 1917, Miller opened his own shop, which he closed temporarily the next year when he enlisted in the U.S. Navy. After the war, Miller returned to lithography and, over the course of the next several decades, printed thousands of impressions for almost every artist-printmaker practicing in New York. See Alfred P. Maurice, "George C. Miller and Son, Lithographic Printers to Artists since 1917," *American Art Review*, 3, 2 (March–April 1976), 134.

28. A letter from Bellows to H. A. Trask at the *St. Louis Post Dispatch* lists six photographic plates of "my most important fight pictures" being sent to the paper. "Preliminaries of the Big Bout" is given the credit line "*Courtesy of Colliers Weekly*." Since the drawing is unfinished—a blank white space exists where there should be a ring, boxers and referee—we can assume he is referring to the lithograph. If *Colliers* had the photo, had they or did they intend to publish it, and in what context? George Bellows to H. A. Trask, May 19, 1924, in George Bellows Papers (Box 1, Folder 14), Archives and Special Collections, Amherst College Library.

29. The drawing was exhibited at Allison Galleries in October 1942, and reviewed in that month's issue of *Artnews*: "The only Bellows prizefight drawing still on the market is at Allison's and a gem it indeed is. . . . The flashy but somehow magnificent foreground figures, the harsh tense atmosphere, the punch of the composition puts this one way up in front." ("The Passing Shows," *Artnews*, 41, 10 (October 1942): 27.)

30. Most of the artist's drawings were done in crayon, or some mixture of media dominated by crayon. Adding to this group all the lithographs, which were also drawn in crayon, it is easy to think of Bellows as a linear draughtsman. A few major wash drawings like *Preliminaries*, for example *Polo at Lakewood* (1910, private collection) and *Luncheon in the Park* (1912, Albright Knox Art Gallery), demonstrate that he was also a master of painterly tone, and that his drawings could be much more than facile illustrations.

31. According to Clinton Adams, longtime lithographer, art historian and resident of Albuquerque, the name of the town in New Mexico is Quemado, not Quevado. It is likely that the mistake originated with the artist. In her 1927 catalogue of the lithographs, Emma Bellows, who compiled her information from her late husband's notebooks, titled the print *Well at Quevado*. (Notes from a conversation between Adams and Sinclair Hitchings, May 3, 1990.)

32. In the first catalogue of the lithographs, Thomas Beer wrote:

> *Seen while motoring from California to New Mexico with George Washington Smith, the architect. Bellows tried this composition in three mediums, oil, water-color and lithography. The lithograph did not satisfy him, so very few prints were pulled.*
>
> Beer and Bellows, 253.

The painting is now in the collection of the Minnesota Museum of Art, St. Paul. The watercolor is in a private collection. The two known impressions of the lithograph are in the Wiggin Collection and the Amon Carter Museum.

33. Lauris Mason, *The Lithographs of George Bellows A Catalogue Raisonné*, revised edition, San Francisco: Alan Wofsy Fine Arts, 1992, 86.

34. Jack Johnson became the first African-American champion in 1908. He successfully defended his title in 1910 against the "great white hope" Jim Jeffries, a victory so controversial it sparked race riots across the United States. See Robert W. Snyder, "City in Transition," in Zurier, Snyder and Mecklenburg, 47. Bellows obliquely referred to the racial tension surrounding boxing in his drawing *The Savior of his Race* published in *The Masses*, May 1915, 11. See the JO Sports, Inc. website for pages of reproductions of the Dana Photo cards: http://www.josportsinc.com/catalog/view.php?a=&cat=87&s_name=&offset=40.

35. See Quick, in Quick, Myers, Doezema and Kelly, 21.

36. The exact ratio specified by Hambidge is $\sqrt{\varphi}$ or 1.272, the square root of the golden section ratio, 1.618. Bellows used the golden section many times before he met Hambidge, and it is possible that he would select its square root for an early experiment with Dynamic Symmetry.

37. See the essays and checklists for the drawings and lithographs by Linda Ayres and Deborah Chotner in Carmean, Wilmerding, Ayres and Chotner, 60, 68, 90, 96, and 98.

38. See Glenn Peck's introductory essays in the catalogues for *George Bellows, Lithographs*, exhibition catalogue, Adelson Gallery, New York, 1999 and *With My Profound Reverence for the Victims George Bellows*, exhibition catalogue, Samuel Dorsky Museum of Art, State University of New York, New Paltz, 2001.

39. Bellows' image is based upon the following passage in Whitlock's article, 17:

> *The subject (of the deported Belgian workers) was ever present with the suffering, the misery, the despair it connoted, and now the reality of it was brought more directly to all of us by the few returning Belgians who had been repatriated by the Germans. They were pitiable objects of German brutality; they were those, for the most part, who had refused to work, or whose physical condition made them useless as workers—and they were brought back to Belgium to die, broken, maimed, helpless, hopeless, pale emaciated men whom a few weeks in the slave compound in Germany had so reduced by sickness, exposure and starvation that they were hauled back home and flung down in their villages to die.*

40. Frederick Keppel & Company, *Original Lithographs by George Bellows*, New York, exhibition catalogue, 1918.

In the late 1940s Emma Bellows wrote about her husband's War Series:

> *To artists who have a constructive sense of life and a love of beauty and order, war is naturally repugnant. Bellows' war drawings were hence an indictment of war in general. In a broad sense the drawings are an attack on the horrors of war and unfortunately are once again very much in touch with the times.* Sieberling, 228

41. Francisco de Goya y Lucientes (1746–1828), painter to the courts of both Charles III and Charles IV of Spain, began producing his thematic series of prints late in his career. *Los Disastres* (1810–20) was the second of five series created between 1799 and 1825. He is often cited in relation to the illustrations of the Ash Can School artists to emphasize their candid portrayals of people outside the upper classes. Henri's students and colleagues would have been familiar with Goya, as Henri had visited Spain three times by 1908. Bellows was quite aware of the connections made between his work and Goya's (see Myers and Ayres, 64, and Eleanor M. Tufts, "Bellows and Goya," *Art Journal* 30, 4 (Summer 1971), 363), as was his dealer, H.V. Allison. In a letter to Albert Wiggin, he describes the drawings for *Dance in a Mad House* and *The Law Is Too Slow* as " . . . superb, as good drawings as ever were made, to me as fine

as Daumier or Goya." (H.V. Allison, Federick Keppel & Co., to A.H. Wiggin, September 30, 1936). Wiggin purchased the latter drawing. The former went to the Art Institute of Chicago.

Thomas Beer, in his introductory essay to the 1927 catalogue raisonné of the artist's lithographs, made an interesting observation about Bellows and the war images:

> *. . . this attack of anger sent him back, as it had sent Manet before him, to effects of Goya. A man in a fine state of anger never can fully exercise his imagination. . . . Bellows, in 1924, referred to his war paintings as "hallucinations" but I do not suggest that he was ashamed of them.* Beer and Bellows, 20.

42. Charles Dana Gibson to George Bellows, August 27, 1918, in George Bellows papers (Box 2, Folder 12), Archives and Special Collections, Amherst College Library. As he implies, Gibson understood the political power of Bellows' images. If they had appeared before the war, perhaps they would have stimulated a quicker response by the United States against Germany. Since they appeared after, they could be instrumental in exacting severe penalties against the German government. See Charlene Stuart Engel, "The Man in the Middle: George Bellows, War and 'Sergeant' Delaney," *American Art* 18, 1 (Spring 2004): 78.

43. In high school, Bellows squared off and exactly copied Gibson's drawings. See Sieberling, 77. For Henri's reaction, see Morgan, 1965, 40.

44. Praise for the War Series has not been universal. Frank Sieberling observed that the images

> *. . . are rooted in the incident and miss the overtones which are the true tragedy of war. They are not unrealistic, but too realistic, pointing up local detail that does not contribute to the idea but only to the act.*
> Seiberling, 116.

Milton Brown wrote that Bellows,

> *. . . carried away by the tales of German atrocities in Belgium, did his famous series of twelve lithographs of the "Huns," a series which is no credit to Bellows either as an artist or as a thinker.*
> Brown, *American Painting, from the Armory Show to the Depression,*
> Princeton: Princeton University Press, 1970, 71.

45. Comparison of the drawing of Base Hospital with the two versions of the lithograph suggests that Mason's entries 51 and 52 should be switched. What she titles *Second Stone* is more likely the earlier version, as it more closely resembles the drawing, especially the treatment of light entering the cathedral, and its reverse orientation suggests the simplest relationship between the two, given the normal reversal that occurs when printing an image from stone.

46. Miss Frick was the daughter of Henry Clay Frick, the industrial magnate. During the war, she served overseas for close to a year, first in helping to repatriate Belgian refugees, the victims of the same invasion depicted by Bellows, and later nursing on the front. After the war ended, in November 1918, working within the Goodwill Section of The Red Cross, New York, she created an elegant and highly successful thrift shop on Fifth Avenue to aid hospitalized soldiers.

> *Knoedler donated paintings, society women tore through their attics and closets, men cleaned out their bureau drawers, cooks parted with equipment, antique dealers gave furniture, and famous jewelers donated fine pieces. . . . Her mother, with the help of Duveen, decorated one room in the style of Louis XVI, named it Pandora's Box, and as the New York Herald describes, it sold "everything from a dollar trinket to a diamond."*
> Martha F. S. Sanger, *Henry Clay Frick: an intimate portrait,*
> New York: Abbeville Press, 1998, 477-78.

In six months, the shop cleared $50,000. According to a thank-you letter from her to Bellows, he donated the proceeds of the sale of the two paintings ($500 each) to The Red Cross Shop. H.C. Frick to George Bellows, March 27, 1919, in George Bellows Papers (Box 2, Folder 12), Archives and Special Collections, Amherst College Library.

Dawn of Peace and *Hail to Peace* are now in the Allentown Art Museum, PA and Scott and White Hospital, Temple TX, respectively. According to Glenn Peck, Duveen specified their unusually long vertical proportions so that they fit a specific wall space in his gallery.

Sometime early in 1919, Bellows printed a small Christmas card based on *Hail to Peace*. Like many of us, he appears to have been late in the making, not to mention the mailing. A listing of his lithographs up to and including the Christmas card was published in Frank Weitenkamp, "George W. Bellows, Lithographer," *Print Connoisseur*, 1924, 225–44.

After the entry for *Hail to Peace*, Weitenkamp noted "Proofs to this point (i.e. from 1916 to 1919) pulled by Edward Krause." This statement is not accurate, as we know that George Miller printed for Bellows between 1916 and 1918, when he enlisted in the United States Navy. Nevertheless, it does provide a possible answer to the question of who printed for the artist during the war, after Miller enlisted in 1918 and before Bellows actively began his collaboration with Bolton Brown in 1920–21. In a letter to Charlene Engel written during her preparation of her thesis on Bellows and *The Masses*, Gordon Allison, whose gallery represented the Bellows estate, suggested that Krause was that printer. See Engel, 1976, 118, n. 6.

In his Introduction to the exhibition *With My Profound Reverence for the Victims George Bellows*, Neil Trager states that Bolton Brown "pulled at least one of..." the War Series lithographs of 1918. (Samuel Dorsky Museum of Art, State University of New York, New Paltz, 2001, 3). Bellows and Brown most likely discussed working with one another in the winter of 1918–19. To collaborate on one of the War images, they would have had to been together no later than early fall of 1918, when the series was exhibited at Keppel Galleries in New York, and more realistically the spring before, when Charles Dana Gibson saw the prints at Keppel's. See note 41 above. I don't know of any evidence specifically linking Bellows and Brown in the spring of 1918.

47. Getting his location wrong, Thomas Beer, in Beer and Bellows, 30, observed that "This 'Legs of the Sea' shows you how Bellows saw the plebians taking the sun on shores of Long Island and New Jersey, not very gracefully but so honestly."

48. Edward Keefe, his studio-mate during their first years in New York and life-long friend, described his visual memory as " . . . so remarkable that he could paint a detailed landscape entirely in the studio, without having made any sketches or graphite notations on the actual site." See Seiberling, 207.

49. The photograph of Emma swimming can be found in the George Bellows Papers (Box 5, Folder 6), Archives and Special Collections, Amherst College Library, and is reproduced with the permission of the Estate of George Bellows.

Other evidence in the Wiggin Collection of Bellows' involvement with photography includes:

- *A Knock Down*, 1910, most likely used photographs of the Jeffries / Johnson fight for the poses of the two fighters.
- As he noted in the entry for the 1918 lithograph *Base Hospital* in the 1919 Rouillier Gallery exhibition, he used a contemporary photograph as the source for this image. Another drawing of World War I, *The Belgian Prisoner*, now in the collection of the Princeton University Art Gallery, also has a photographic feel to it.
- *The Appeal to the People*, 1923 is based on a photograph with the caption "Eamon De Valera speaks in County Clare 1923" a copy of which is attached to the mat of the drawing in the Boston Public Library.

- *The Deadline*, c.1923, contains several figures taken from a 1913 photograph of a Pennsylvania mining accident.
- *Auntie Mason and her Husband*, 1923, appears to have been based on a family photograph.

Despite this evidence, little attention has been paid to the topic. Thomas Craven, in his assessment of Bellows just after his death, offhandedly observed that the figures in the lithographs "... have the unreality of photographs and occasionally appear as if they were actually made from photographs." Thomas Craven, "George Bellows," *The Dial*, 80, 2 (February 1926), 136.

50. Morgan, 1965, 206 and 239. See also Glenn Peck, *George Bellows Paintings, Drawings and Lithographs, An Exhibition in Memory of Gordon K. Allison* (1904–1984), exhibition catalogue, Hirschl and Adler Gallery, New York, 1984.

51. Charlene Engel nicely summarizes the nature of the genre:

> *Illustration is a theatrical art form. The illustrator creates a stage, places his characters on it, and tells their story. Bellows was a good illustrator because he was able to identify with the characters and stories he portrayed, to animate and energize them, and to involve the viewer.* Engel, 2004, 86.

In these abilities, Bellows was not unique. A number of his Ash Can colleagues had worked as newspaper illustrators, "visual reporters ... trained in topicality, human interest, and speed." See Brown, 1970, 9. A few pages later, 21–22, Brown, identifies what he considers the central weakness of the Ash Can approach:

> *Each incident remains interesting as an incident and not as art. This ability to recall the normal events of living without interpretation, except perhaps for a bit of humor and irony, is characteristic of the journalistic style.*

Brown echoes a contemporary criticism of Bellows' approach:

> *So far as I grasp his intentions, he merely wants to reproduce what he sees, never bothering his head to discriminate, sympathize with or rearrange, intruding the merest casualy upon you with the drums and trampling of the epic. He suggests to me the alertness of American journalism turned painter, the reportorial spirit armed with the palette and brush.* Charles Buchanan, "George Bellows, Painter of Democracy," *Arts and Decoration* 4 (August 1914): 371-2.

Elizabeth Mongan, curator of prints for Lessing J. Rosenwald and later his print collection at the National Gallery of Art. approached the same issue more positively:

> *George Bellows, was primarily an illustrator. His published drawings are the best examples of American graphic reporting done between the two great wars. He used, in a perfectly legitimate way, the shock value of realistic scenes of prize fights, slums, social injustice, and the brutality of war. Also, he was by instinct an inheritor of the odd American sense of caricature and drollery.* Smithsonian Institution, *George Bellows Prints and Drawings*, exhibition catalogue, Washington D.C. 1957–58, 6.

52. The crowd may have judged Dempsey sense of patriotic duty unfairly.

> *Dempsey always paid dearly—too dearly, perhaps—for staying out of the war, even after a San Francisco jury took but ten minutes to clear him of the charge of evading the draft. Dempsey's first wife, Maxine Cates, fifteen years his senior, was the government's star witness in that 1920 trial. Listed as a wartime dependent of Dempsey's even though the brief union hadn't survived that long, the woman swore that she had paid her own way. Dempsey always insisted this wasn't so but it wasn't crucial to the case in any event, for white-haired Cecilia Dempsey testified that her son was indeed the sole support of a large brood—his own family—come on hard times in 1917 and 1918. Beyond that, the fighter produced evidence that the Secretary of the Navy had asked him to stay in civilian clothes because he could do more good for the war effort that way; he had raised $200,000 for the Red Cross. What hurt Dempsey,*

down through the years, was a wartime publicity photo showing him supposedly at toil in a Philadelphia shipyard. He had overalls on but his feet were shod in patent leather. The picture, naturally, was published very widely. Nat Fleischer, Dempsey's biographer, always defended him on the slacker charge but conceded in later years that many boxers had ducked World War I. "They considered a bayonet a poor substitute for the padded glove and were loath to risk life and limb in a quarrel without gate receipts," said the candid Fleischer.

Dempsey had to wait a quarter of a century to redeem himself. In World War II, as a Coast Guard commander detailed to the physical training program, he went into Tarawa under fire—an "old man" in his late forties among a bunch of boys. Paul Sann, *The Lawless Decade*, http://www.lawlessdecade.net/new1921-1.html

53. Bellows was commissioned by Herbert Bayard Swope (1882-1958), editor of the *New York World*, Pulitzer Prize recipient in 1917 for his reporting during the Great War, and owner of Land's End, the Long Island estate generally considered the model for Tom and Daisy Buchanan's mansion in F. Scott Fitzgerald's novel *The Great Gatsby*. The Carpentier—Dempsey match, the first match to gross over $1 million and the first to be broadcast live on radio, was one of a series of heavily promoted prizefights during the 1920s which brought professional boxing to its greatest popularity. Since many newspapers ran large photo spreads on the day after the event, Swope did not need Bellows' drawing as a record of what happened, and was more likely capitalizing on his fame as the artist of once scandalous boxing pictures. Bellows, judging from the humorous title he first wrote on the sheet and then erased, saw through the hype boxing promoters and popular media gave to the spectacle, yet wasted no time developing a lithograph based on his drawings of the match, the only time he and Bolton Brown worked together in Brown's studio in Woodstock. According to Brown, it was "printed to perfection." See Clinton Adams, *Crayonstone: The Life and Work of Bolton Brown With a Catalogue of His Lithographs*, Albuquerque: University of New Mexico Press, 1993, 113 and Brown, Bolton, "My Ten Years in Lithography," Part II, reprinted in Adams, Clinton, ed., *The Tamarind Papers*, 5,2 (Summer 1982), 39.

54. Morgan, 1965, 247. See also Linda Ayres, "Bellows: the Boxing Drawings" in Carmean, Wilmerding, Ayres and Chotner, 61.

55. Sieberling 211–212.

56. Brian Oswald Patrick Donn-Byrne (1889–1929) was an Irish-American novelist and poet. For a brief biographical summary, see http://www.geocities.com/Athens/Forum/1333/byrne.html

57. Mason, 223.

58. See Braider, 131, and cat. no. 6, *Night at Petitpas*. In a letter to his close friend Joe Taylor, Bellows commented on the Century project:

> *Starting with April number the Century will run Donn Byrnes new serial story The Wind Bloweth, a fine piece of literature I think, well worth a good reading, some parts superb, Fifteen drawings by yours truly. My job for this winter, and one I liked supremely well. Drawings in first issue are the poorest. Had I been given time would have made them over.* George Bellows to Joseph Taylor, March 16, 1922, in George Bellows Papers (Box 1, Folder 14), Archives and Special Collections, Amherst College Library

59. The sale of *Club Night* was made by Marie Sterner, one of the artist's dealers and wife of the artist and lithographer, Albert Sterner, who introduced Bellows to the printer George Miller. It was re-titled *Stag at Sharkey's* after its purchase by the museum. According to his income ledger for 1908–24, Bellows earned just over $11,000 in 1922, his third highest annual total at that point in his career. That amount is equivalent to about $135,000 today. Forty percent of that total came from income received that year for the *The Wind Bloweth*, *Men Like Gods* and *Club Night*. Prior to building their own, the Bellows family had spent two summers in Woodstock in a rented house. They continued to vacation there through

1924. After the artist's death in early 1925, Emma Bellows and her two daughters returned each summer for many years.

60. See the drawings *The Donkey Cart* and *Girls by a Lake* reproduced in Royal Cortissoz, "George Bellows and His Draughtmanship", *New York Herald Tribune*, October 4, 1936, 3–4.

61. Herbert George Wells (1866–1946) was an English novelist, journalist, sociologist, and historian best known for his works of science fiction: *The Time Machine* (1895), *The Invisible Man* (1897), and *The War of the Worlds* (1898).

62. Evidence indicates that Bellows wanted to illustrate the hardcover edition. In May 1923, he wrote a highly complimentary, deferential letter to H.G. Wells, and sent him a series of proofs and one original lithograph. In March 1924, Bellows instructed Weil Perrin, Art Editor at Hearst to send the plates of the Wells illustrations to Alfred Knopf. George Bellows to Wells, May 8, 1923, Bellows to Knopf, March 8, 1924 and Bellows to Perrin, March 10, 1924, in George Bellows Papers (Box 1, Folders 8 and 15), Archives and Special Collections, Amherst College Library.

63. Jay Hambidge, *Dynamic Symmetry in Composition as Used by Artists*, New Haven: Yale University Press, 1923, 22, gives a lively account of Bellows' first visit. For concise descriptions of the systems of compositional design Bellows used, see Henry Adams, "The Paintings of George Bellows," *American Artist*, 56, 600 (July 1992), 57. For a longer discussion, see Michael Quick, "Technique and Theory: the Evolution of George Bellows's Painting Style," in Quick, Myers, Doezema and Kelly, 63–65. For the viewpoint from someone within the school of Dynamic Symmetry, see H.J. McWhinnie, "A Review of the Use of Symmetry, the Golden Section and Dynamic Symmetry in Contemporary Art," *Leonardo*, 19, 3 (1986), 242.

Bellows utilized theories of composition other than Hambidge's, for example Hardesty Maratta's Compositional System based upon the equilateral triangle and the ratio of the Golden Section, before being converted to Dynamic Symmetry in late 1917. See Quick, 21–33 and 38–42.

Critics generally disapproved of these theoretical compositional systems. The arch-conservative Thomas Craven, writing shortly after the 1925 memorial exhibition at the Metropolitan Museum of Art in New York, considered Bellows' enthusiasm for systems a sign of his lack of discrimination:

> *It is also true that he was easily imposed upon by the manufacturers of formulae, and that not infrequently his adaptations resulted in mere smartness and prestidigitation. . . . Having a limited critical faculty, he was open to the bad as well as the good, and theories like those of Hambidge and Maratta were swallowed with the same gusto as the sounder influences of good painting.* Craven, 133–34

In 1946, writing about the monumental exhibition at his museum, Daniel Catton Rich, director of the Art Institute of Chicago, sympathetically understood the context and motivation for Bellows' susceptibility:

> *Why, with such remarkable gifts, did Bellows slowly but unmistakably surrender a number of them and become a self-conscious stylist? The answer is not only to be found in his ambition (no one was more ambitious) but in his response to the revolutionary doctrines exposed in the Armory Show. Much has been written of the public's amazement at this revelation of advanced European art, but how did the artist feel? How did a man like Bellows, brought up on what he believed to be the most advanced tendency of his day, self-expression applied to the problems of contemporary life, react when suddenly confronted with the fauvism of Matisse and Rouault, the cubism of Picasso and Braque? We can imagine the bewilderment, self-questioning, the determination not to be swept off one's feet. . . . So we find Bellows turning away from the organic vigor of his early work and seeking theories and formulas which would resolve the conflict.* Daniel C. Rich, "Bellows Revalued", *Magazine of Art*, 39 (April, 1946), 140–41.

Rich's connection between Bellows' obvious penchant for artistic theories and his supposed response to the most avant-garde work in the Armory Show laid the foundation for later critical opinion. Noting a comment the artist made to a reporter regarding cubism's ". . . merely laying bare a principle of construction which is contained within the great works of art which have gone before," the modernist advocate Milton Brown, "Twentieth-Century Nostrums: Pseudo-Scientific Theory in American Painting," *Magazine of Art*, 41, 3 (March, 1948), 288, gave Bellows' response a more negative spin: "Bellows was led by the challenge of Cubism to investigate pseudo-scientific alternatives which proved a hindrance rather than a help." Building on Rich and Brown, Suzanne Boorsch, "The lithographs of George Bellows," *Artnews*, 75,3 (March 1976), 60–62) applied the idea of Bellows' faltering self-confidence to her frank and refreshing assessment of the widely varying quality within his body of almost two hundred lithographs. Coming from an entirely different tradition, Joyce Carol Oates, *George Bellows*, 1995, x, freely admitting she was not a critic or art historian, thought that "his numerous theories of composition and color" marked him ". . . as one of the most restlessly intellectual of American artists, of his time or any other."

It is important to separate what is known from what is assumed, however likely those assumptions might be. We know the artist enthusiastically studied and applied Hambidge's system to his work. His behavior in this regard seems entirely consistent with his usage of other compositional systems at other stages of his career. We can see the obvious effects that Dynamic Symmetry had on his paintings, drawings and lithographs after 1917. We don't know that Bellows experienced a crisis of confidence after the Armory Show, and we don't know if he embraced Dynamic Symmetry, or any other theory, as a solution to this possible but so far undocumented crisis. Finally, we can observe in the Wiggin drawings done between 1918 and 1925 the artist moving in and out and finally beyond his infatuation with this system.

64. Bellows' illustrations for *Men Like Gods* did not receive critical approval, either during his lifetime or after. In 1925, the *New York Times'* generally positive review of a memorial exhibition of his drawings and lithographs at the Keppel Galleries commented:

> *With the exception of a few romantic illustrations containing nude figures wandering about the landscape and illustrating a story which apparently was never very clearly visualized by the artist, nearly all of the works shown are favorably representative of Bellows's gifts.*
>
> "Vivid Black and Whites by Bellows," *New York Times*, April, 1925, from a clipping in Bellows Papers, Box 4, Folder 13, Archives and Special Collections, Amherst College Library

In 1936, Keppel presented another exhibition of drawings. Ann Brewer, writing for *Artnews*, reached an almost identical conclusion:

> *The show is a fine testimony to the artist's ability as a master draughtsman and only occasionally, as in the case of some of the fairy tale illustrations, is one irritated by the flawlessly smooth technique.* Ann Brewer, "A Fine Showing of Some Bellows Drawings", *Artnews*, 35, 1 (October 1936): 6.

Thirty years later, in another generally positive *Times* review, this time of the 1966 Bellows show at the Gallery of Modern Art, John Canaday wrote:

> *Afraid of being a literal realist, he prettified his style in an effort to illustrate the fantasy of H.G. Wells "Men Like Gods" and produced the only really bad drawings of his career.* John Canaday, "George Bellows and the End of a World Picasso Never Knew," *New York Times*, March 13, 1966, 135.

65. Mary Johnston, "Nemesis," *Century* magazine, May 1923, 3. Note that, in this case, the magazine published the lithograph instead of the drawing. Since the Wiggin Collection of drawings was formed to complement his earlier complete collection of Bellows lithographs, also given to the Boston Public

Library, it provides many opportunities to observe the fluidity Bellows maintained between media. While they are different in their technical details, his style of drawing and lithography were both based upon the same process of creation—using a black crayon on a smooth surface.

By early 1923, Bellows was thoroughly engaged with his third master printer, Bolton Brown (1865–1936), probably the most skilled lithographer then working in the United States. The two men were in the middle of an enormously productive three years, 1921–24, during which they printed at least one hundred and twenty-five editions. Circumstances were most conducive to his choosing the lithograph over the drawing for submission to the magazine. As Brown put it: "By this time, [we] had worked so much together that each knew precisely what his part was and how to play it. We made a gorgeous team." (Clinton Adams, 113).

Whatever Bellows and Brown thought, later critics found fault with this particular translation from drawing to print. A review of the 1936 Keppel Galleries exhibition of Bellows drawings and prints noted that:

> *Naturally his lithographs are known to most. But the drawings are another matter and give particular interest to the present display. For here are the original studies for some of his famous prints, showing the changes he made on second thought, and not always for the best, some are inclined to hold. Take the original drawing for his lynching print, "The Law Is Too Slow," for example. In the original drawings the night effect is more subtly and suggestively handled and the drawing has an atmospheric quality that has been sacrificed in the lithograph to a more crude and violent contrast of blacks and whites.*
>
> "Bellows's Art To Fore Again," New York Sun, September 26, 1936, from a clipping in George Bellows Papers, (Box 4, Folder 13), Archives and Special Collections, Amherst College Library

Another review of the same show called the drawing for *The Law Is Too Slow* " . . . another fine example of Bellows' feeling for atmosphere and sense of design." (Brewer, 6.)

66. Morgan, 1965, 31 and 259. After the artist's death in 1925, the lithographic version of this image played a prominent role in the anti-lynching movement. It was used as the frontispiece for Walter White's 1929 book, *Rope and Faggot*. Six years later, White, the Director of the National Association for the Advancement of Colored People, organized the exhibition *An Art Commentary on Lynching*, February 15–March 2, 1935 at the Arthur Newton Galleries in New York City. *The Law is Too Slow* hung in the exhibition and was reproduced on the second page of the accompanying catalogue. See Helen Langa, "Two Antilynching Art Exhibitions: Politicized Viewpoints, Racial Perspectives, Gendered Constraints," *American Art* 13, 1 (Spring 1999), 20.

67. Speicher in Sieberling, 219.

68. George Bellows to Edna S. Pratt, March 10, 1924, in George Bellows Papers (Box 1, Folder 9), Archives and Special Collections, Amherst College Library.

69. In the letter cited above, Bellows describes Auntie Mason and her husband as the people "with whom my father lived when he was building the old high school or there abouts."

70. Mason, 201.

71. Attached to the mat protecting this drawing is a photograph cut from a review of Mary C. Bromage's *De Valera and The March of a Nation* (Horace Reynolds, "A Source of Argument," *New York Times Book Review*, March 24, 1957, 22). The photograph is not reproduced in Bromage's book, and its origins have yet to be identified. The Clare County Library web site has a concise biographical sketch of De Valera http://www.clarelibrary.ie/eolas/coclare/people/eamon.htm

72. William Glackens (1870–1938), George Luks (1866–1933), Everett Shinn (1876–1953) and John Sloan (1871–1951) all worked as newspaper illustrators in Philadelphia, where, with Robert Henri's encouragement, they developed themselves as artists and eventually moved to New York to pursue their careers. See Judy L. Larson, *American Illustration 1890–1925 Romance, Adventure, and Suspense*, exhibition catalogue, Glenbow Museum, Calgary, University of Chicago Press, 1986, 65.

73. Mason, 217, cites the photograph and its caption. A drawing, probably taken from the photograph, shows miners' families gathered at the entrance to the Cincinnati Mine following the explosion on April 28, 1913. See http://patheoldminer.rootsweb.com/wascincinnati.html.

74. Morgan, 1965, 40, quotes Henri: "Draw your material from the life around you, from all of it. There is beauty in everything if it looks beautiful to your eyes."

75. *I am going to Woodstock in just a week. . . . I would have to ask you, I think, to get me a number of photographs of Salvation Army accoutrements. I haven't got time while in town to find any Salvation Army model to make any drawings from. I shall have to ask you to get me this material.*

George Bellows to W.V. Curtis, May 19, 1924, in George Bellows Papers (Box 1, Folder 6), Archives and Special Collections, Amherst College Library.

76. Agnes Tait McNulty to Emma Bellows, March 4 and 31, 1943, in George Bellows Papers (Box 3, Folder 8), Archives and Special Collections, Amherst College Library. For a discussion of the sitters' identity see Marjorie B. Searl and Ronald Netsky, *Leaving for the Country / George Bellows at Woodstock*, exhibition catalogue, Memorial Art Gallery of the University of Rochester, 2003, 73, 90. Mason, 198, dated to lithograph to 1921, but noted conflicting evidence and allowed that it could have been printed in 1924.

BIBLIOGRAPHY

Adams, Clinton, *Crayonstone: The Life and Work of Bolton Brown With a Catalogue of His Lithographs*, Albuquerque: University of New Mexico Press, 1993.

Adams, Henry, "The Paintings of George Bellows," *American Artist*, 56, 600 (July 1992): 52.

Albert Roullier Art Galleries, *Catalogue of an Exhibition of Original Lithographs by George Bellows N.A.*, Chicago, exhibition catalogue, 1919.

Art Institute of Chicago, *George Bellows / Paintings, Drawings and Prints*, exhibition catalogue, 1946.

Beer, Thomas and Bellows, Emma S., *George W. Bellows: His Lithographs*, New York: Alfred A. Knopf, 1927.

George Wesley Bellows Papers, Archives and Special Collections, Amherst College Library, Amherst, Massachusetts

Bellows, George, "The Big Idea: George Bellows Talks About Patriotism for Beauty," *Touchstone* 1 (July, 1917): 269–275.

________, "The Relation of Painting to Architecture," *The American Architect*, 118, 2349 (December 29, 1920): 847–851.

Boorsch, Suzanne, "The Lithographs of George Bellows", *Artnews*, 75,3 (March 1976): 60.

Boswell Jr., Peyton, *George Bellows*, New York: Crown Publishers, 1942.

Braider, Donald, *George Bellows and the Ashcan School of Painting*, New York: Doubleday and Company, 1971.

Brewer, Ann, "A Fine Showing of Some Bellows Drawings", *Artnews*, 35,1 (October 1936): 6.

Brown, Bolton, "My Ten Years in Lithography," Part II, reprinted in Adams, Clinton, ed., The Tamarind Papers, 5, 2 (Summer 1982): 36–54.

Brown, Milton, "Twentieth-Century Nostrums: Pseudo-Scientific Theory in American Painting," *Magazine of Art*, 41, 3 (March 1948): 98.

________, *American Painting, from the Armory Show to the Depression*, Princeton: Princeton University Press, 1970.

________, *The Story of the Armory Show*, New York: Abeville Press, 1988.

Buchanan, Charles, "George Bellows, Painter of Democracy," *Arts and Decoration* 4 (August 1914): 370.

Burns, Sarah, *Inventing the Modern Artist Art and Culture in Gilded Age America*, New Haven: Yale University Press, 1996.

Cahill, Holger and Alfred Barr, *Art in America: A Complete Survey*, New York: Reynal & Hitchcock, 1934.

Canaday, John, "George Bellows and the End of a World Picasso Never Knew," *New York Times*, March 13, 1966, 135.

Carmean, E.A. Jr., John Wilmerding, Linda Ayres and Deborah Chotner, *Bellows The Boxing Pictures*, exhibition catalogue, National Gallery of Art, Washington, 1982.

Collier's New Photographic History of the European War, New York: P.F. Collier & Son, 1916.

Columbus Museum of Art, *George Wesley Bellows, Paintings, Drawings and Prints*, exhibition catalogue, 1979.

Cortissoz, Royal, "George Bellows and His Draughtmanship", *New York Herald Tribune*, October 4, 1936, 3-4.

Craven, Thomas, "George Bellows," *The Dial*, 80, 2 (February 1926): 133.

Crowninshield, Frank, "An Appreciations of the Life and Work of George Bellows", *Artnews*, 23, 15 (January 1925): 6.

Doezema, Marianne, *George Bellows and Urban America*, New Haven: Yale University Press, 1992.

Eggers, George W., *George Bellows*, American Artists Series, New York: Whitney Museum of American Art, 1931.

Engel, Charlene Stuart, "George Wesley Bellow's Illustrations for the Masses and Other Magazines and the sources of His Lithographs of 1916–17." Ph.D dissertation, University of Wisconsin, Madison, 1976.

__________, "The Realist's Eye: The Illustrations and Lithographs of George W. Bellows," *Print Review X* (1979), 70–86.

__________, "The Man in the Middle: George Bellows, War and 'Sergeant' Delaney," *American Art* 18, 1 (Spring 2004): 78.

Fairman, Deborah, "The Landscape of Display: the Ashcan School, Spectacle, and the Staging of Everyday Life", *Prospects*, 18 (1993), 205.

Fitzgerald, Richard, *Art and Politics: Cartoonists of the Masses and Liberator*, Westport, CT: Greenwood Press, 1973.

Gombrich, Ernst, *Art and Illusion*, New York: Bollingen Foundation, 1961.

Green, Catherine, *George Bellows Works from the Permanent Collection of the Albright-Knox Art Gallery*, exhibition catalogue, Albright-Knox Art Gallery, Buffalo, NY, 1981.

The Grunwald Center for the Graphic Arts, *The American Personality The Artist-Illustrator of Life in the United States, 1860–1930*, exhibition catalogue, University of California at Los Angeles, 1976.

Hambidge, Jay, *Dynamic Symmetry in Composition, as Used by Artists*, New Haven: Yale University Press, 1923.

Hapgood, Norman, "To Artists," *Harper's Weekly*, (August 16, 1913): 3.

Haywood, Robert, "George Bellows's Stag at Sharkey's: Boxing, Violence and Male Identity," *Smithsonian Studies in American Art*, 2, 2 (Spring, 1988): 2.

Henri, Robert, *The Art Spirit*, Philadelphia: J.P. Lippincott, 1923.

Hunter, Robert, "The Rewards and Disappointments of the Ashcan School: The Early Career of Stuart Davis" in Sims, Lowery Stokes, *Stuart Davis American Painter*, exhibition catalogue, Metropolitan Museum of Art, New York, 1992, 31.

Hutton, Molly S., *"The Ashcan City: Representational Strategies at the Turn-of-the-Century,"* Ph.D. dissertation, Stanford University, CA, 2000.

Jaffe, Barbara, "Jackson Pollock's Industrial Expressionism", *Art Journal*, 63, 4 (Winter 2004): 68.

Frederick Keppel & Company, *Original Lithographs by George Bellows*, New York, exhibition catalogue, 1918.

Langa, Helen, "Two Antilynching Art Exhibitions: Politicized Viewpoints, Racial Perspectives, Gendered Constraints," *American Art* 13, 1 (Spring 1999): 10.

Larson, Judy L., *American Illustration 1890–1925 Romance, Adventure, and Suspense*, exhibition catalogue, Glenbow Museum, Calgary, University of Chicago Press, 1986.

De Leiris, Alain, *The Drawings of Edouard Manet*, University of California Press, 1969.

M., F.J., "The Independent Artists," *The Nation* (April 7, 1910): 360.

Mason, Lauris, *The Lithographs of George Bellows A Catalogue Raisonné*, revised edition, San Francisco: Alan Wofsy Fine Arts, 1992.

Maurice, Alfred P., "George C. Miller and Son, Lithographic Printers to Artists since 1917," *American Art Review*, 3, 2, (March–April 1976): 133.

McWhinnie, H.J., "A Review of the Use of Symmetry, the Golden Section and Dynamic Symmetry in Contemporary Art," *Leonardo*, 19, 3 (1986): 241.

Charles Morgan Papers, Archives and Special Collections, Amherst College Library, Amherst, Massachusetts.

Morgan, Charles H., *George Bellows Painter of America*, New York: Reynal and Company 1965.

__________, *George Bellows Paintings, Drawings, Lithographs*, exhibition catalogue, Gallery of Modern Art, New York, 1966.

__________, *Drawings of George Bellows*, Alhambra, CA: Borden Publishing Company, 1973.

Myers, Jane and Linda Ayres, *George Bellows, The Artist and His Lithographs 1916–1924*, Amon Carter Museum, 1988.

National Gallery of Art, *George Bellows—A Retrospective Exhibition, Jan 19–Feb 24, 1957*, exhibition catalogue, Washington, D.C., 1957.

Naves, Mario, "Glackens, Sloan and friends: the Ashcan Artist' New York", *New Criterion*, 14, 10 (June 1996): 48.

Oates, Joyce Carol, *George Bellows*, New York: The Ecco Press, 1995.

Peck, Glenn, *George Bellows and the War Series of 1918*, exhibition catalogue, Hirschl & Adler Galleries and the Museum of Fine Arts, Springfield, 1983

__________, *George Bellows Paintings, Drawings and Lithographs, An Exhibition in Memory of Gordon K. Allison (1904–1984)*, exhibition catalogue, Hirschl and Adler Gallery, New York, 1984.

__________, "About the Artist," *George Bellows, Lithographs*, exhibition catalogue, Adelson Gallery, New York, 1999.

__________, "George Bellows on the Conflicts of His Age," *With My Profound Reverence for the Victims George Bellows*, exhibition catalogue, Samuel Dorsky Museum of Art, State University of New York, New Paltz, 2001.

__________, *George Bellows' Catalogue Raisonné*, H.V. Allison & Co. (http://hvallison.com/home.aspx)

Phillips Memorial Gallery, Washington, D.C., *George Bellows Drawings and Lithographs*, exhibition catalogue, 1945.

Quick, Michael, Jane Myers, Marianne Doezema and Franklin Kelly, *The Paintings of George Bellows* Amon Carter Museum and Los Angeles County Museum of Art, , exhibition catalogue, New York: Harry N. Abrams, Inc., 1992.

Rich, Daniel C., "Bellows Revalued", *Magazine of Art*, 39 (April 1946): 139.

Ries, Estelle H., "The Relation of Art to Every-day Things", *Arts & Decoration* (August 1914): 158–159, 202.

Robertson, Bruce, *Reckoning with Winslow Homer: His Late Paintings and their Influence*, exhibition catalogue, Cleveland Museum of Art, 1990.

Sanger, Martha F. S., *Henry Clay Frick: an intimate portrait*, New York: Abbeville Press, 1998.

Sann, Paul, *The Lawless Decade*, http://www.lawlessdecade.net.

Searl, Marjorie B., and Ronald Netsky, *Leaving for the Country / George Bellows at Woodstock*, exhibition catalogue, Memorial Art Gallery of the University of Rochester, 2003.

Seiberling, Frank, Jr., "George Bellows, 1882–1925 / His Life and Development as an Artist," Ph. D. dissertation, The University of Chicago, 1948.

Setford, David and Wilmerding, John, *George Bellows: Love of Winter*, exhibition catalogue, Norton Museum of Art, West Palm Beach, 1997.

Shepard, Lewis, *George Wesley Bellows*, exhibition catalogue, Mead Art Building, Amherst College, November 1–20, 1972.

Sloan, Helen Farr, notes recorded in Moore College of Art, *John Sloan / Robert Henri, their Philadelphia Years, 1886–1904*, exhibition catalogue, Philadelphia, 1975.

Smithsonian Institution, *George Bellows Prints and Drawings*, exhibition catalogue, Washington D.C. 1957–58.

"The Passing Shows," *Artnews*, 41, 10 (October 1942): 27.

Sweet, Frederick, "Bellows: Twenty-three Years after Dempsey and Firpo," *Artnews*, 44, 19 (January 15–31, 1946): 12.

Tufts, Eleanor M., "Bellows and Goya," *Art Journal* 30, 4 (Summer 1971), 362–368.

Watrous, James, ed., *Pennsylvania Academy of the Fine Arts 200 Years of Excellence*, Philadelphia: Pennsylvania Academy of the Fine Arts, 2005.

Weinhardt, Carl, *The Drawings of George Bellows in the Boston Public Library*, unpublished manuscript, 1973.

Weitenkamp, Frank, "George W. Bellows, Lithographer," *Print Connoisseur*, 1924, 225–44.

Whitlock, Brad, "The Crowning Crime," *Everybody's Magazine*, (December 1918): 9–17.

Wilentz, Sean, "Low Life, High Art," *The New Republic* (September 28, 1992): 41–44.

Young, Art, "Clash of Classes Stirs 'The Masses'," *New York Sun*, April 8, 1916, 6.

Young, Mahonri Sharp, *The Paintings of George Bellows*, New York: Watson-Gupthill Publications, 1973.

Zurier, Rebecca, *Art for the Masses (1911-1917): A Radical Magazine and its Graphics*, exhibition catalogue, Yale University Art Gallery, New Haven, 1985.

__________, "Hey Kids: Children in the Comics and the Art of George Bellows," *Print Collector's Newsletter*, 18, 6 (January–February 1988): 196.

Zurier, Rebecca, Robert W. Snyder and Virginia Mecklenburg, *Metropolitan Lives The Ashcan Artists and Their New York*, National Museum of American Art, Washington D.C., November 17, 1995–March 17, 1996.

INDEX

PHOTOGRAPHY CREDITS

FRONT FLAP:
George Bellows.
Courtesy of the Estate of George Bellows

PAGE 4:
George, Anne and Jean Bellows, c. 1918.
Courtesy of the Estate of George Bellows

PAGE 31:
Schematic of Elinor, Jean and Anna According to Dynamic Symmetry, from Jay Hambidge, *Dynamic Symmetry in Composition as Used by Artists*, New Haven: Yale University Press, 1923, p. 24.
Courtesy of Hambidge Center for Creative Arts and Sciences

PAGE 47:
Splinter Beach.
Private Collection

PAGE 56:
I Was Beatin' 'is Face.
The Nelson-Atkins Museum of Art, Kansas City, Missouri.
Gift of Mr. and Mrs. Herbert O. Peet, 58-31

PAGE 76:
Johnson/Jeffries Fight, Dana Photo no. 12;
Johnson/Jeffries Fight, Dana Photo no. 82.
Collection of Craig Hamilton, JO Sports, Inc.

PAGE 86:
Church Field Hospital.
Courtesy of *Collier's New Photographic History of the European War*, New York, 1916

PAGE 94:
Emma Bellows Swimming.
Courtesy of the Estate of George Bellows

PAGE 128:
Miner's Families at the Cincinnati Mine Entrance, after the April 28, 1913, Explosion.
Courtesy of the U.S. Department of Labor, Mine Safety and Health Administration, National Mine Health & Safety Academy